Additional Praise for
RETAIL'S SEISMIC SHIFT

"A smart and insightful look at the so-called retail apocalypse. This book goes beyond the rise of e-commerce to truly understand the macro and sociological forces driving the changes and ultimately what these changes say about where we are as a society."

—LAUREN HIRSCH, M&A/Retail correspondent, Reuters

"A terrific job of capturing the seismic changes taking place in the retail landscape. Dart and Lewis's insights provide a framework for understanding who will be the winners and losers in the new world of retail."

—STEVE SADOVE, former chairman and CEO, Saks Inc., and chairman, National Retail Federation

RETAIL'S SEISMIC SHIFT

Also by Michael Dart and Robin Lewis

The New Rules of Retail: Competing in the World's Toughest Marketplace

RETAIL'S SEISMIC SHIFT

HOW TO SHIFT FASTER, RESPOND BETTER, AND WIN CUSTOMER LOYALTY

MICHAEL DART
WITH ROBIN LEWIS

St. Martin's Press
New York

www.stmartins.com

Library of Congress Cataloging-in-Publication Data

Names: Dart, Michael, author. | Lewis, Robin, 1940- author.
Title: Retail's seismic shift : how to shift faster, respond better, and win customer loyalty / Michael Dart with Robin Lewis.
Description: First edition. | New York : St. Martin's Press, [2017] | Includes bibliographical references and index.
Identifiers: LCCN 2017023623| ISBN 9781250142856 (hardcover) | ISBN 9781250149725 (ebook)
Subjects: LCSH: Retail trade. | Retail trade—Management. | Consumer satisfaction. | Customer relations.
Classification: LCC HF5429 .D2495 2017 | DDC 658.8/7—dc23
LC record available at https://lccn.loc.gov/2017023623

Our books may be purchased in bulk for promotional, educational, or business use. Please contact your local bookseller or the Macmillan Corporate and Premium Sales Department at 1-800-221-7945, extension 5442, or by email at MacmillanSpecialMarkets@macmillan.com.

First Edition: October 2017

10 9 8 7 6 5 4 3 2 1

*To David, Alison,
and Janine*

To Martha and Cloe

CONTENTS

SECTION 3

WHAT WILL THE FUTURE LOOK LIKE?

SECTION 4

HOW TO WIN

SECTION 5

VIEWS FROM THE TOP

INTRODUCTION

RETAIL'S SEISMIC SHIFT

For creative entrepreneurs, there has never been a better time to start a retail business. Opportunity abounds, as we shall show. For established retailers, the challenge to change has never been greater or more needed. For many, the shifts in our society we identify will prove to be too much. Extinction looms large—over stores, brands, and many consumer-facing businesses—even over the very words, language, and vocabulary of the entire retail ecosystem. The words "store," "retail," "wholesale," even "brick-and-mortar" will cease to exist. They exist now only on top of fragile fault lines that are moments away from completely fracturing.

To fully understand a society, you must understand retail (commerce in its broadest sense). To understand retail (or to win in retail), you must also understand society and where it is going.

Archaeologists and historians often focus on shopping habits when seeking to describe far-away cultures or those lost in time. Exploring what, why, and how we buy offers a unique understanding of a society. From ancient Greece and Rome, where the markets became places not only of commerce but political ferment; to the Silk Road in Asia, where the spread of commerce also spread new intellectual ideas (including Buddhism from India to China); to the early markets of the Middle Ages, which revealed tight-knit localized communities, the study of retail and the consumer provides us a unique glimpse of life.

Today is no different.

Circa 2016, the earth cracked. The extreme pressure from the collision of two tectonic plates, an excess of supply and plummeting demand, triggered and accelerated what will be looked upon as the biggest and most profound economic shift in the history of the retail and consumer-facing industries. For businesses to survive the chaos and earth-shaking effects of this shift, they must fundamentally transform their business models, objectives, and strategies. Those who succeed in doing so will create a profoundly different economic and retail landscape for the twenty-first century. Those who fail to change will fall through the cracks, never to be seen again.

From a positive perspective, the shift is exciting because of the enormous opportunity to recreate the retail landscape for the better. However, it is also an enormous challenge because the changes will be hugely difficult and costly to implement. But there are no options. It is do or die.

We felt and recorded the earlier rumblings of this seismic shift in the second edition of *The New Rules of Retail*, published in 2014, and realized that retail would soon feel the full impact of the quake. We began to explore its genesis: the convergence of an emerging new consumer, empowered like never before on the steroids of technology and the Internet, with unlimited and instantaneous access to anything they desire.

So, when one CEO said to us, "I can't believe that everything changed in August 2016, but it sure felt like it. Wow, nothing has been the same for us since then," we realized the early tremors were indeed erupting.

The general and business media were just beginning to report on some of the symptoms of the shift. *The Atlantic* ran a lengthy article titled "The Great Retail Apocalypse of 2017." Likewise, *The New York Times*, *The Wall Street Journal*, CNBC, Bloomberg/Businessweek and various other publications all piled on the news of massive store closings, from Macy's to Payless Shoes to Sports Authority to American Apparel, and dire sales and earnings reports. However, they were mostly reporting the news and facts surrounding the events. All these reports indicated that major changes to the industry were afoot, yet they failed to explain the reasons driving the change, the results, what the future looks like because of these trends, and any suggestions about what retailers could or should do about it.

This book does all that and more. We share a vision of the future and the emerging new business models that will help retailers thrive in it.

It's Not Just Technology or the Internet

What's causing these changes?

Contrary to common belief among consultants, academicians, economists, and business executives, this seismic shift is not being driven solely by the Internet and technology. While they are powerful elements of the disruption, and will be major enablers of the changes that retailers must make, there are even larger, more dominant, forces that few have recognized. We have analyzed all of them but determined one to be the single most powerful and enduring factor driving the shift.

We believe that the disequilibrium of supply and demand—namely, an extreme and perpetually oversupplied marketplace—is the primary driver of consumer behavioral change and how technology and the Internet will be used by consumers and companies alike; this disequilibrium will essentially play the major role in how new business models must evolve.

Defying Gravity

The global supply of material possessions is growing much faster than the demand for them. This phenomenon started in Western developed nations and has slowly spread around the globe, as the sheer amount of supply continued to increase unabated. It happened quietly, unnoticed by most, and is continuing to grow. Even the most extreme anti-globalists will not be able to stop it. We will explore these global supply-and-demand dynamics in greater detail in the subsequent chapters, but let us be clear about the result: as the storehouse of virtually everything we buy—from the shirt on your back to the phone in your pocket to the food in your fridge—continues to grow, the prices of those items will continue to decline. Everything is headed awfully close to being free.

Basic economics tells us that the prices we pay for goods and services reflect a relative equilibrium between supply and demand. This predictable pricing is necessary to sustain healthy, growing economies. If either supply or demand overshoots the other for a prolonged period, bad things happen. Too much supply can drive deflation, and too little supply can drive inflation and economic bubbles, which will ultimately deflate. At the very least, such a huge distortion will drive equally huge strategic and structural shifts in commerce and the economy. For example, the already massive levels of discounting we see. Perhaps more important for workers and bosses alike is that, when supply exceeds demand for any extended period, companies' profitability falls precipitously, forcing the demise of those with the least competitive business models.

We'll go into more detail shortly, but global overcapacity has reached its tipping point, driving companies in a variety of sectors to search for new strategies and business models to regain healthy, profitable growth. Prices continue to drop yet supply only increases.

And this superabundance of material goods has also dramatically changed the way *customers* value things. We see among all generations the emergence of a new attitude toward material goods, marked by a greater emphasis on experiences and meaning, a massive increase in the value put on convenience, a shift away from ownership and toward collaboration (or what is being called a "sharing economy"), and an increasing desire to be understood as an individual. In this book we will show that these attitudinal shifts amount to *the end of rampant consumerism as we know it, as consumers seek greater meaning in their lives, use their time for endeavors other than shopping, and shift away from ownership.*

We are also entering an era when competition will be based on (1) values—understanding the moral values of younger generations and building retail strategies around those values, as reflected in consumers' lifestyles, experiences, and meaning; (2) distribution—those companies that are able to provide fast, frictionless, and highly convenient commerce; and (3) experiences.

This will be very much a winner-take-all economy: those business models caught in the middle will quickly join the losers on the bottom.

That's where the marketplace is now.

We'll begin with a more in-depth explanation of why this perpetual supply-and-demand imbalance exists and will continue, and we will discuss its powerful role in driving the seismic shift. From there we will explore the increasingly fragmented nature of Western society and how technology is magnifying and shaping these trends and creating new businesses. By under-standing the links between all these, you will be able to see how consumer psychology is changing and what consumers are searching for now. Then we will explore what it will take to be successful in consumer-facing businesses.

Let's get started.

SECTION 1

THE CAUSES

CHAPTER 1

THE SUPPLY-DEMAND IMBALANCE

The one hundred top-selling retailers and restaurants averaged a *12 percent* loss in market value between August 2015 and October 2016, according to the National Retail Federation. Amazon's stock rose nearly 45 percent during that period. This is just the beginning.

We like the earthquake metaphor because we believe developed economies around the world are experiencing a seismic shift, driven by an underlying collision of too much supply and too little demand for traditional products (mostly things like apparel, food, toys, electronics, household goods, and shoes). The net result is good news for consumers—a proliferation of choices and better prices—and bad news for retailers and manufacturers: rapidly falling prices and declining profits. This oversaturation is an almost inevitable consequence of companies' seeking perpetual growth. Constant growth demands constant increases in capacity combined with efficiency gains, which in turn drive down costs. This dynamic also results in the commoditization of goods and services—that is, products that have no

real differentiation among brands, leading to significant competition on price. If consumers can't tell the difference between
two items or services, they will almost always choose the less
expensive or more convenient one.

This process has been going on for a long time, even if the
cracks have only just begun to show. The International Monetary
Fund reported, "There has been a downward trend in real commodity prices of about 1 percent per year for the last 140 years."[1]
Our ability to use less, produce it more efficiently and create alternatives has driven the cost of inputs down and down. Even the
recent oil price decline is a result of this, as innovation in frack-
ing techniques has increased supply. Every manufacturing and
information technology process has had a sustained learning
curve, creating evermore efficiency in the production of goods
and lower prices over time. For example, in supercomputing,
in 1968 one dollar bought you one transistor. In 2002, one dollar
bought you ten million transistors—and today it buys you close
to one billion!

Examples exist everywhere. Compare the cost and quality
of the color TV set you purchased only ten years ago to what is
available today. Now look further back, to the early days of tele-
vision. In today's dollars a 1939 RCA TV would cost $10,539, ten
times more than a modern TV with features like 3-D viewing
and Internet readiness.[2] If we drill down on this one example, we
see lower commodity costs for things like metals, plastic, and
glass, and accelerated learning curves for technology companies
and ever more manufacturing capacity (with countries like China,
Japan, and South Korea continuing to churn out ever-greater
numbers of sets). Add to this an ever-increasing number of
distribution points (retail stores, websites, delivery vehicles, and
more), and it's clear how lower prices have increased the supply

of every material thing. Indeed, the long-term trend for material goods is approaching a price tag that says FREE! We know this sounds crazy, but this is the trend (obviously, in any given year the possibility of disruption as a result of political activity, strange weather, stock market volatility or any other unknown factor may cause prices to rise, but it will not break the long-term trend). However, it is worth thinking about the consequences of a world in which the price of many material possessions is essentially free. In this world consumers' attitudes and desires for material possessions, ownership and brands—to name just a few things— will all change.

It's important to note here that the only elements of the retail ecosystem that cannot be commoditized are experiences. Starting in chapter 7, we will explore this point in depth.

So we begin our story with this supply-and-demand thesis.

What Caused the Imbalance and When?

The imbalance in supply and demand began full force with the rise of globalization and the movement of manufacturing to low-cost countries. This has combined with a dramatic decrease in the costs of both global distribution and local fulfillment.

In the first nine months of 2016, China produced 170 billion feet of clothing,[3] or roughly twenty-one billion t-shirts, and that's despite many companies' turning toward lower-wage countries. To put that in perspective, with roughly five hundred million people in the world's developed economies (we assume some of this clothing will be consumed by China's growing middle class), each of them would have to buy roughly 350 feet of clothing every year, or almost forty t-shirts, for China alone to sell everything it produces—never mind any of the other dozen or so clothing-producing countries. And all this new clothing needs to find a place in a crowded wardrobe that contains last year's 170 billion feet of clothing. The same is true in footwear, household goods—nearly everything we wear or use on a daily basis.

Indirectly, the move toward higher wages in China has generated even more supply, as manufacturing gets pushed to more and more lower-cost locations. A World Bank analysis suggests apparel exports from South Asia to the United States will increase 13 to 25 percent for every 10 percent increase in Chinese apparel prices, while exports from Southeast Asia will increase 37 to 51 percent as a result of the same Chinese price hike—so as labor in China becomes more expensive, manufacturing moves to lower-cost countries, which then send the West even more products.[4] Supply keeps increasing despite the true level of demand. Yet there's often nowhere for this massive supply to go. For example, the global auto industry manufactured 72 million cars in 2016, or roughly one for every one hundred people on the planet, even though nearly half live on less than $2.50 a day.

There is no end in sight for this productivity explosion. By the time China starts to confront labor shortages, Indonesia, India, and Malaysia will fill the void, and after them the massive populations in Africa and South America will be available to continue the perpetual cycle of lower costs and deflating value. Capital will flow to build low-cost manufacturing capacity wherever it can be found. For as far into the future as we can see, the proliferation of supply against stagnant to decreasing demand will continue.

It's important to note here that a logical question is: If demand is decreasing so that suppliers are not able to sell all their products or services, won't suppliers cut their production and retailers reduce their inventory? Wouldn't supply and demand thereby regain some equilibrium? The logical answer is yes. However, lumpy investment decisions (big factories are built years in advance in many separate geographies), unforeseen demand changes, technological innovations that increase efficiency, and incredible access to capital all mean that capacity will keep increasing. A globally efficient market in equilibrium will take a long time to arrive—if ever.

The illogical pushing of more and more stuff out into a marketplace that with insufficient demand to consume it all is perpetuated by the captains of commerce, all of whom are committed to infinite growth. And, of course, the ever-decreasing costs of production allow them to continually decrease their prices, which needlessly revs short-term demand.

Exhibits 1.1 and 1.2 provide a closer look at the underlying country data behind this macro trend and reveal how this process has led to an incredible growth in income in China and, to a lesser extent, in India and the rest of Asia, and in Latin America and the Caribbean, while growth in the United States has remained mostly stagnant. Exhibit 1.2 also shows the next location of great middle-class wage growth: India and the rest of Asia, and sub-Saharan Africa.

It is also important to remember that the costs of distributing and moving goods have gone through their own productivity explosion. During the twentieth century the real cost (inflation adjusted) of moving goods fell by 90 percent. The cost to fly, float, or drive all sorts of food, drinks, clothes and everything else we use on a daily basis around the world has fallen dramatically. We no longer find it funny or unusual when our waiter in a nice New York restaurant says tonight's special is fresh fish from Turkey.

The really interesting question is this: What happens when everything moves close to free?

We are often asked whether the current antiglobalization, anti–free trade movement will decrease global production, fueling a corresponding decrease in global supply. For a variety of

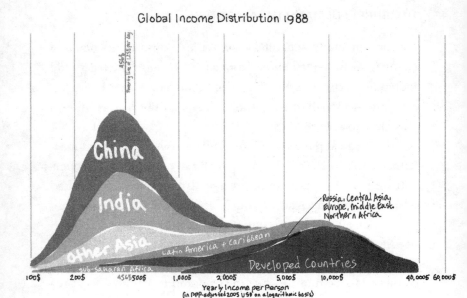

Exhibit 1.1. Distribution of Global Income, 1988

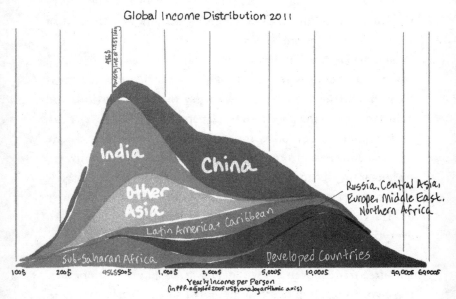

Exhibit 1.2. Distribution of Global Income, 2011

reasons, we do not expect this will happen. The biggest reason is that the current flows of global capital have already created the infrastructure for more supply in many developing countries. The productive capacity is already built. Unless we have a full-on trade war, these goods will reach the developed economies. Even a trade war will not change the picture because trade barriers will create unemployment in developed markets and further depress demand—sustaining the imbalance. Further, the trend toward on-shoring production in developed economies (to reduce lead times and now to counter political pressures) will increase supply. For "fast-fashion" items, items that are not labor-intensive to produce and those that sell better with a MADE IN THE USA tag, the expansion of sources of production is under way. Finally, 3-D printing will not only increase the amount of supply but will move a lot of production to local markets, even to individual homes (more on this later). This technology has the potential to revolutionize our production processes and global distribution.

The key takeaway here is that even if countries pursue more protectionist policies, global demand will not keep up with perpetually increasing supply. As the imbalance continues to widen, the impact on the strategic and structural models of all consumer-facing businesses will be enormous.

So who buys all this excess supply? The short answer is nobody. Much of it just gets wasted. In fact, the US Environmental Protection Agency says we throw out roughly 12.8 million tons of textiles, such as clothing and shoes, every year—or more than eighty pounds per person.[5]

Despite this monumental waste, Western consumption-driven economies, with their easy credit and spending power, do their best to cram more and more goods into closets and kitchens and garages. The United States leads the way here by a significant margin. Controlling for purchasing power, Britons consume only 85 percent of what Americans do, while people in Germany, France and Japan buy only 70 percent as much.[6] This is a big reason for our trading imbalance. "They" produce and "we" consume. But the problem is "they" can now produce more and more, at lower and lower cost, than even "we" can or want to consume.

Our consumption fails to keep up with production (or supply) for several reasons we have already noted; a few more are worth highlighting.

First, a number of major trends that supported demand have now ended. While the growth in production was occurring (both in developed economies and in the early days of offshoring to Asia), an increase in dual-income households was increasing spending power. From 1960 to 1990 the number of dual-income households rose from about 25 percent of US households to 60 percent, where it remained at least through 2012.[7] With more women in the workforce and more consumers feeling pressed for time, more income and more demand were chasing consumer household products—especially those products that saved time or otherwise made life easier. But the growth of this trend leveled off and can no longer be counted on to fuel even bigger growth in consumption.

Another one-time trend occurred in the late 1990s and early 2000s. Baby boomers hit their peak spending years, and with their large numbers—seventy-six million Americans—they drove even more demand. Buying more clothes, getting the second house equipped and the first remodeled, and buying multiple cars to transport all members of the family to their various daily activities propped up demand, keeping it reasonably aligned with increasing supply. Closets grew in size and number, and storage locker rentals boomed.

In this environment, businesses found it relatively easy to stimulate or create demand for their products. The focus on classic creative advertising and marketing, lifestyle branding, and new product development and proliferation increased and helped drive consumption. The constant push for growth led companies to create more and more, intensifying competition across every category. Porsche and Coca-Cola started selling clothing, Ross and T.J. Maxx began filling their checkout lanes with candy and snacks, and Oreo introduced a Peeps-flavored variety (one of more than one hundred iterations of the classic cookie), moves that were emblematic of the lengths to which companies would go to drive growth.

But by 2016, boomers were still feeling the sting of the Great Recession and, with retirement looming, had stopped their rampant spending. Much of their disposable income shifted to spending on travel, leisure, entertainment, health, and welfare. They didn't need or desire more stuff,

Real income growth (as a result of productivity growth in the 1990s) also maintained reasonable levels of consumption. Now, however, labor productivity is slowing down around the globe, further eroding the growth in living standards. In the United States, labor productivity grew just 1.3 percent from 2005 to 2016, compared with 2.8 percent over the previous ten years. This has been happening across dozens of advanced economies, at a loss of $2.7 trillion loss in GDP since 2004.[8] Few economists predict any near-term increase in productivity.

If anything, economists are pessimistic that global productivity will ever again (or at least in the next few years) reach historic levels. The Princeton economist Robert Gordon has argued convincingly that technology is actually leading to declining productivity growth. To state the argument simply: When electricity was first being harnessed, dark evenings and nights became productive; high-rise elevators changed how people lived; factories became automated and developed new production methods; trains, cars, and planes changed how goods and people moved from place to place; much backbreaking labor disappeared; and all sorts of major household labor-saving devices emerged. The impact of that innovation and three other factors (urban sanitation, chemicals, and pharmaceuticals) fueled growth between 1870 and 1940 that drastically reshaped lives to a degree not seen since. While people today would find a 1950s household relatively livable, conditions in 1900 would be far from tolerable to a modern traveler. Before 1900, for example, parts of New York's Financial District were seven feet deep in manure. In comparison the Internet's impact on economic growth and living conditions in the West is relatively muted (at least to date), largely affecting how we shop, order taxis, and entertain ourselves. We are actually optimists about the long-term impact of technology on health, longevity, and knowledge formation, but we do not see significant short-term growth in productivity.

When productivity growth and incomes slowed, consumption was initially buoyed by easy access to credit through home equity loans, mortgage loans, and ubiquitous credit cards. Consumers mistakenly believed they could support real increases in their standard of living with credit, not income. Financial institutions, with complicit central banks, supported this lie. In 2008, the bubble burst, causing the Great Recession, and the music stopped. As depicted in the movie *The Big Short*, the housing crisis and recession made a fortune for many, but it changed a generation's attitude toward and desire for credit. The notion of using debt as a cost-free route to living above your means had been thoroughly discredited.

It is clear that recent years have seen no substantial growth in demand for almost all consumer products in the developed economies. Desperate attempts to stimulate demand with monetary policy have been marginally successful (the bubble costs of this policy are not yet clear), but all the underlying drivers of demand have slowed. If anything, demand has been in a gradual decline.

The Internet, Technology, and the Smartphone

Another critical element to the seismic shift is the massive increase in both the number of points of distribution and their increasing level of fluidity (more on this idea later).

Major retailers and brands have been able to control the flow and distribution of goods for large parts of the buildup in supply that we have described. Everyone knows there has been a relentless and sustained increase in retail square footage during the last five decades. From 1983 to 2009, US retail square footage per capita shot up 30 percent.[9] It's slid 3 percent since then: the seismic shift's first victims have started to fall through the cracks and shut their stores.

For several years, retailers were able to maintain relative control over product sales by using more, but managed, promotions and price reductions. As they gradually felt the pressure of the growing level of supply, retailers and brands developed the strategy of price discrimination and began opening outlet stores and the off-price model (significantly discounted name brands). Outlet stores grew by using inconvenient locations to sell goods at a lower price than traditional retail stores to consumers who would not otherwise (the outlets hoped) have bought the product. At first, this worked nicely. At the same time, excess production was also sent to off-price retailers who sold the products at significantly discounted prices. Again, the hope was that new consumers would be attracted to the somewhat disorganized "treasure hunt" shopping experience. But what these channels really accomplished was selling ever-increasing amounts of excess product, driving prices ever lower. It worked for a while—from the mid-1990s to around 2010, these retailers were able to manage the price declines and grow by serving demand in different markets. The most successful of them, T.J. Maxx and Ross Stores, grew into monster retailers. Coach grew by increasing its number of outlet stores. But eventually the excess supply tarnished the brand with too much ubiquity, and Coach, like many others, found itself in trouble until it started paring back its distribution.[10]

Attempts like these to manage excess supply through different distribution channels were then thoroughly blown apart by the Internet and the appearance in the early 2000s of e-commerce, the smartphone, and related technologies. The multiplicity of new websites appearing daily, each offering a better-discounted deal than the one before it, or selling "pre-used" goods or just plain "swapping," and literally millions of apps and other innovative ways to market more goods faster and at a lower price blew open the spigot of supply. If customers living in Manhattan no longer had to travel fifty miles to the Woodbury Common outlet mall, why would they?

How big a hole did this new means of distribution open in the world of commerce? Piper Jaffray analysts concluded that the e-commerce penetration rate across retail is much closer to 40 percent than the 10 percent figure currently floating around.[11] Piper Jaffray analysts arrived at a "more realistic" e-commerce penetration of 37.4 percent by including an estimated $146 billion in traditional retailer e-commerce sales that the company claims are underreported, excluding categories that are not commonly sold online—food and beverage stores, building materials and garden equipment, stores, and gas stations—and by using gross merchandise value instead of revenue as a better proxy for online sales. And this penetration rate will only continue to grow as some household and personal care items, such as those commonly sold at food and beverage stores and gas stations, continue to fall victim to "subscribe and save" models.

E-commerce also has eroded retail margins by creating ultimate price transparency, forcing investment in expensive technologies and ramping up distribution costs. Even more concerning is that, while the majority of retailers still rush to implement these big-ticket systems, it may already be too late. The top twenty-five store-based retailers saw their e-commerce sales growth slow to just 10 percent in 2015, down from 25 percent just three years earlier, while Amazon's gross merchandise value continued to grow at 30 percent or higher in the same time period.[12]

But every sector is being affected. Think of any type of product, and the web has produced at least one—and probably dozens—of ways to access it. Food? Instacart, Deliv, Caviar, Munchery, Blue Apron, and so many more. Beauty products? Birchbox, Julep, Ipsy, and many others. Electronics? NewEgg, Enjoy (which also delivers an in-home experience). We could go on, but you get it.

As we've discussed, a seismic shift in our economy has opened up a deep chasm between supply and demand. This supply-demand imbalance has driven down prices and led to an immense loss of market value across much of the retail and consumer products space. Supply has skyrocketed, thanks to globalization and the movement to low-cost manufacturing countries. Meanwhile, demand in the United States and other Western countries has plummeted because of aging populations, a lack of growth in disposable income, and a growing emphasis on experiences and shared goods rather than ownership, among other factors. Adding technology to the mix provided countless new distribution

Exhibit 1.3. Supply/Demand Imbalance

points for this massive product wave, and the result has been an irreconcilable gap between supply and demand.

The consequences of this gap, or imbalance, are going to be immense and require a complete rethinking of retail and consumer strategies. *Many companies will fail during the next few years.* Overhead structures built to support the retail industry, including stores and the associates who staff them, are too large and cannot be supported by the ongoing price deflation that is occurring. Consumers' expectations of the retailer and the brands it sells are going to change fundamentally. The ever-persistent push for growth by opening stores will end or has already ended—closures have to come next. The metrics used to evaluate a successful retailer will change—from total sales growth (especially from new stores or points of distribution) to margin expansion or return on capital. The value will shift from selling commodity products to those who own the point of distribution. The number of retail jobs will shrink radically, re-placed by delivery jobs.

The inevitable shakeout will escalate the need to put more meaning in the product or experience. The need to build more information into retail or consumer organizations will acceler-ate (in our conclusion we predict a shift in the meaning or pur-pose of business). In fact, everything is changing, all because of the simple concept of supply and demand and the growing gap between them.

And this gap will only continue to grow because of a variety of key and dramatic trends that we will explore in the chapters that follow. We begin with the important concept of dematerial-ization.

CHAPTER 2

DEMATERIALIZATION

The concept of dematerialization—critical to understanding the seismic shift—is multidimensional, its impact felt in significantly depressing the demand for material goods.

The first element of dematerialization is that it now takes less and less physical matter to produce the goods we consume. As Kevin Kelly points out in his book *The Inevitable*, "In 1870 it took 4 kilograms of stuff to generate one unit of the U.S.'s GDP. In 1930 it took only one kilogram. Recently, the value of GDP per kilogram of inputs rose from $1.64 in 1977 to $3.58 in 2000—a doubling of dematerialization in 23 years."[1] The obvious reason for this is the vast improvement in manufacturing technology and use of materials. The result is the ability to produce more and better products at lower cost. It also means that less of the US GDP is now going to products that have physical matter at their core. People are spending their dollars on things that do not contain physical atoms.

The first of these types of nonphysical products are digital products. The massive increase in consumer spending on technology and digital products shows no sign of abating. US consumer spending on media and technology rose 7 percent in 2015 and globally is expected to achieve a compounded annual growth rate of 7 percent between 2015 and 2019, hitting $2 trillion in 2019, double the level of 2009 spending.[2]

Also, the digital shift is changing the consumer mind-set from one of ownership to one of access. Consumers, particularly millennials, are no longer interested in owning everything they desire. However, they do want access to physical products as well as digital services and products—whenever and wherever they need or want them. Many millennials would rather have access to even the material goods they do want—through sharing and swapping—than by purchasing and owning. Thus, the rise of the sharing economy. This is yet another factor that diminishes traditional demand for products.

The second area of increased spending is on experiences. This trend also dovetails with the rise of millennials as we discussed earlier—72 percent of millennials say they would rather spend money on experiences than products.[3] This trend is aligned with a wave of recent psychological research showing that experiences bring people greater happiness than material objects.[4] So it's no surprise that from 1987 to 2016, the share of consumer spending on live experiences and events relative to total US consumer spending increased 70 percent. We will return again and again to the growing desire for the unique, satisfying nature of experiences that are hard to commoditize. Experiences tend not to require extensive amounts of material, so part of the shift in the US economy is the continuing increase in spending in these areas.

One type of experience that consumers do value highly but that remains open to commoditization is the convenience, speed, and price of the delivery process—perhaps because speedy, convenient delivery gives time-crunched consumers more time for experiences they actually value. As goods become more abundant and less expensive, the opportunity to add value through convenience and distribution becomes paramount in differentiating the retail experience. Amazon has led the way, but consumers will see more and more innovative delivery mechanisms that will further uproot traditional retail models. When the product contains less and less material and takes a smaller percentage of the wallet, value starts to increasingly shift to the point and method of distribution.

Another element of this concept is the shift in consumer attitudes toward owning lots of possessions. The trends suggest a significant move toward owning fewer things, accessing those that you need only when you need them, and decluttering (driven in part by moves to cities and smaller living spaces—86 percent of millennials live in cities and so do 83 percent of the Gen Xers who came before them. Thus it's no surprise that since the Great Recession, construction of single-family homes has hovered at decades-long lows while multifamily housing has boomed).[5] Uber and bike sharing are the most prominent examples, but others are Airbnb, Getaround, and companies that provide coworking spaces, like WeWork.

The last aspect of dematerialization is the growing focus on health and wellness combined with the rising costs of health care. Since around 2007, people have been increasingly interested in extending their longevity and improving their health and wellness. Many factors drive this trend, including aging boomers looking for healthier living and more active retirements. Their healthy living goals have spread to all segments of the population. This has in part fed the desire for less consumption overall; the trends toward organic and natural foods, which are also perceived as less environmentally wasteful and are consumed in smaller quantities; and the ubiquity of gyms and personal training services, and the accompanying growth in leisure-time athletics. It has also fueled more spending on health care, and that, combined with a largely dysfunctional health care system, has led to large increases in the percentage of national income consumed by health care.[6] The net result is once again a shift from products to services.

But this growing obsession with a healthier lifestyle wasn't the only factor pushing up health care spending at the expense of traditional consumer goods: many consumers are giving an increasingly large share of their paychecks to basic medical services. In fact, in 2014, 8 percent of consumers' spending went to health care, compared with 4.8 percent in 1984. The difference was even more stark when it came to spending on health insurance, which made up 5.4 percent of total spending in 2014 compared to just 1.7 percent in 1984.[7] As Exhibit 2.1 shows, consumers are also spending more on housing and entertainment now, leaving less money for apparel, food, and personal care products.

Thus, dematerialization is an additional constraint on demand for physical products, and, despite low interest rates and promotional sales, increasing demand to meet the growing supply is simply impossible. The result will be a continuing drop in prices.

We believe that by 2016 the markets were beginning to feel the painful impact of the increasing oversupply and deflating prices and value. But the increasing pressure to achieve growth in this massive downward vortex simply exacerbated the tendency to seek the path of least resistance: to sell more stuff. Thus, promotional pricing and discounting, which once was a weapon of choice, is now a weapon of necessity. The often-heard laments that "this year was exceptionally promotional" or "we had to

Percent distribution of expenditures for all consumer units, 1984 and 2014 annual averages

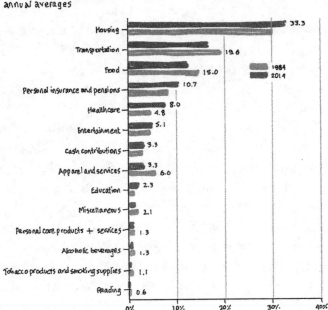

Source: U.S. Bureau of Labor Statistics.

Exhibit 2.1. Distribution of Expenditures for Consumer Units, 1984 and 2014

discount early to beat competitors" are not going away. If anything, expect to hear this more often. In fact, as promotions become more ubiquitous—companies now spend $1 trillion a year on discounting—these sales and gimmicks are also becoming less efficient. A full two-thirds don't even break even, and the average discount now results in a product's being sold for 66 cents on the dollar, compared with 77 cents in 2012.[8]

However, the ultimate outcome of this dynamic, in the aggregate, is depressed material demand and even more excess supply.

A famous French economist, one of the leaders of classical economics, Jean Baptiste Say, once said that supply creates its

<u>dematerialization</u>

amount of physical matter to create GDP :

1930

1980

100mg
△
today

≡<u>DRIVERS</u> : ○ productive efficiency / capacity
 ′ ′ ′ ′   ○ technology
          ○ health + wellness
          ○ services
          ○ entertainment

Exhibit 2.2. Dematerialization over the decades

own demand. Well, we say, "Oh, Say, can't you see" the trillions of tons of food, apparel, and consumer goods that are wasted every year? We're sorry to say that Say's Law, as it was called, is being debunked every day and has been for the last half century. To give the great economist his due, he did make his declaration about supply and demand about 1803, more than two hundred years ago. Do you think Jean had any inkling of what the modern industrial revolution would do to his law?

CHAPTER 3

THE GREAT
DEMOGRAPHIC SHIFT

One especially big drag suggests the gap between desire and quantity will only continue to exacerbate the supply-demand imbalance. That drag is a demographic cliff—aging populations and low birthrates—that has negatively affected all developed economies, including that of the United States. Quite a few trends are important to consider in relation to these economies' failure to replace graying workers and consumers.

First, fewer workers will be supporting more retirees. In many of the world's wealthier economies, fertility rates have been below the replacement rate for decades. As Exhibit 3.1 shows, all twenty countries with the top nominal GDPs in 2016 (as ranked by the International Monetary Fund) have seen their birthrates tumble since the mid-1970s. So even if people weren't living longer, the elderly still would be accounting for a larger percentage of the population in most developed countries.

The issue of depopulation in developed economies is one of the most significant and least mentioned global trends today. We approach the issue from that of consumption and the demand for material goods, but the potential political and social upheavals

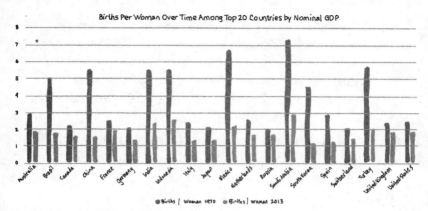

Exhibit 3.1. Births Per Woman over Time
Across continents and cultures, women are having fewer children—in many
cases, the birthrate is below the replacement rate.

that this suggests are immense. It is not a coincidence that the areas that voted for Brexit and Trump were those with aging populations and a rapidly fleeing group of younger people. For many, the psychological impact of seeing their areas depopulated of young people and immigrants entering and taking low-paying jobs to fill the void has helped fuel the so-called populist movements. It is too soon to say what the inverted population pyramid means for China, as well as eastern Europe and Russia, but it is likely to have a profound impact on all of them.

For retailers, brands, and investors in countries with fast depopulation, the economic risks are increasing and in some cases may be substantial.

All this means fewer workers and consumers. In 2016, advanced economies' combined working-age population declined for the first time since 1950, and by 2050 it will shrink another 5 percent, according to the United Nations.[1]

The story is the same around the globe. According to the United Nations, by 2050, the working-age population will shrink 26 percent in South Korea, 28 percent in Japan, 23 percent in Germany and Italy, and 21 percent in Russia and China. And although the working-age population of the United States is projected to grow 10 percent by 2050, thanks in large part to immigration (the forecasts for which now look increasingly optimistic), it will still shrink as a share of the total population—from 66 percent to 60 percent. If immigration rates into the United States were to become dramatically lower (given the current political climate), we would be facing challenges to our long-term consumer demand similar to what the other countries are anticipating.

The "share of population" figure is critical—it's about not only the number of workers but the number relative to nonworkers—older adults and children. We first saw how crucial "share of population" can be when the number of workers per total dependents started plummeting in Japan in 1990, precipitating an economic crisis (or at least correlated with an economic crisis). And the same thing is now happening in the West. In the United States, the number of workers per total dependents peaked at just above two in about 2005 and has been falling ever since. It is now on a long-term decline, forecasted to reach 1.5 by 2050. Census data reveal that between now and 2026, ten thousand boomers will reach retirement age every day. Note that both the US financial crisis (2008) and the European debt crisis (2009) also correlated roughly with this demographic turning point, where the number of working individuals fell relative to the number of dependents.

And in Europe, the number of workers per total dependents peaked in about 2009, and the Continent has been struggling with low or no growth, deflation, and high unemployment ever since. Almost one in five western Europeans was sixty-five or older in 2014, a relationship that will grow to one in four by 2030—creating a situation even more dire than in the United States. And early retirement ages, pay-as-you-go pension systems and low labor participation rates even among nonseniors many European countries just add to the dilemma.[2]

Simply stated, more people were earning money and consuming goods in 2010 relative to the number of dependents (children and elderly) than anyone is likely to see again for the next forty years.

All this matters for the US consumer economy because, of course, working is closely tied to spending. The peak age for spending in retail stores (for material possessions) tends to be roughly between forty-four and fifty-four years of age, with the average head of household spending $70,000 a year. Among those aged fifty-five to sixty-four, spending falls to $59,000 annually before really tumbling off a cliff: people sixty-five and older spend just $45,000 annually. In the United States, 2005 was, roughly speaking, the year with the greatest number of people at top spending age.[3]

Boomers were able to spend even more during their prime spending years because of their relatively low number of dependents (fewer children than the replacement ratio and few elderly parents). The data show that boomers upgraded their houses, bought vacation homes, and filled out wardrobes (with branded apparel and footwear) for themselves and their one or two children to the tune of $3.2 trillion annually—greater than the total GDP of Brazil, Russia, or the United Kingdom.[4]

During these years, the savings rate declined. In 2005, the US personal savings rate dropped to 2.6 percent, the lowest rate since the government started collecting these data in 1959, capping off a decades-long slide from its peak of 13.3 percent in 1971.[5] The historic low was down from 4.6 percent the year before and climbed back above 4 percent only in 2008, the general level it has held ever since. Clearly, during peak spending years, preparing for retirement was not a top priority. Spending was fun. Lots of fun, until it wasn't, as we hit the demographic tipping point just as the globe was plunged into recession.

Since then, the JPMorgan Chase Institute has found that year-over-year change in everyday spending among seniors fell a full 7.6 percentage points between 2014 and 2016, more than the spending slowdown among younger consumers.[6] And some of the spending we might expect to return among all age groups isn't happening at all as the saving rate increases.

This problem of demographics and spending has hidden dimensions as well. In 2016, the current median balance of a US 401(k) account held by a household near the retirement age was $104,000.[7] That's right: the entire balance is just over $100,000, which suggests, under normal withdrawal guidelines, an income of just $4,000 per year. While boomers are certainly counting on Social Security to fill some of that void, it's also likely that the diminishing number of workers with aging parents may have to provide income support from their earnings. If that is the case, these workers will have less to spend on themselves than previous generations, and the retired certainly don't have any surplus cash to continue to fund high levels of discretionary consumption.

We note too that since the Great Recession, young people are living at home (with their parents) at higher percentages than ever before. Many expect this trend to reverse and that we will see a boom in household formation. But we think another scenario will play out: the young will take over running the house with the retirees still living with them. This approach would reduce or eliminate child care expenses, living expenses for the aging and the transaction costs of buying a house—all things that millennials care about. We call this the Italian scenario.

Is it possible to predict the size of the economic drag from these demographic trends?

Well, no one is trying to figure out what our Italian scenario means, but economists are concerned about the larger trends. The Federal Reserve recently detailed its findings on the demographic trends and argued that their effect is a 1.25 percent reduction in the economy's annual growth from what it would otherwise be. The Fed's report concludes: "Our results further suggest that real GDP growth . . . will remain low in the coming decades, consistent with the US economy reaching a new normal."[8]

The reduction in annual growth that this implies is equivalent to roughly $220 billion in purchases that American would otherwise have been made. To put that in perspective, the United States is staring down a decline in demand that is equivalent to nearly half of Walmart's annual sales. Or twenty times the annual sales of The Gap.

Not everyone agrees with this dire forecast. A popular alternative suggests that "seventy is the new sixty-six," that is, the US retirement age would be pushed back as those with low pension reserves keep working. If a high percentage of boomers keep working until seventy instead of retiring, they would help smooth the demand curve instead of sending it off a cliff.

Japan, which fell off the demographic cliff before the United States, is already putting this into practice—roughly 20 percent of Japanese seniors work, which is almost double the average of working seniors in the advanced economies that make up the Organisation for Economic Co-operation and Development.[9]

And in the United States this trend is emerging, for example, among people in the top income bracket. As of 2013, 61 percent of those in the top fifth of wage earners were still working at age seventy (versus 99 percent of forty-five-year-olds in that bracket).

Those with no or low savings will probably continue to work, if they can, by preference if not necessity. But even if they are able to work, these employed older adults are likely to spend their earnings at rates well below historic levels. In fact, all consumer and retail organizations should be focused on creating more job opportunities for those older than sixty: it's good for their business and great for the economy.

But while greater employment opportunities for older adults might help mitigate the anticipated consumption decline, they will not stop it. Indeed, older adults are likely to increase their savings, not go on a spending spree.

Another alternative theory is that, although boomers and older adults own 63 percent of American wealth, a coming transfer of wealth to a younger generation will drive new consumption.[10] In fact, the opposite seems to be happening. Census data show that between 2000 and 2011, every age group except those sixty-five and older had significant decreases in median household net worth, while those sixty-five and older saw their net worth grow by 17 percent.[11] Because people are living longer, there is no obvious reason to believe that the transfer of wealth between generations will occur before 2022. If anything, as we have said, more millennials (maybe even millennial families) will be living in their parents' home or renting small spaces in cities while waiting to inherit the house.

The bottom line is that demographics suggest a continued decrease in the overall level of consumer demand in the United States. With the trend repeated across all developed economies, excess supply has no obvious, equally demanding or affluent consumer markets to which to flow. It will take a long time for a middle class to develop in the emerging economies and longer still for mature economies to fill the gap the boomers leave behind.

So, with companies desperate to sell their excess stock, the path of least resistance is to further drive down prices, continuing the downward vortex of value and the race to the bottom. Since the production of goods is unabated, and these most likely are still flowing into the United States, the only sales lever retailers can still pull is price, leading to another wave of special offers, flash sales, loyalty card promotions, the opening of more and more outlet stores, and every creative discounting idea imaginable.

The other implication of this demographic shift is the change in the goods that will actually be in demand. Boomers are now spending 4.7 percent less on apparel and 3.8 percent less on home furnishings than they were in 2005. Meanwhile, data from the US Bureau of Labor Statistics show that people fifty-five and older spending on clothing and transportation decreases and health care spending increases.[12]

How much more do older adults spend on things like health care? The typical American older than sixty-five funnels 13 percent of her total spending to health care, compared to just 6 percent among thirty-five- to forty-four-year-olds.[13] So not only do older adults spend a lot less when they retire but spend it on all sorts of health-related products and services—not just on retirement homes or medical services but on a plethora of products, including vitamins, creams and support braces, to name but a few. At this stage of life the absolute value of any purchase has to be high to induce people to spend. Gone are the impulse items, the extra piece of clothing or the fashion accessories. Fitness classes, maybe a gym membership, or travel are still attractive and will grow as a percentage of this group's expenditures. Boomers and seniors aren't immune to the trend of spending more on experiences. In fact, seniors are spending more on hobbies, education and entertainment than they did in 1990. For people aged sixty-five to seventy-four, spending in certain categories has grown: miscellaneous entertainment (9.8 percent), pets and hobbies (5.2 percent) and education (14.3 percent) since 1990.[14]

How about housing and technology?

Housing is the single greatest expense in terms of total dollars and as a share of total expenditures—making up a third of all spending by people aged fifty-five and older.[15] So the mortgages that exist will continue to take their fair share or more of seniors' wallets in the near term. In the long run, seniors' houses may become a source of cash again as they are sold or used to obtain reverse mortgages.

As for technology, the boomer generation considers the access and connectivity provided by the smartphone to be as important as any other age group does. Also, the psychological attitudes of the elderly are younger than ever. The participation rates for those older than sixty on Facebook, Twitter, and even Snapchat, while lagging behind those for Gen Z, are still remarkably high—83 percent of boomers use Facebook, 31 percent use Twitter, and 9 percent even use Instagram.[16] Expect an unprecedented amount of any available dollars to go to technology and away from other categories for spending disposable income.

All in all, we think a compelling case can be made that the level of demand is structurally depressed because of the aging population and depopulation.

The example of Japan, which went through this demographic wave earlier than any other country, adds an additional (daunting) perspective on what the future might hold for the United States.

Japan's Graying Population

Twenty-five percent of people in Japan are sixty-five or older, compared with just 15 percent of Americans. And even though older Japanese people are more likely to work than their American counterparts, Japan has just 1.6 working-age adults to support each senior, or child younger than fifteen. That imbalance is already unsustainable, and the situation will only worsen. By 2050 Japan will have only one working-age person for every senior or child. During a high-growth period in the 1980s, the ratio was about 2:1, roughly the same as the current US level.[17]

We see in Japan a warning sign of what might happen to the United States. The Japanese population reached its peak age-driven spending level, which tends to be between forty-five and fifty, around 1995. That year, Japan's GDP per capita (as measured in current US dollars) reached its second-highest all-time level before flatlining as Japan struggled through an economic crisis. GDP resurged in 2012 before totally falling off the cliff. Since 1995, Japan has seen GDP growth stagnate, on average, at less than 1 percent annually; even as we write this in 2016, the nation is fighting further challenges from deflation. Without any immigration into Japan, the economy has been on a sedative and has seen no impetus that would drive growth or demand. Japanese corporations full of cash have been looking overseas for investment opportunities because they see few prospects to earn a return in their home market.

Around 2005, the United States reached that same age spending peak. Since 2005, GDP growth has averaged just 1.4 percent. The US course is likely to be different because the United States still has a relatively robust immigration pipeline—unless the spigot of legal immigration is turned off, we are likely to fare better—albeit with less demand than during the boom consumer years. Consumer-facing companies can expect another economic benefit from immigrants: to build their new lives they also often have to purchase many things when they arrive.

Japan's story offers many lessons. An important one is how work takes on a greater meaning in one's life and in society. The Japanese word for the level of meaning in work is *shokunin*, and it conjures up ideas of mastery and constant improvement. No matter how menial the job is, individuals have an opportunity to demonstrate mastery, pride and satisfaction in their work. Society provides much respect for anyone who does any task with this attitude.[18] In a low-growth economy, such a mind-set may be critical. Certainly, it is a notion all lower-growth businesses should consider as they look to motivate and retain their best employees.

But Japan's story has another important facet: the elderly are dominating society in both Japan and the United States, and both societies also are becoming younger. By this, we mean two things. The first is that with increases in life expectancy, the distance between age fifty and death is increasing, a trend that will continue, given the projected increases in longevity and improvements in health care. On average (a dangerous concept but relevant here), someone who is sixty-four today already enjoys approximately the same health of a fifty-eight-year-old in an earlier generation. This is why we see health foods, pets, education, fitness, and travel as sustainable spending categories for boomers.

The second aspect of being younger is attitudinal. Boomers want to be involved in the mainstream entertainment world—movies, sports, and music. Expect this age group to value experiences, meaning, and community as much as any other age group. The only catch is that boomers will be much more selective in where and how much they spend than they were just a few years ago.

We'll further explore this last point in section 2. But the lesson of the demographic shift is clear: despite all the talk about the importance of millennials and Gen Z, the boomer generation is still going to be driving major trends for the foreseeable future.

And of even greater significance is that the "great demographic shift" will act simply as another accelerant of the growing imbalance of too much supply and too little demand.

Indeed, as the populations of many huge markets around the world age, their spending slows as they face shrinking incomes and retirement savings. Younger generations, even if they were as populous as their older counterparts, are increasingly unable to make up the difference as they plow money into caring for these elders, as well as managing their own depressed incomes.

Age has, of course, always played a role in explaining spending

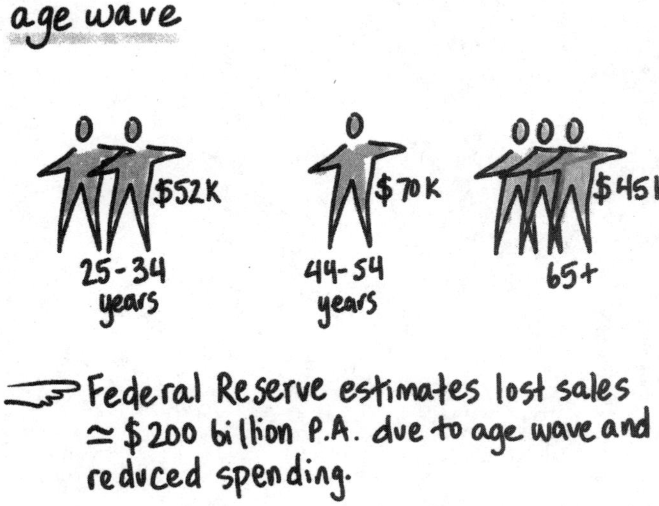

age wave

$52K 25-34 years

$70K 44-54 years

$45K 65+

☞ Federal Reserve estimates lost sales ≃ $200 billion P.A. due to age wave and reduced spending.

Exhibit 3.2. Age Wave

differences. But its impact is now more acute than ever. In fact, the impact of many thousands of demographic and societal differences are a powerful driver of the reshaping of the retail landscape. In the next chapter we explore some of these millions of tiny cuts that may kill even the biggest retailers.

CHAPTER 4

THE GREAT FRAGMENTATION

If you think of yesterday's mass market as a nice glass bowl, that market today is shattered into a thousand small fragments of glass.

In the mid-2010s, and for many decades before that, the idea of the "must-have toy" (or must-have latest fashion attire, TV set, or shoes) fascinated retailers and consumers alike each holiday season. There would be lines, perhaps even fights in the aisles, to obtain the items. Nowadays, industry—and, more importantly, consumers—seem not to have the same consensus about the identity of a must-have item. Driving this lack of consensus is the incredible consumer fragmentation that is occurring, and it is critical for two reasons. First, it is impacting supply and demand—dampening demand (e.g., in the absence of major trends consumers feel less compulsion to buy) and, with the emergence niche markets, enabling start-up companies to satisfy these idiosyncratic tastes, which once again increases supply. Second, the lack of consensus is also leading to significant shifts in the pattern of consumption.

Exhibit 4.1. The Great Fragmentation

This hyperfragmentation of consumers across almost every important dimension is becoming a significant challenge for retailers. People's lifestyles, cultural traits, attitudes, preferred products, services and experiences in different regions, countries and even cities are rapidly becoming distinct, separate and definable microcommunities. Their tastes, expectations, and purchasing behaviors are diverging in multiple directions. This fragmentation is also characterized by an increasing disparity in how these diverse groups define and live their lives.

For many years, the prevailing theory has been that mass brands can serve mass markets. For every Sam Adams or local craft beer drinker, there would always be a large group of people for whom a mass-marketed cold Bud or Miller Lite did the trick. But available data suggest this is no longer the case, that the move is toward an infinite number of discrete consumer segments. People will look for niche brands that are intensely relevant to their needs and provide a clear emotional connection. In fact, a by-product of the growing oversupply is that new, so-called brands are appearing almost daily, thus redefining what a brand is. Unlike megabrands of the past, such as Levi's jeans or Budweiser beer, these brands and retailers will be multifaceted and diverse—each with a distinct position and set of identifiers—to target a smaller and smaller niche of consumers. Among these identifiers will be: showing an understanding of people's lifestyles and everyday pressures, being environmentally friendly, creating a sense of a tribe around a brand, and connecting people with others who like the same music, go to the same events, and share the same aspirations.

By definition, these niches will be more personal, more authentic, and therefore also smaller and smaller in size. Think of the disappearance of logos that once were prominently displayed on everything—at their peak in the 1990s, branded logo goods accounted for more than 40 percent of fashion purchases, but that fell to less than 10 percent by 2014, a factor in the struggles to survive of such leading and/or once-big brands like Lacoste, Juicy Couture, American Eagle and Abercrombie & Fitch. A&F even removed its signature logo from its clothing in 2014.[1] These are symptoms of a move away from conformity.

Several drivers of this fragmentation—among them, societal changes (economic and demographic), experiential (how people live), psychological (people's desire for self-esteem and individuality), and political (greater levels of freedom to express yourself)—suggest that it will not end anytime soon. The trends in fragmentation pose a direct threat to every mass market—and the supply chains designed to fulfill them. It is worth emphasizing that a core part of our thesis is that we see the end of mass markets because of these trends.

Psychological Drivers

We think the most important contributor to the great fragmentation of markets is the underlying psychological force that governs purchasing behavior and attitudes. That driver is the need for high self-esteem—and one major component is the need for social status. Put in simple terms, social scientists have long argued that social status directly affects how individuals feel about their lives. In highly conformist societies with a clear hierarchy, the social pecking order is well established and changing your social status is difficult. However, an environment in which you can use fashion and products to separate yourself from members of other groups is likely to have smaller hierarchical structures in which more people believe they are at the top or otherwise belong. One example is the use of fashion to express what is cool. The rebellion that is part of youth culture is a direct expression of this psychological need.

Punks did not want to be regarded as just another part of the hippie movement so they created their own expression and fashion. In doing so, new punk rockers immediately had status within their group (status is achieved by both the expression of an idea and the importance the group places on you—so new members always get higher status).

From there, punk splintered into new wave, grunge, indie rock, and more. All individuals had the ability to move up the social hierarchy of their splinter group and avoid being characterized as having low status as part of greater whole.

Fashion is the same—the desire for rebellion and status is driving the need for a constant flow of new brands that capture a unique identity. As soon as a brand gets too big, new members or fans lose the ability to achieve status and go looking for something new. This cycle of creation and decline is deeply embedded in our psyches and drives consumer and brand fragmentation. It stretches from beer to chips to shoes to coffee.[2]

Since we are on the subject of freedom of expression and identity, it's worth mentioning sexuality. Americans have never had the freedom to express their sexual identity that they have today. Probably no other aspect of our identity has gone through such fragmentation (at least in terminology, if not in absolute numbers). Today people identify with such terms as the now almost-dated *queer* (a slur reclaimed by some to reflect a range of nonheterosexual identities), *transgender, gender fluid, intersex,* and *transsexual*, to name a few. The ability to be open about one's identity (here, sexual identity) is allowing people to find both others and groups like themselves but also to feel free to stand out

Exhibit 4.2. Psychological Drivers.

against the mass (or dominant) identity. In turn, this allows for more freedom of expression in the clothes, food, and music one consumes—if I no longer feel the need to pretend I'm part of any sexual mainstream, I'm also much less likely to feel constrained to wear the clothes or eat the food that signifies that mainstream. The impact of homosexuality on fashion and retail has been almost incalculably immense. This expanded freedom of expression is opening the door to many new creative opportunities.

Five Generations Under One Roof

The second clear-cut trend is that we are entering a period when (for arguably the first time in history) the marketplace and workforce will be hosting five distinct generations with considerable purchasing power and different life experiences at the same time. From the silent generation to Gen Zers, the marketplace has more segments than ever before—and that's just taking age groups into account. (See sidebar.)

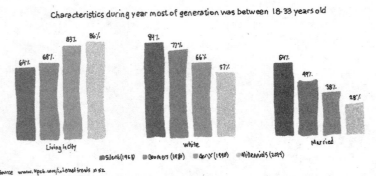

Exhibit 4.3. Characteristics of the 18- to 33-Year-Old Generation
Generations became more urban, less white, and less likely to get married.

The Five U.S. Generations in the Marketplace and Their Differences

- The silent generation—people born between 1928 and 1945. During their peak adult years (eighteen to thirty-three), they were less likely to live in a city, more likely to be white, and more likely to be married than the generations that came after them. By 2026 only about fourteen million people will remain from this generation, and 75 percent of them will be white.[3]
- Baby boomers—people born between. 1946 and 1964. Boomers represent the beginning of a shift toward more diversity, more female employment, and a host of other societal changes. Those changes will continue for the next ten years (through to 2026), when only sixty-six million boomers will be alive, only 65 percent of them white.
- Gen X—people born between 1965 and 1980. Although this generation likes to complain about being lost between the large boomer and millennial groups, sixty-five million of them—the same as the number of boomers—will be alive in 2026. Gen Xers continued the trends toward urbanization and diversity and away from traditional households and gender roles.
- Millennials—people born between 1981 and 1996. This generation is the nut almost every retailer is trying to crack today. Millennials were the first generation to grow up with much of the technology that is reshaping society and retailing today.
- Gen Z—people born after 1996. Although often overlooked, this generation should be on every company's radar. They will be eighty-two million strong by 2026 and the first "majority minority" generation, with only 48 percent of Gen Zers identifying as white.

Here are some of the experiences that separate these generations:

- In the mid-1980s, young adults in many countries (boomers) earned more than the national average—and now millennials and Gen Zers earn as much as 20 percent less than the national average. In the United States that translates to a 9 percent decline in household disposable income versus the national average growth rate in

[Cont.]

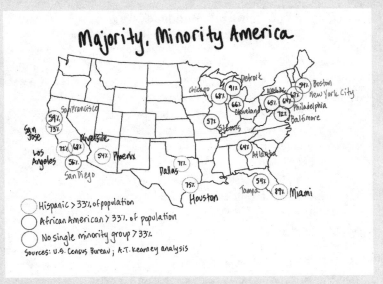

Exhibit 4.4. Majority, Minority America

household income.[4] That means that millennials' disposable income is only slightly more in real dollars than it was for their age peers thirty years ago.

- Twenty-eight percent of millennials and Gen Zers were raised by single parents, whereas this was the case for only 9 percent of boomers.[5]

- More than 60 percent of the forty-seven thousand drug overdose deaths in the United States in 2014 involved an opioid, and most experts think the problem has worsened.[6] The opioid crisis has generated shocking headlines about the rising death rates among white middle-aged Americans, in contrast to those in every other age and ethnic group.[7] Opioid addiction started in rural, poorer parts of the country, such as Appalachia, northern New Mexico, and Utah—where jobs involving physical labor left workers vulnerable to injury, and thus painkiller addiction—and has since spread significantly throughout the West, Northeast, Oklahoma, Kentucky, Tennessee, and Florida, fueled by the introduction of superpowerful fentanyl and a rise in heroin use when people cannot obtain opioids. If you live in a city, you would most likely not have experienced this phenomenon, but in more rural communities people can't avoid it—if not personally, then seeing a friend, neighbor or relative who is addicted. While this is a political issue, it does reinforce the fragmenting nature of the experiences in the United States.

- Opioids represent just one in a series of dire changes in the experiences of low-income, middle-aged white men. Since 1970, their workforce participation has slipped 18 percent to just 79 percent, while their marriage rate has fallen to 39 percent. An important point is that men typically build a career and family during middle age. The dramatic change in the marriage rate for this group of men is only now starting to affect the broader US society and culture. Suffice to say that alongside the rejection of these norms is a concurrent rejection of consumer culture. Lack of income might explain some of this rejection, but it is deeper than that—these men no longer aspire to high levels of material ownership. They reject typical media campaigns.

However, it is also true that to understand the real level of fragmentation in the market, it is necessary to recognize that age is not the only driver of attitudes. Our attitudes are like the remix of a Top 40 hit with layers of new beats that leave the original riff noticeable but the song completely different.

One characteristic of the boomer generation is a phenomenon called the "millennial mind-set" that exists in the boomer generation. The mix of old and new attitudes are layered atop each other to create something distinctive in both age cohorts. These older consumers can be seen in the latest ripped jeans, drinking at trendy coffeehouses and moving quickly from Facebook to Snapchat. Even more important is that many boomers live by some of the "experiences over stuff" credo popularized by millennials.

(We will discuss the influence of each new generation on the preceding ones in more detail in chapter 10—especially in the context of Gen Z.)

But there are also clear differences in these age cohorts. The Harris Poll lists just one of many: 47 percent of millennials have a tattoo versus just 13 percent of boomers—but that is still quite a lot of older folks who have this similarity to the younger cohort.[8] The key point here is that even within large, clearly identified age cohorts, different attitudinal and behavioral subsegments are looking for ways to express their uniqueness—and are able to do so with all of today's selection of products and experiences.

A Widening Income Divide

But fully understanding Americans' current level of fragmentation does not end with exploring generational differences. Another important factor is the growing level of income inequality.

As Exhibit 4.5 shows, the gap between the richest 1 percent and all other Americans continues to grow. This is important for many reasons beyond the obvious ones related to human well-being. The propensity to consume more goods drops as you get wealthier, and consumers on the poorer end of the wealth gap are finding it increasingly difficult to purchase everything they need. The result: the rich get richer, the poor get poorer, and neither group is buying much, creating another factor that depresses overall demand.

Also, the wealthy and the middle class consumer a different mix of products, so the pattern of demand changes as well. The bottom 10 percent of Americans by income devote 42 percent of their spending to housing and 17 percent to food. In contrast, the

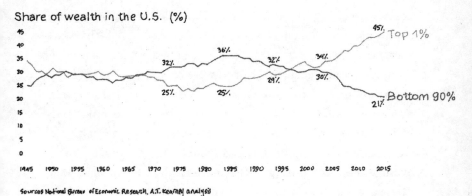

Share of wealth in the U.S. (%)

Exhibit 4.5. Share of U.S. Wealth
Since the Great Recession, income inequality has widened.

wealthiest 10 percent of Americans dedicate only 31 percent of their spending to housing and 11 percent to food. The poorest Americans also spend more of their income on transportation than do the wealthiest. So what do top earners spend more on? They put 16 percent of their income away for retirement, whereas the poorest Americans save only 2.6 percent.[9]

Finally, the push to serve the top 1 percent is the reason behind the creation of so many new business ideas. It may be that this group will build and sustain the home delivery of groceries— they have the resources to pay for the service and highly value the savings of their time.

Hidden in the bottom 90 percent are the long-suffering middle- and lower-income groups—those earning an average of $30,438 in 2012 dollars.[10] Nationally, the median income of middle-income households decreased 6 percent from 1999 to 2014, while incomes of lower-income households fell 10 percent.

And many people are dropping out of the middle class altogether. As a recent report by the Pew Research Center noted, the share of American adults living in middle-income households shrank from 61 percent in 1971 to 50 percent in 2015.[11] This stark statistic illustrates a trend that has accelerated but one that many Americans only recently became aware of.

Although incomes fell in almost every metropolitan area, as we have said, consumer experiences vary quite dramatically by locality. The ten metro areas that took the biggest wealth hits from 2000 to 2014 have one factor in common: a greater-than-average reliance on manufacturing. Most are in the Rust Belt. These areas generally saw a steep drop in the number of manufacturing jobs from 2000 to 2014, an employment sector that contracted 29 percent nationally. Making matters worse, the jobs lost in manufacturing were not always replaced by others, as overall private sector employment fell in these ten areas, with declines ranging from 3 percent to 25 percent. This is compared to a 5 percent overall *increase* in private sector employment in the United States as a whole.[12] What has made this even more difficult for these regions is that available jobs have almost all been at lower income levels and in service industries.

These regional differences help explain the anger expressed in the 2016 presidential election and are a reminder that retailers and brands speaking to a national market are likely to miss regional and community differences. In these markets many consumers felt the retailers who served them did not understand what was going on. Instead of spending money on a new pair of premium skinny jeans, these buyers may have been more likely to part with their declining wages to pay for health care or housing.

Income inequality shows no signs of abating. In fact, it's increasing. Between 2016 and 2026, the share of households earning $25,000 or less a year—putting them below the median household incomes of countries like Mexico, Venezuela and Romania—will increase by five million people, to twenty million.

Within the United States, this means a population that is more reflective of emerging markets. This bottom 15 percent will be largely new immigrants and those who have been unable to find new regular skilled employment.[13] They will fuel the continued demand for thrift stores, grocery discounters and extreme off-price retailers. The only good news for this group is that, at least in the world of products, a lot of low-priced goods will be available. In the world of services, especially health care, low-priced options will be scarce.

Income inequality is growing between generations as well. Demographics, globalization, the aftermath of the Great Recession, unemployment and underemployment are conspiring to keep millennials' wages down. This of course has significant implications for consumer spending, especially as it also dovetails with a reduction in home buying, marriage and having children, as well as what millennials expect from retailers.

Another important part of the income gap between generations has been the number of people today who are earning less than their parents did. Only 50 percent of Americans born in 1984 earned more at age thirty than their parents did at that age, down from 92 percent in 1940.[14] This has a significant influence on how individuals think about their careers, lives and ability to spend on consumer goods. The idea of being relatively poorer than your parents makes you challenge their values and goals and probably the importance you place on material possessions— something boomers valued highly.

A "Majority Minority" Nation—In More Ways than One

Often closely linked with income inequality is the growing diversity of the United States, with many nonwhite groups bearing the brunt of the impoverished conditions we have described. The implications of an increasingly diverse country in many ways dictate what is bought and where—a challenge for retailers now and in the future.

Already, many large cities are "majority minority," meaning that the nonwhite population is more than 50 percent of the total, or that no one ethnic group has a majority.

And the nation will only get more diverse with time. As we note in the sidebar to this chapter, Gen Z is the first majority minority generation—by 2026 only 48 percent of Gen Z will be white, whereas 27 percent will be Hispanic, 14 percent black, and 6 percent Asian. Ninety-five percent of population growth between 2016 and 2026 (an increase of twenty-six million) will be driven by nonwhite ethnic groups. The retail implications of this shift are extremely significant—in 2015, nonwhites accounted for 26 percent of US buying power, or $3.5 trillion, a figure that is expected to hit $5.9 trillion by 2026.[15] And of course these groups will have a concomitant social and cultural impact.

Another significant change accelerating among younger generations is the number of nontraditional households. Younger generations are less likely to get married and have kids and more likely to live alone. The United States is also seeing an increase in the number of single parents, many of whom put a premium on convenience. Time-starved single moms (predominantly) are looking for retailers and brands who understand the pressures in these women's lives. This experience has shaped many of these peoples' attitudes, and our conversations with them have revealed that these experiences have made these people more frugal in their spending patterns and more eclectic and individualistic in their fashion tastes.

Younger consumers are also more likely to live in cities, driving an overall trend toward urbanization. The United States is in the midst of a wave of migration to cities at levels not seen since the Census Bureau started tracking these data in 1970—among young, educated, relatively high-income people and older empty-nesters.[16] A hidden trend is behind this movement: the breakdown of traditional work-life styles. The classic nine-to-five job in an office has given way to a more dynamic gig economy that has more networked forms of production organized around on-demand, on-location activities. In accordance with this, we anticipate that the societal definition of "household" will be redefined to support lifestyles sustained by anytime, anywhere work and play. With work being done in so many different ways by people with less rigid lifestyles, the distinction between home and work, and even between home and work and places for socializing, will collapse. The "third place" between home and work that Starbucks defined may now become the first place people go.

This urban migration is driving up overall income levels in cities across the country and spurring a new wave of development, including retail and restaurants.

Cities overall are also becoming bigger and more dense. Urban density (people per square mile) for the fifty biggest cities in the United States has already grown 28 percent since 2006 and is expected to grow 10 percent more by 2026.[17] With this increasing density and purchasing power, cities are ground zero for successful new distribution models. People expect to see localized stores with merchandise specific to their community's wants and needs within their neighborhoods. Local stores will become distribution centers, making home delivery a given in densely populated areas.

Another emerging trend is the increasing density of the areas surrounding cities—not necessarily the suburbs (although it is happening there as well) but the immediate environs that commuters used to bypass. Driven by high property prices in cities, people are looking to build these communities so they can be closer to the cities at more affordable levels. In the Bay Area of San Francisco, Dallas, Salt Lake City, Phoenix, Nashville and Houston, this phenomenon is increasing urban sprawl.[18]

A Socioeconomic Trip Across the Country

The differences in peoples' attitudes about life and how they are manifesting themselves in identifiable behaviors also are factors creating the imbalance in supply and demand. We'll highlight a few interesting aspects of these attitudes that show the differences—a variety of socioeconomic measures that are highly indicative of attitudes and reflective of the experiential fragmentation of the United States.

We'll start with how purchasing behavior varies by location. "It turns out that relative market shares for the leading brands of widely purchased and consumed super market products, such as beer, coffee, mayonnaise and soft drinks, vary considerably throughout the US," David Bell reports in his 2014 book, *Location Is Still Everything*.[19] He provides an interesting example of how loyal people in the Northeast remain to Maxwell House coffee versus Folgers coffee, which is much more popular in San Francisco. It turns out that Folgers was introduced in San Francisco and Maxwell House in the Northeast. Decades later, you would think people had forgotten that and competition would level the playing field between the brands, but that hasn't happened.

The same is true for many brands—think Coke's popularity in Atlanta versus Pepsi's: Coke is so dominant that people call any kind of soda, or pop, "Coke." What we thought most interesting was Bell's finding that even when people move from Boston to San Francisco, for example, their preference for their original coffee remains strong, even after twenty years, than locals (never mind that most taste tests reveal that few people are able to distinguish between brands). The interesting point here is that long-held purchasing behaviors are heavily influenced, maybe even determined, by the attitudes and preferences of the communities that we live in (the advice and opinions of friends and neighbors), the historical roots of the products, and the area's cultural roots. This is happening even though all these communities are diverging and fragmenting, which will ultimately have an enormous impact on the strategic and structural transformation of all consumer-facing industries.

Married same-sex couples, for example, are clustered along both coasts and in urban areas. In fact, same-sex married couples cluster in clearly defined pockets, and their numbers are drastically lower in all other parts of the country. Retailers and brands that tend to do well in those communities are both innovative and often somewhat antiestablishment. It is no surprise that many of the new digitally native (born online with an e-commerce website or mobile app) retail start-ups do well in those areas, only to find that customer acquisition stalls when they try to grow elsewhere. Change-embracing cultures are open to having a mattress or pair of glasses delivered without having tried them out—but people elsewhere? Not so much.

Another example is retailers in rural counties who are more focused and serve niches; these businesses tend to cater to a more rugged, individualistic consumer, offer security, and do well. A perfect example is Tractor Supply, the home improvement and lawn and garden retailer, which tends to open stores in rural communities with a broad product range—including guns, pet supplies, and rugged footwear. The retailer offers a psychologically supportive environment to those in communities that identify as libertarian and are concerned about their personal defense and freedom. Tractor Supply grew by taking share from its specialty "category killer" competitors. Unlike many brands, it offered a community of brand enthusiasts and everything they need to live and work.

This broad assortment and tribal feel are even more important in the Internet age, when consumers can be even pickier about finding just what they're looking for and support brands that align with their views. For example, if you came from England (as Michael does) and lived in a town with stores that did not sell your favorite English products (think Yorkshire tea), you tended to buy Lipton's and become part of the mass market. But now, with the endless cyberaisle you can search for the products you like, you have no need to go to the common denominator in the brick-and-mortar store. The mass market has eroded and Michael gets his pick-me-up cup of tea. This new ability to access any niche thing, anytime, anywhere is true not only for hard-to-find brands but also for people's attitudes and opinions.

The essential point is that local attitudes and values have been diverging quite dramatically across the country, further fragmenting the marketplace. These divergent behaviors are clearly noticeable and are continuing to increase. People are having different experiences based purely on where they live. The thought that a flat world (one that's increasingly globalized, interconnected, and fast-paced) meant that our experiences would converge is proving to be wrong.

We see it in politics and news—but also in the proliferation of food trends: a growth in popularity of vegetarianism, the surge in veganism, a growing gluten-free movement, a focus on organic and local foods—all generally happening among higher-income Americans. Juxtaposing these against lingering food deserts, where many of the poorest Americans can't buy produce or other healthy foods of any kind in their neighborhoods, shows how fragmented these trends are. Even in the realm of health we see a dramatic difference across regions.

Even something as simple as smoking varies dramatically by region. Smokers are more likely to be male, young, have a low amount of education, live in the South or Midwest and live below the poverty level.[20] This group has interesting and views on brands and retailers, which can be characterized broadly as traditional, conservative and adverse to change. One example: they love Levi's jeans but hate the brand's current marketing, which they view as an attempt to change its historical identity. The question is whether these traditional attitudes will become mainstream in the same way hip-hop music and attitudes have evolved. Few retailers or brands speak directly to this group, but they are out there with distinct needs and desires—and incomes.

Polar Opposites

One thing all these trends have in common is that they're happening in pockets—not to everyone, just to certain groups in certain places. For example, people are increasingly surrounding themselves with others who look and think like them and have similar incomes.

People are separating themselves physically and psychologically from those who are not like them. Between 1970 and 2012, many families moved out of middle-class neighborhoods and into affluent ones, further sealing themselves off from the rest of the country. During that time, the percentage of families with kids living in very affluent neighborhoods—defined as those with a median income more than 1.5 times that of the metropolitan area in which they're located—more than doubled, and the majority of those gains came at the expense of middle-class neighborhoods. In 1970, 64.7 percent of families lived in one of these affluent neighborhoods compared with only 40.5 percent of families in 2012.[21]

So when boomers grew up, the vast majority of kids lived in neighborhoods full of people solidly in the middle class, and (despite income differences within the middle class) they had access to the same schools, friends and social activities. That is not the case anymore. The wealthy spend more money on private schools, private sport teams, tuition, and social activities than ever before—dramatically so in fact—but fewer and fewer members of the diverging middle class join them. From 1990 to 2012 the average private school tuition, as measured in 2012 dollars, went up 116 percent. Sports are also becoming more expensive and attracting fewer and fewer blue collar fans—pro football ticket prices have gone up more than 50 percent since 2006, while pro hockey tickets became 17 percent more expensive in the same time period. No wonder a third of these fans, compared with just 19 percent of all Americans, earn more than $100,000 a year.[22]

The same is true when it comes to education—more people with college degrees are living next to each other than ever before.[23] They are also marrying others with college degrees (and from similar universities) at a higher rate than ever before. People are clearly marrying others from their socioeconomic group (education level and background) at unprecedented rates. Gone are the days when the boss married his (or her) secretary or assistant. The concentration of married couples living in communities with other married couples is increasing (all these are correlated with income as well).[24]

The same is true of race. While the segregation of African Americans has declined significantly since 1960, they are still nearly three times as segregated from whites as are wealthy and poorer Americans of any race. Meanwhile, immigrants, Latinos,

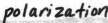

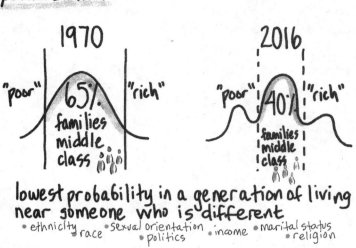

polarization

1970   2016

"poor" 65% "rich"   "poor" 40% "rich"

families middle class

families middle class

lowest probability in a generation of living near someone who is different
• ethnicity • race • sexual orientation • politics • income • marital status • religion

Exhibit 4.6. Polarization

and Asians have all become more segregated over time.[25] The bottom line is that whether you are walking out your front door, attending a kids' sports event, or going to a social activity, the probability of meeting people who are different from you is at its lowest level in a generation. Our society is fragmenting into like-minded niches.

Retail Implications

As we have said, the fragmentation we have identified here is inhibiting the ability of retailers to drive mass demand and is increasing the supply of many niche brands or products. Why? Because of the incredible segmentation in the consumer base across almost every dimension. The implications for retailers are clear. First, they must cater to changing demographics. For example, the growth in sales of tomato ketchup averaged

-0.2 percent from 2011 to 2015, whereas niche brands of chili sauces have seen 7.1 percent growth on average as the US Latino population continues to flourish and foodies expand their taste buds.

Brands will also have to reckon with a fast-proliferating set of consumer preferences that are creating an infinite number of finite markets. For example, the grocery category has been shifting from Kraft Foods to craft foods. Huge food companies are losing significant market share to start-ups, organic and localized brands, and smaller grocery stores that are buying from local farmers. For example, the domestic organic food market grew 12 percent nationally from 2014 to 2015, according to the US Department of Agriculture, and local food sales hit $12 billion in 2014, up from $5 billion in 2008, an average annual growth of about 7 percent.[26]

Meanwhile, niche players are thriving. Campbell's Soup Company lost 13 percent of its market share from 2005 to 2014, while Amy's Kitchen, a family-owned producer of organic and non-GMO frozen foods, saw its share grow 175 percent, according to Euromonitor International, a market research company. Amy's is just one of many small, authentic players all pecking away at pieces of traditional brands' markets, forcing them to figure out how to create their own special niches across their enormous enterprises. Another example is the explosive rise of craft beers, which in 2015 accounted for 12 percent of the US beer market. That year, the number of American breweries grew 15 percent, the biggest growth at any time in US history, according to the Brewers Association.[27]

Even an iconic American brand like Levi's has fallen victim to this trend. The company was flying high with $7.1 billion in sales as recently as 1996—making it bigger than Nike at the time. But its consumers were picked off by a host of smaller competitors coming from all sides—superpremium brands like 7 for All Mankind and True Religion attacked from the top while more value-oriented brands like Lee and Wrangler nibbled away at the bottom. Levi's sales bottomed out at $4.2 billion in 2003 and haven't grown much since, hitting $4.5 billion in 2015.[28] And it's not just jeans—the khaki icon Dockers, also owned by Levi's, finds itself newly on the defensive from upstart brands like Bonobos, which Walmart appears to believe can be taken to the mass market,[29] and which grew more than 200 percent in its early years.[30] Brands like Levi's, though still benefiting from strong loyalty, will have a hard time finding growth in the saturated, fragmenting US market.

Retailers are rushing to adjust to this new reality. Many mass retailers are applying this approach to niche segments—see Whole Foods's efforts to locally source 15 to 30 percent of its products in any given store and its more recent efforts to appeal to a younger, lower-income demographic with its 365 stores (maybe a big reason Amazon likes them!). While such initiatives have had some success across the retail industry, retailers will need to do even more to make themselves compelling and convenient to an increasingly diverse set of niches. Retailers have found vastly different preferences by neighborhood—even within the same city—for things like convenience, ethnic foods, and healthy product offerings, demonstrating that fragmentation drives real purchasing differences.

Americans are now living in the fragmented states of America, and the implications for retailers and brands are life altering. Next we will explore one of the primary engines driving the changes we discussed in this chapter, which is not only driving more overcapacity, shifting patterns of demand, and increasing fragmentation but is also providing a way to address them. We refer, of course, to technology.

CHAPTER 5

THE TECHNOLOGY CATALYST

Obviously, technology has been a key vehicle in increasing the supply of goods coming to market with new delivery and sales channels. It also has created a whole series of new business models that are still in their infancy and are reshaping the retail landscape. Finally, technology has changed the retail experience for consumers in their everyday lives, and this is both stealing time from traditional shopping trips and radically shifting why people come or will come to stores in the future.

Why Early E-Commerce Failed and Today's E-Commerce Won't

The networked world first came into Americans' consciousness with a huge bang and then seemed to disappear with a whimper. In the late 1990s, the first dotcom bubble seemed to offer a lot of promise about the potential of the newly emerging Internet to reshape commerce. But within a few short years, most of the businesses promising to do this had failed.

Early efforts at e-commerce were doomed to fail for two big

reasons: a lack of excess supply and technological hurdles yet to be cleared, namely, the infrastructure.

First, businesses were not experiencing today's level of excess supply of goods looking to get to market. In the 1990s, rival companies, such as Petstore.com and Pets.com or Furniture.com and eToys.com, were unable to get the products that would make their business models sing. Brands, packaged goods companies and retailers were all aghast at the thought of Internet start-ups and simply refused to sell to them. The business risks of annoying their established channel partners was too great, so the idea of an endless aisle was a dream because only a few products were readily available to the consumer.

An early tour through the websites of that era, courtesy of Internet Archive, shows storefronts that had relatively few product choices and unimaginative presentation (see Exhibit 5.1 for Amazon's early look). Low prices were the main purchase driver for these sites, and many had distribution models that were either nonexistent or overly ambitious, with companies like Kozmo and Urbanfetch both promising free delivery of books, music, movies, electronics, personal care items, food, and more in less than an hour. Few people thought that this new Internet sales craze was going to yield much after the massive dot.com bust in early 2000.

One infamous example of this era was Webvan, a grocery home delivery service. The company went from a value of $1.2 billion and forty-five hundred employees to liquidation in less than two years. Within eighteen months of opening for business, it had spent more than $1 billion on a series of warehouses at $30 million each in its rush to rapidly expand and simultaneously into multiple US cities; it went public and raised almost $400 million dollars. But the lack of selection, high costs, and low customer density (which meant distribution was not economical) made Webvan's model one of the most public failures

Welcome to Amazon.com Books!

One million titles, consistently low prices

SPOTLIGHT! -- AUGUST 16TH

ONE MILLION TITLES

EYES & EDITORS, A PERSONAL NOTIFICATION SERVICE

Exhibit 5.1. Welcome to Amazon
Amazon's first homepage is a far cry from its current selection and personalization.

in an era of many failures. If you don't have good products, you can't satisfy the consumer. But a few business models did survive despite the lack of access to product.

Amazon's ability to survive rested largely on its choice of a category (books), which was highly vulnerable to online competition because of commoditization, the ease of offering a large assortment, availability and relative economy of distribution networks (US Postal Service, UPS, FedEx), and no need for a consumer to try anything on. Amazon's original name was Cadabra, but Jeff Bezos changed it because it sounded too much like *cadaver*. Bezos's parents were the company's first two investors in 1995, and its initial public offering came two years later, just as it introduced one-click shipping. It survived and slowly began to expand its offerings of items other than books.

EBay, another survivor, offered peer-to-peer sales and a marketing and distribution approach that also allowed it to use existing inventory and delivery infrastructure. Clearly, as the examples of eBay and Amazon show, early web successes made the limited access to product and the physical world work to their advantage. Amazon leveraged a vulnerable category and exploited the existing distribution networks, whereas eBay relied on millions of products their owners no longer wanted.

However, as product supply increased during the next two decades, so did the pressure to find new distribution avenues for the growing supply of product. By 2008, the pressure was becoming more intense, and online was becoming an increasingly attractive channel for distribution. Online sales totaled $141 billion in 2008, or just 3.6 percent of total retail sales. During the next eight years online sales would rise fourfold, to $420 billion and 8.4 percent of total sales by 2016.[1] In the fall of 2016 and into early 2017, the online world exploded even more.

Why did this happen? For one thing, the consumer got comfortable with ordering online. The Great Recession created such an excess of supply that every retailer or brand rushed to sell their products—at almost any price and anywhere. Technology had provided a new channel that, given the level of excess supply that businesses needed to sell, could not be ignored. Enter Gilt Groupe, Groupon, Rue La La, and numerous other discount sales channels. Enter Amazon, which was offering consumers almost any product in any category through its store, and now the supply lines opened up. Enter all the existing retailers trying to unload their stagnant inventory through their own websites. The online retail world was achieving scale—but not quite the velocity it needed for liftoff. That would take a little longer.

This new technology and disruption might not have made such a big difference in consumer and retail markets if the existing players had been able to control those markets. After all, large incumbent retailers had little incentive to unleash the full power of the Internet—they rather liked a controlled and measured way to grow their stores, increasing their sales by managing pricing. But a series of start-ups had the incentive to use the new aspects of technology and that proved highly disruptive. Start-ups flourished and were able to capitalize on the increasingly networked world because from 2010 to 2016 a series of conditions favored fast, nimble competitors.

What were these conditions? The first and perhaps most crucial was the almost unlimited access to capital for funding unprofitable start-ups (even Amazon). We leave why this occurred to a study of the financial industry.

However, we will explore three other factors that also were critical: the rapidly changing or fragmenting consumer preferences, the emergence of new distribution mechanisms, and a dramatic change in the cost of acquiring customers.

First, as we discussed in chapters 2 and 3, there's no doubt the United States is witnessing a once-in-a-lifetime shift in customer preferences, fueled in part by changing attitudinal, demographic, societal and geographic factors.

All these changes have offered nimble competitors opportunities to win customers. Tastes in food, cosmetics, and drinks are also shifting and fragmenting. People are looking for products that closely match their specific tastes, as evidenced by the growth of emerging food brands; drinks, such as the wave of cold-pressed juices, kombucha and natural soda like Zevia; the popularity of Greek yogurt led by Chobani, which went from zero to $1 billion in less than five years; and the host of new all-natural beauty brands like Axiology and Aster & Bay. Hot chili sauces, new soups and organic foods all have exploded. Even Twinkies have roared back. All this fragmentation favors start-ups as the big brands try to continue to use scale with mega-brands.

The second change wrought by technology is the creation of new distribution mechanisms. A simple and obvious example is books, which are now (because of technology) both ordered and delivered physically from Amazon and through new digital platforms to Kindles and iPads. As the networked world has further developed and linked to the physical world, the variety of new distribution options is expanding. Amazon, eBay, and Alibaba have provided instantaneous access to a large market for almost any new product or service. Instacart, Google Express, Blue Apron, Postmates, Grubhub, Eat24, Caviar, and a host of others will bring food to consumers. The crowdsourcing model of Deliv provides all small-scale independent retailers with the ability to offer home delivery, so even the newest, smallest retailers can efficiently reach their niche consumer base. Technology has dramatically changed the consumption of media, with Amazon and Netflix now both producing content as well as distributing it.

In a world of superabundance and price deflation, the ability to compete on distribution becomes increasingly critical. Convenience is at the forefront of the consumer's mind. The new ability to buy product online or by using mobile devices and quickly receive it at home offers all sorts of other benefits to the consumer that stores struggle to match.

The final ingredient that has favored new start-ups is a radical shift in customer acquisition costs. The arrival of Google, Facebook, and other social networking sites created a short-term opportunity for new, agile companies to reach millions of potential customers. With the large brands slow to react, these ad spaces were initially mispriced, and start-ups exploited that advantage to reach new customers at low cost. For example, Bonobos's Facebook campaign was so successful that the social network at one point drove 10 percent of the clothier's site traffic. Meanwhile, Burt's Bees used video on Facebook to garner hundreds of thousands of new likes—and sales. And the fashion site HauteLook used Facebook to advertise exclusive sale items, generating 10 percent of sales and doubling conversion rates.[2] All the while incumbents were asleep. The ability of brands like Warby Parker (inexpensive glasses), Gilt Groupe (providing low-cost access to brands), Groupon (discounted services and products), and many others to grow rapidly is a direct result of their exploitation of digital marketing and access to social media. Many large retail and consumer companies missed out on using social media and digital advertising for a long time.

The purveyors of every consumer and retail brand suddenly realized that they also had to develop their own technology and increase the number of ways in which to serve their customers. This has meant excess supply is now getting to market through more avenues and faster than ever. The Internet has broken the ability of retail stores to bottleneck the amount of product that gets to market and they will never recapture it.

So every retailer has dashed to create an online presence. The hockey great Wayne Gretsky claimed that his success owed to his ability to go to where the puck was going to be, not where it was. If this applied to retailers, they would all belatedly be dashing to where the puck already is: online. The trouble is that now are all spending a lot of money trying to make the online world work. The net increase in investment this requires, its corrosive impact on total margin, and the impact on store traffic have caused further confusion and panic in the retail world.

The problem is that for every sale that moves from an existing retail store to the same retailer's e-commerce business, margin deteriorates. That's right: by selling online the exact same product sold in a store, every existing business loses some profit.

So the actions of existing retailers are attacking their entire business model. This is retail executives' single biggest frustration today. How is it possible for start-ups to achieve huge valuations while making no profit by selling online, yet established businesses lose value when they do the same?

Exacerbating the problem is that most retailers' supply chains were built for mass efficiency, not small online orders and high return rates. The costs of trying to change this or manage the activities of each channel are enormous. For example, having store labor pick and pack an item to ship from the store or for the consumer to pick up in-store, or to handle online purchases returned in-store, is costly and complicated. In fact, the levels of investment required to achieve full channel integration—that is, to give consumers the same experience online and in-store—and support online sales doesn't make economic sense for most retailers yet apparently must be done. Suffice it to say that achieving full channel integration requires a complete redesign of the overhead structure, supply chain and customer acquisition process.

The end result is a massive increase in supply and easy access for the consumer. All at an increasingly low and known price. That's right, technology has also destroyed retailers' ability to control price.

One big ramification of the Internet is that it has radically changed the way the consumer behaves. Obviously, by shopping online, searching ahead of buying, and getting peer and expert reviews, the consumer is using technology at every step. Technology has upended assumptions long held by behavioral economists about the "irrationality" of the consumer.

Price is one of those assumptions. Today, because of the digital revolution, consumers will increasingly find online the absolute value that they place on a product and will not be manipulated to pay more. Recent studies describe an experiment that asked which consumers to choose one of two shredders: one costs $20 and shreds seven sheets at a time, and one that costs $50 and shreds eleven sheets at a time. With just these two options, people are more likely to perceive the $20 shredder as the better value. But if you add a third shredder for $95 that can handle twelve sheets, suddenly the $50 shredder seems like a better value. People actually chose that option more frequently. Then add technology to the mix. Researchers ran the same experiment in an "Amazon-like" environment that offered consumers a variety of options and prices, as well as consumer reviews. This time the $20 shredder did as well at its more expensive counterpart, even with the introduction of the $95 shredder.[3] In other words, the tests that once supposedly proved consumers' irrationality do not reflect the new real world in which people seek out other options and opinions, discuss things in chat rooms and compare prices. Consumers are becoming smarter and less open to easy manipulation.

As this experiment shows, the ability to manipulate consumer behavior to drive incremental profit or purchases is, and will become, increasingly more difficult, if not impossible. In fact, such manipulation will end up eroding the consumer's trust unless retailers are transparent about why they are making changes in their offerings.

Right now, dynamic online pricing may provide an opportunity for short-term gain, but consumers eventually will recognize, dislike and spread the word about this gaming. Many consumers have already become frustrated with Amazon's frequent price changes, and entrepreneurs such as the minds behind Tracktor.com and Keepa.com have developed ways to track these price changes. Amazon changes its prices an estimated 2.5 million times a day—affecting 15 to 20 percent of its inventory—compared with the perhaps 50,000 changes made by a traditional big-box retailer in a month. Amazon's changes also hit when consumers are more likely to be shopping in a particular category, for example, video games in the evening. Amazon generally prices its best-selling big ticket items below the competition's but increases prices for less expensive but related items, such as cables for a TV, betting that consumers won't bother to comparison-shop smaller purchases.[4]

All this should sound a warning to those analytic groups looking to use pricing to increase profit in their store pricing. Assuming that historic elasticities (the rate at which sales are gained or lost as a result of price changes) will hold is a big leap of faith; thanks to the smartphone, peer commentary, and expert opinions, consumers know you are trying to exploit them. So as prices fall because of supply exceeds demand, retailers will not be able to charge higher prices. Technology will also ultimately drive shipping costs to zero as well—thanks in part to the self-driving car's capacity to make deliveries constantly, efficiently, and without costly labor.

New Business Models

The API (application programmable interface) is a layer of software that enables every device to communicate with every other device. It also defines the nature and structure of that communication. Think of it as the air traffic controller that determines both which planes (information) land where and when, and which ones take off (which information is shared). As we've discussed with experts at the Institute for the Future, a nonprofit think tank based in Palo Alto, California, the API is why so many new business models that have developed and are changing the way we consume and what we buy.

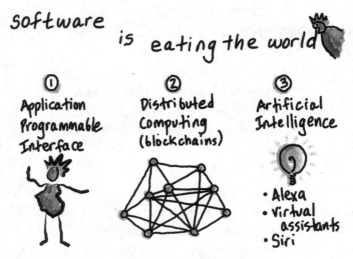

Exhibit 5.2. Software Is Eating the World

As the world has become increasingly networked, the need to manage communications and data flows has become dramatically more important, which means that APIs play an outsized role in the modern world. APIs are essential for sharing data—they make Facebook, Google Maps, and smartphones work. They make possible the massive scale of content on YouTube, dispatch the car for Uber, make rooms available for Airbnb, manage Amazon's internal systems, and on and on. We now take for granted that Instagram uses Foursquare's API to provide location tagging and opens its own API up to other apps, and that Uber, Lyft and Airbnb use Google Maps's API to show the locations of their cars or rental properties. But if you think back to 2008—the last year of George W. Bush's administration, the year the Great Recession hit in full force—these uses were only in their infancy.

Salesforce, today a $6 billion cloud-based company that manages customer relationships, launched what may have been the first big API in 2000, giving customers the power to share data across different platforms. EBay soon followed with its own API, making it easier for third-party partners to integrate with the site and helping both parties grow.[5]

Many of the properties that exist because of this new and easy programming interface are driving the retail revolution and emergence of new business models. How do they do this?

First, because of their nature, once APIs solve a problem, that solution is suddenly readily available to everybody (APIs cannot yet be patented). So once Google created Google Maps, all sorts of businesses—from Waze to Yelp to Disney—could build on that and create their own functionality. From local store websites that now can give you directions to their stores to some of the most important new businesses (Uber and Airbnb), all are rapidly enabled by APIs. Once Uber figured out how to place cars on Google Maps, the next layer of development occurred— Instacart, Deliv, and others arrived and placed grocery stores and delivery vehicles on the map. APIs are enabling the rapid proliferation of new business models.

APIs also made it possible for communications to become two-way. Suddenly, consumers and producers were interchangeable—their data are equally important to a company's success. Think about how Uber's success hinges on having lots of drivers and lots of passengers (and being able to connect them). This technology has singlehandedly uprooted traditional organizational models, from cabs to hotels to restaurants, while allowing a whole new array of relationships to develop. Because of this ability to enable two-way communications, APIs also help create businesses that thrive on the network effect of simultaneously increasing producers and customers (or drivers and passengers in the case of Uber). Network effects are typically defined as those businesses that create value in direct proportion to the number of participants within the system.

They can and likely will change multiple aspects of a business, such as who controls what is said about a brand, designs a product or decides when to work. The new flow of information makes the answer to those questions uncertain, but it is highly unlikely that they will be driven from the top down. An API allows Harley-Davidson to help riders plan trips, find cool stops along the way and share them with their friends, inspiring greater connectivity among members of the Harley tribe. This simply wasn't possible before the API existed. And so as a result of APIs, companies will be able to better engage with their customers and have their customers better engage with each other and the larger brand.

Another key feature of the brave new networked world made possible in large part by APIs is that underused assets have suddenly become valuable, whether that's a spare bedroom, a parked car, space in a store, or relationships. As tech experts at the Institute for the Future told us, "When they [APIs] enter a new sector, they lower the overhead of signaling and delivering information and services to just about zero. Now this is kind of a subtle point, but it means that most of you probably have idle assets or underutilized capacities that you could offer to others at almost no cost to you, by allowing APIs to negotiate and dispatch them for you. And you don't even necessarily need to know what the use case is for your asset."

But the impact of the rapid development and application of APIs does not end there. They help tight communities of users move seamlessly through the world without friction. A good example is Disney's MagicBands in its theme parks—wristbands that let users enter the parks, unlock their rooms at the resort, buy food and merchandise, and get access to customized experiences. Using sensors scattered around the park, Disney can keep track of everyone within it, and, of particular interest to the company, all of its customers can spend money with the quick flick of a wrist. Other examples already live inside the pockets of most people and/or on their wrists: smartphones and smartwatches. The ability to eliminate frustrating frictions has allowed a whole new level of convenience and a chance to connect with consumers on a more meaningful level.

Retailers have yet to fully explore APIs' ability to reduce friction. APIs could lead to great new ways to transact and allow stores to create entirely new experiences by building on the layers of technology others have developed—say, a seamless checkout with the swipe of a wrist, interactive displays based on anything from your inbox to your Netflix queue and more. They enable the creation of new spaces for people to communicate and develop ideas free from commerce and controlled by the community (Wikipedia). They are even uprooting the world of money by giving users the ability to create whole chains of verified transactions to facilitate payments. Bitcoin and its operating system, Blockchain, is doing just that. In doing this, APIs will also enable a whole new world of "dark commerce" in the darknet (the system designed by the Defense Advanced Research Products Agency, which also devised the Internet, that provides a more secure and selective platform because it is outside the view, or beyond the control, of central authorities). Paradoxically, in low-trust environments, such as among drug dealers or weapons smugglers, APIs can create high-trust networks. The power of Bitcoin and other payment systems means that money could become obsolete—with whom people trade and how they get paid may all be handled by an API.

In fact, block chains are coming and will have a big impact on retail. Still in its infancy, the block chain is a publicly available "distributed ledger" that allows for immediate authentication of who owns which assets, performs certain tasks or has paid their bills is currently in its infancy. Block chain was formed to make Bitcoin work, but it has since evolved far beyond a singular purpose. It's a way to distribute but not copy information—think the same spreadsheet copied across thousands of computers, and one click of a button updates them all. Because block chain has something to offer everyone (easier to manage and less expensive for businesses, secure and collaborative for consumers), it will become popular and have a profound effect on the way people work and live. Today it is hard to imagine the gig economy will ever be more than Uber and similar companies, but in the future people will be able to form unique groups that perform all sorts of tasks or living arrangements by validating each other through public block-chain records. All this will make moot the need for centrally controlled and managed databases. Banks spend an estimated $200 billion a year on information technology and fees; block-chain technology offers the ability to drastically cut this amount. Nearly every bank will start a block-chain project in the near future. This will accelerate block-chain development and its adoption into the broader economy. With the power of distributed computing and block chains' ability to enable secure, trusted collaboration and commerce, a whole new wave of technology that connects people is coming: peer-to-peer commerce.

As computing power increases, especially for hand-held devices, individuals will be able to transact with one another on a one-to-one basis with increasing ease. No one will control a central server—block chain will handle the payment method, verify the transaction and vouch for the reputation of the particpants. This entire approach will challenge the big platforms that exist today (like Amazon and Uber). Its impact won't be felt for many years, but the potential for a postplatform or centralized retail world is emerging. Take a look at Openbazaar.com, a de-

distributed computing

blockchains
+
massive hand-held computing power
=
peer to peer commerce

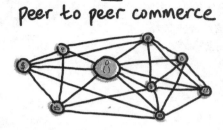

Exhibit 5.3. Distributed Computing

centralized online market where users can buy from or sell to one another—with no fees or restrictions—using Bitcoin, and ask yourself whether this is likely to be as revolutionary as Amazon was in 1995.

Even today, there is a platform version of the future. Amazon's Firefly app lets users take a photo of an object, and the app instantly brings up a description and link to purchase it on Amazon, making our entire world into one huge store. This also makes the effect of wanting to belong in a certain community even more pronounced—now, people can see someone cool wearing or using a certain product and buy it on the spot.

It's impossible not to conclude that these new business models have destroyed the bottlenecks that once controlled what was produced, marketed and sold and by whom. The retail world that existed since early in the twentieth century was centrally built for the car and is now being reconfigured for software in an

Exhibit 5.4. Virtually Intelligent New Paths

increasingly fragmented and decentralized manner. This insight is a big one. The industries and companies that are most susceptible to radical change because of this software are those with a bottleneck, some part of their process or system that prevents them from scaling quickly and effectively. In retail, one such bottleneck is the merchandise buying, planning, and assortment function—and that's why the creation of the endless aisle is so powerful. The ability to break the grip of a planner who determines what you can see or buy has made that function and control point much less valuable. The ability of APIs to make it possible to do that job better is at the heart of the digital revolution. It is also at the heart of our thesis about how oversupply is gaining rapid access to the consumer.

Another technology we must discuss is artificial intelligence, since it will power another wave of disruptive technology that will cause even more dislocation. These technologies include personal assistants and speech recognition devices like Echo or Alexa by Amazon. The technology has matured enough that it soon will be possible to have an assistant for every aspect of your life—from personal coaching to healthy eating and fitness to managing your day and appointments and buying things for you (without your asking).

These devices will learn about you and become the basis for true personalization. Their disruptive power in regard to shopping behavior will be immense because the power of your habits today will be reflected in these devices, and those companies that own the interface will probably own your wallet. If your device, with all its knowledge, suddenly suggests that you should try a new shampoo, has found a great offer for it, and is ready to order it for you, will you refuse? Some companies already are pushing this envelope: Messenger's Chat SDK (Facebook's intelligent as-

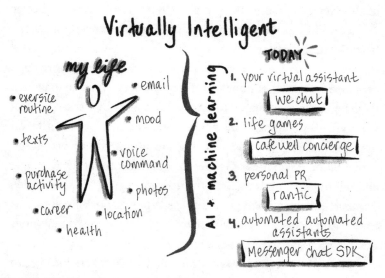

Exhibit 5.5. Virtually Intelligent My Life

sistant), WeChat Secretary (offering advice to foreigners in Beijing), and Cafe Well Concierge (which is beginning to offer health advice).

Retail also is likely to see a major disruption from the creation of new business models that harness the network effect, giving them competitive advantages over the existing retail network. What do we mean by that?

To review: Network effects are typically defined as those businesses that create value in direct proportion to the number of participants within the system. An easy example is eBay. EBay depended on both sellers and buyers on the site to make it function. As more sellers put goods up for sale, more buyers came to eBay instead of other sites, which in turn led to a virtual cycle. In the early days of the Internet, more sellers putting goods on the site made eBay the only place to auction items and later just to buy and sell.

This effect is especially prevalent in technology-inspired businesses—the same is true for Uber (more drivers=better service=more customers=more drivers want to work for Uber); Airbnb (more renters=better place to post your room=more rooms=more renters); the iPhone (more customers=more apps developed for the iPhone=more customers want to have an iPhone). Google was able to dominate search by using the network effect—its algorithm incorporates the number of links on any given web page and information about where people go (more Google searches=Google knows more about what people are looking for=better search results=more people use Google). The first-mover advantage for these types of businesses is immense and helps explain why there is typically only one winner in a technology-driven category.

This insight is immensely important for retailers looking to compete online. The reason is quite simple. Amazon benefits from the network effect, which makes it almost impossible for others to catch up or compete. Why, over time, will you ever bother with a local store's online site or even a big-box site if Amazon offers the same product? You already go to Amazon for almost everything, so why divert your spending to another site? It's just not worth the effort, especially because you'll find less selection and probably a clunky performance anywhere else. Maybe Walmart.com with its Jet.com purchase and scale can compete, but few others are able to. Amazon today is almost eleven times larger than Walmart.com—the next biggest online business—which is itself two to three times larger than the next on the list—Target.com.

On top of the consumer-driven effect (more customers on Amazon mean you need to sell on Amazon, which attracts more customers to Amazon) are the supply-driven economies of scale (the ability to spread a huge distribution investment across especially high volumes). Amazon can provide lower-cost delivery than anyone else because of classic scale economics. The ability to manage delivery fleet capacity and costs and therefore offer "subscribe and save" purchases (with delivery windows of a few days) should send shivers down the spine of all retailers who assumed they were immune to online orders because of delivery costs. Walmart will be next to build this capability.

One other great advantage is buried inside Amazon: its ability to eliminate frustrating frictions. The wonders of the simple payment system, the beauty of Prime, excellent customer service and the vast array of products make it a frictionless site that others cannot compete with. If you suddenly want to buy laundry detergent, soap, or your groceries, for example, why would you go to the local store's website or the big-box website and enter all your data again instead of going to Amazon? You won't. Of course, all those stores will get customers and their business will grow at first, but they will likely never achieve economies of scale. As a result, every retailer should be asking: Will my e-commerce business ever provide a return on the capital invested? The bottom line is that the network effect of technology-driven businesses makes the purely off-line retailers' push into online a long, hard road—unless of course you sell products that have no competition on Amazon or your business itself can take advantage of technology.

A couple of examples exist. First is Under Armour with its big push into data, tracking performance and nutrition with the acquisitions of MapMyFitness, MyFitnessPal and Endomondo. Nike is doing the same with its connective technology. Starbucks's rewards app and innovative partnership with the superpopular Pokemon Go game help draw and reward consumers. All these will help sell the physical product and may create their own network effects. The problem is that most businesses do not have the opportunity to do this. So the questions become: How can you play with Amazon? How should you invest in your own site? How likely are you to lose money (and how much) in the process?

Retailers and consumer brands face one other big challenge in regard to technology-related innovation: the incredible benefits that accrue from being located in a center that has a technology focus—something most retailers are not. The loose, collaborative corporate culture of Silicon Valley helps companies learn from each other and fosters better, more universal products—in contrast to the more hierarchical structure of many companies. For example, many companies' technology efforts mirror those of Boston's Route 128, an early tech outpost like Silicon Valley that quickly fizzled because of a lack of idea-sharing by firms.

As a study by the regional development expert AnnaLee Saxenian suggested,

> [Silicon Valley's] dense social networks and open labor markets encourage entrepreneurship and experimentation. Companies compete intensely while at the same time learning from one another about changing markets and technologies through informal communication and collaborative practices. . . . In contrast the Route 128 region is dominated by autarkic corporations that internalize a wide range of productive activities. Practices of secrecy and corporate loyalty govern relations between these firms [employees] and their customers, suppliers, and competitors, reinforcing a regional culture that encourages stability and self-reliance.

Even the buildings of successful tech companies are designed to foster collaboration. Take Apple's new headquarters, a glass-wrapped donut nicknamed "the Spaceship," that was designed to encourage mingling and conversation across various departments.

Because most retailers don't have the benefit of being located in Silicon Valley, Seattle, or a similarly nurturing environment, most retailers will not be able to use and keep up with the latest technology innovations and must always anticipate being a buyer of these services. This is not to say that retailers or brands cannot deploy technology well, but their ability to make technology a true competitive advantage is limited. Most likely, true technology breakthroughs will come from start-ups. The speed with which technology will evolve means retail has a great need for collaborative partnerships but also a realistic assessment of the economic returns of technology.

Changing Consumer Behavior

Technology has created one of the biggest changes in the way people allocate their time. Recent studies have shown that people have allocated a substantial amount of time to going online at the expense of other activities, particularly going to the mall. Indeed, a recent Pew study found one-fifth of Americans report going online "almost constantly."[6] Meanwhile, from June 2015 to June 2016, monthly mall visits were down an average of 4.5 percent year-over-year.[7] They haven't increased since a brief blip in 2012. The reality is people now have so much freshness, personalization, and entertainment at their fingertips that a trip to the traditional mall or store is totally uninspiring or plain boring. Reinventing the mall and the store is the next great retail challenge.

Final Observations About Technology

The Internet as we know it is broken. With so many recent data breaches—Netflix, Yahoo, eBay, LinkedIn, Dropbox, and many more—it's clear that Internet security is fractured. It is only a matter of time before even more massive attacks occur on the network using both artificial intelligence and the large number of devices now connected to it. Every retailer is exposed and the risks are only increasing. The true risks and costs associated with online transactions are not reflected in their operating economics. The ability of organized crime to further disrupt the web will escalate so significantly that the Internet will probably have to be completely redesigned or transactions will move onto the darknet, which provides a more secure and selective platform— which is of course why there is so much illegal activity there. You must prepare for this event. For it is likely to shake your world in the future.

Since we are on the subject of the darknet, it is worth noting how technology is disrupting even the illegal retail world. The drug trade is being uprooted. A business based on local territory (markets) and governed by intimidation and violence is going online, where the price, customer service, quality of the product (all verified by reviews today and block-chain systems later) will be offered from remote locations and delivered to your post office box. The lack of records, inability of law enforcement to keep tabs on the millions of transactions, and a fragmented production base will make the local drug lords of today soon feel like every other sector of retail—they will be lamenting the "unfair nature" of the web (darknet in this case). If you are interested, take a look at Torrentfreak.com or Popcorntime.ws.

Next we turn to the implications of this new world.

CHAPTER 6

THE STORY SO FAR . . . EVERYTHING HEADING TO FREE AND VOLATILITY

As supply and demand imbalances drive prices to zero, the entire basis of competition in retail and consumer-facing businesses radically shifts. Suddenly, one of two things drives success in the retail world: distribution or a new deep relationship with the consumer. When this happens, the price of entry for retailers and brands will be well beyond the right product, at the right place with the right price. Now, providing the product in the most convenient manner at the right time wherever the consumer is located and with the right experience will be the new point of entry for retailers and brands. Most existing retail structures, behaviors and assets are now incompatible with this new set of requirements. Retail is entering a prolonged period of restructuring and asset reallocation. And the process will be painful, with large numbers of retailers and brands disappearing.

Another implication that emerges from this thesis is slightly more obscure but no less significant—the death of mass markets. The dramatic shattering of mass markets into thousands of microniches, combined with the decentralized power of emerging

implications

"Everything is heading to free."

SALE   30% OFF   everything 40% off   SALE

basis of competition shifting to <u>new</u> customer values

distribution   experiences

BUT...

Exhibit 6.1. Implications Everything Is Heading to Free

technologies, means all consumer businesses will face a dramatically higher levels of market volatility.

All the technologies we have discussed so far have the effect of giving consumers greater control in commerce and forging stronger connections between otherwise distant people. And for this reason these technologies will mean greater volatility on a number of fronts: economic, societal and political. Further, because of the mind-boggling pace of technological change, it will be difficult (for even the biggest beneficiaries of network effects) to predict where this volatility will lead, which in turn will drive more uncertainty and volatility.

Historically, macroeconomic shocks like wars and trade embargos have produced the most volatility, but today it is coming from the decisions of millions of individuals who can suddenly create a powerful collective effect. The effect of this individual decision-making power is that predicting or forecasting any major trend is difficult.

A look at key financial metrics shows that this has already started. Volatility in corporate profits has increased by 60 percent during roughly the last fifteen years, compared with the period from 1965 to 1980.[1] Fashion cycles and trends will be short and explosive as technology spreads—and quickly kills them. People will have more careers with more unexpected twists and turns than ever before. More people will move across the country, around the world, and away from their families, as the cost of travel drops and technology helps unlock opportunities elsewhere. The twenty-four-hour news cycle and social media will create a volatile, short societal attention span that brings every previously unnoticed incident to the fore—but only for a short time before people turn their attention elsewhere.

When we look at retail structures around the world, we see that in those regions that are highly volatile and have been historically unpredictable—like large parts of Africa or Indonesia—the retail structure that has developed features a lot of small independent stores, few big chains, and few economies of scale—meaning the risk of a major shift is distributed across thousands of small businesses. It's relatively easy for these businesses to adjust to new circumstances, because they hold low levels of inventory, can quickly switch products and, with almost no overhead, keep themselves afloat throughout a downturn. Larger retail formats, however, find volatile environments hard to manage, likely leading to periods of high losses.

So the best system for managing a big increase in volatility is one that has a distributed network of connected but separate components that can move quickly and easily but not necessarily together. Amazon, with its ability to take in an order and fulfill it from one or several independently operating distribution centers, is a good example so long as it does not build large rigid supply chains. Structures that cannot bend or quickly and efficiently transfer the energy of a major fluctuation across a network—dissipating its power—will tend to break and collapse.

The political, social, and economic worlds also require stability and predictability for large institutions, companies, and organizations to flourish. In business, these conditions are especially critical to justify investments in economies of scale. In the United States and most of developed Europe, the historic stability of their economies and major demographic and homogeneous attitudinal trends have created the ability to support large-scale and highly efficient retailers and consumer packaged goods companies.

The seismic shift we have outlined is turning all this upside down. We focus on this point because, while we explore in this book many implications of the seismic shift, *the increase in volatility and the pressure it places on the benefits of economies of scale are at the heart of everything taking place today.* Together, they represent an *existential* threat to every major retailer and consumer-facing company—from department stores to packaged goods to media and entertainment to financial services to hotels and to transportation. Once we have explored how to win loyal customers, we will return to the strategic choices retailers can make to navigate this new world.

SECTION 2

HOW TO ATTRACT LOYAL CUSTOMERS

CHAPTER 7

MASLOW'S HIERARCHY REVISITED

All the changes that we have just explored have begun to affect both the values and behaviors of the consumer. To explain what is happening, we need to delve into the realm of psychology and the emerging science of behavioral economics.

We start with psychology and revisit an old theory that helps explain the human motivation—Maslow's hierarchy of needs. In 1943, Abraham Maslow wrote a highly influential paper that laid out the different stages of human psychological development and satisfaction. He developed his ideas further in the 1954 classic *Motivation and Personality*.

Maslow believed people are motivated by factors other than rewards or unconscious desires. He categorized needs by importance and developed a pyramid reflecting five stages of development, as shown in Exhibit 7.1: at the base of the pyramid were physiological needs like food and water, then safety, on to self-esteem and self-actualization. Maslow later added a sixth stage (not reflected here) that he termed *self-transcendence*, which included the effect that one has on others and the world.

In *The New Rules of Retail*, our first book (2010), we argued that "many consumers are now able to achieve the pinnacle of Maslow's hierarchy of needs: self-actualization. Their material desires are being satisfied and they are able to move toward maximizing their human potential: to seek knowledge, peace, aesthetic experiences and so forth." This idea now requires further exploration.

For our purposes the hierarchy offers insight into key changes in the consumer's psychology since the late twentieth century. First, with an overabundance of material possessions, many Americans have moved up Maslow's hierarchy.

One immediate manifestation of this shift is that people no longer value spending time looking to satisfy their more basic physiological or material needs: this explains how important convenience has become to consumers, giving them more time to pursue self-actualization by helping others, being creative, and developing personal relationships. Today many regard time as the most precious commodity—and the value of time has been increasing. Americans are going through a period when

Exhibit 7.1. Maslow's Hierarchy of Needs

people are being offered products that are highly affordable, exceptional in performance, can be purchased in a great environment, and will arrive on their doorstep through an easy and hassle-free process. These factors are driving the location of smaller local stores that are well designed and are easy to get to and to leave.

Trader Joe's effectively exploited this desire with neighborhood stores that offer great value and an edited assortment (the only inconvenience is long lines because the stores are so popular). As the population of urban areas continues to grow, and the costs and amount of time required to drive to the mall or the big-box store increase for the consumer, the neighborhood part of this equation will become increasingly important.

The importance of convenience is also driving the relentless growth of Amazon and other online stores. The ease of ordering online is constantly improving, making the trip to a store harder and harder to justify—especially for basic products. Even if (or when) the online price rises above the store price, the consumer is not going to go back to buying at the store—the inconvenience is just too great. Store traffic will continue to fall.

Nor are bulk purchases from club stores immune to this trend. For now, the bulk value and fun of the trip to Costco and others is worth the trip, but at some point they too will start to see the number of stock-up trips decline as consumers shift to the most convenient option. Jet.com is trying to create a club-like model in the digital space. And why not? Is the treasure hunt experience going to be worth the trip if you can easily get most of what you need delivered?

With their basic needs fulfilled, 80 percent of consumers have increasingly been looking for more rewarding, highly experiential and meaningful purchases. This has also influenced how consumers want to be treated in their interactions with retailers and the services they provide.

Of course, the other 20 percent of Americans are still struggling to meet their basic needs and have different priorities. For this group, the trip to the store will persist, and above all they will be looking for the best price. Hard discounters, close-out formats, and off-price retailers with private-label products at lower prices will win these shoppers for the foreseeable future. Even here, though, the in-store experience (and ways to elevate it) will become increasingly important.

The 80 percent who are better off will seek higher and higher levels of emotional satisfaction in their daily lives. All retailers and product categories have seen this, with companies that offer higher levels of emotion tending to perform better—think samples and fun products at Trader Joe's or the Genius Bar at the Apple Store. In fact, a recent *Harvard Business Review* study found that companies that connect with consumers on emotional factors have higher net promoter scores (the proportion of consumers likely to recommend a brand to others compared to those who would not recommend it) than brands that connect on only a functional level.[1] The link to revenue growth is obvious.

This search for greater levels of meaning and self-actualization in people's relationship to products and services has fueled the spike in spending on experiential purchases. Since 2001, discretionary spending on goods like cars and furniture has shrunk as a percentage of total spending, while spending on travel, recreation and eating out increased about 13 percent in the same period. And this trend is only likely to intensify: as we have already noted, 72 percent of millennials surveyed recently said they preferred to spend money on experiences rather than products.[2]

This emphasis on experience is even more important because recent research suggests that people at different ages and life stages endow different parts of the pyramid with different levels of importance.[3] In other words, the progression up the pyramid is not linear and indeed at different times in your life the order may be quite different.

Maslow appeared to recognize this, writing, "We have spoken so far as if this hierarchy were a fixed order but actually it is not nearly as rigid as we may have implied. It is true that most of the people with whom we have worked have seemed to have these basic needs in about the order that has been indicated. However, there have been a number of exceptions."[4]

Maslow then offers a number of different circumstances in which individuals make trade-offs different from what the static pyramid might imply. The image that comes to our mind is the starving artist who forgoes basic needs to fulfill his urge to create art—his urge for self-actualization is so great that he all but forgets about his needs at the bottom of the pyramid. Anyone who has participated in an extreme sport or devoted themselves to a lifelong passion will immediately identify with this. We also see this theory come to life in the resurgence of craft, or artisanal, jobs, including barbering, butchering, bartending, distilling, coffee brewing, and furniture making. While these jobs have always been poorly paid, they now have cachet and provide higher-end services and products. Young people are drawn to this work because it feels authentic, and they're liberated to pursue quality for quality's sake, serving a crowd of consumers equally obsessed with quality and authenticity.[5]

This fluid interpretation of Maslow's hierarchy is a useful way of thinking about consumer behavior for two reasons. First, this expanded view of his theory suggests that people value different things at different life stages, and this is important in how they spend their time and money. For example, younger people naturally tend to value love and self-esteem more than the basic motivational elements of food and shelter, whereas older people increasingly need security. Another interesting aspect of this fluid approach is that it suggests that the value placed on an item depends on the context in which it is obtained and its level of availability. For example, it appears that when an element is in abundance, individuals who provide a higher rating to other parts of the pyramid tends to further devalue the plentiful item. So, to return to one of our main points—the massive increase in material goods—individuals are devaluing both products and material possessions. It is interesting that because of the great material abundance that exists, people are placing a decreasing value on these items. The need to own a lot of material goods is almost laughably different between generations—someone who grew up during the Great Depression would often collect everything lest they never be able to obtain it again, whereas a millennial sees little value in owning almost anything.

Also, because of the growing influence of millennials, a larger number of consumers are in age cohorts that tend to place greater value on self-esteem and love. A Pew survey found that millennials were much more likely than other generations to describe themselves as confident and placing high value on relationships with family and friends.[6]

While we're on the subject of millennials and relationships, let us briefly discuss an often-heard idea, that technology has made people value relationships and personal contact less than before. While it is undoubtedly true that people spend more time on devices (even in the presence of their friends), our research suggests that people have not lost the desire to be part of a community and be recognized and valued. The quest for authentic, intimate relationships is undiminished even if the way that friendship is expressed is different than it used to be and the number of people who are involved has increased. In fact, Pew data show that mobile phone, Internet, and social media use are associated with larger and more diverse social networks.[7]

The net result is that consumers want to spend in areas that align with their values. So, the growth in retail and consumer products overweighted toward products and services with attributes that are at the top of the pyramid and provide or offer a combination of self-transcendence and self-actualization to millennials and security to boomers, whereas competing products satisfy bottom-of-the-pyramid basic needs without any emotional or personal attachment.

The second reason that this framework is useful is that it helps explain the impact of the Great Recession on the consumer psyche. There is something of a paradox about the recession and how consumers' values shifted. After the recession you might expect that consumers would value material purchases more than before, since a loss of jobs and income, repossessed houses, and increased anxiety would make people concentrate on the bottom of Maslow's pyramid.

But our research, based on multiple discussions with consumers and consumer groups, suggests a more nuanced outcome. We heard people say that the recession made them want "less stuff" and that it was not "worth the debt to just buy more." In fact, people appeared to want to spend more on things that have meaning in their lives and "fun experiences with their friends and family."

The data bear this out as well. Data from the US Bureau of Labor Statistics on the relative importance of certain spending categories—basically, how consumers divide up their spending among categories—show that spending on food and travel in 2013 (during the recovery) surpassed spending during 2007 (during the boom), while spending on cars, furniture, and appliances had not recovered.[8]

For boomers the recession raised fears about security for their future but did not make them want more material goods—they instead saw one of the largest increases in their spending on eating out. Millennials, facing 182 percent more college debt than people their age did in 1995, as well as fewer promising job prospects, have allocated their spending to purchases at the top of the pyramid—eating out, traveling, shopping at farmers' markets, drinking craft beers, eating organic foods and buying brands associated with their values.[9] And because many millennials are putting off marriage and home buying—and some are still living with their parents—spending on home goods and furniture is down. We hear Gen Zers saying that they don't "want to get into debt like our parents, who bought too much."

Another big consequence of the Great Recession was a large drop in trust not only for political institutions, financial institutions and the "system" but also retailers and consumer packaged goods companies. The perception lingered that easy credit offered by banks and retailers to stimulate purchasing was creating unnecessary debt and helped fuel the crash. As a result, the percentage of Americans younger than thirty-five with credit card debt has fallen to its lowest level since the Federal Reserve started keeping track in 1989. But it's not just debt that younger generations are trying to avoid—it's the temptation. In fact, a whopping 63 percent of millennials aged eighteen to twenty-nine told a Bankrate survey they don't have a credit card, whereas that was true for only 35 percent of adults older than thirty.[10]

Few brands or retailers are viewed as being highly trustworthy or as acting in their consumers' best interest. Apple and Nike are the exceptions, but many brands are now perceived as almost being at odds with the consumer. For example, recent soda taxes in several cities across the country have stirred up intense battles between retailers, beverage companies, and the public, while more and more consumers believe food companies adulterate food with harmful ingredients—from adding addictive amounts of salt and sugar to genetic modification. In fact, 57 percent of consumers believe GMO foods are not safe to eat.[11]

Again and again we have heard from consumers who believe companies always put profit ahead of customers' well-being. Companies "just try to get you to spend more on things you don't need," and these companies "are not really interested in helping you." Placing racks of impulse candy at the checkout at children's eye level may boost sales but has left many a parent arguing with their kids. Placing critical items (e.g., milk) in hard-to-reach places in a store undermines consumer trust. It is no wonder that as choice has increased and pricing has made all sorts of new options available, consumers show little loyalty to stores that have behaved in this manner. This perception has been particularly prevalent among millennials, who have led the movement to buy local, avoid big chains, and support natural and organic products and ethical businesses. The quest for authenticity and trust is increasingly spilling over to products and where people shop.

So a fluid interpretation of Maslow's hierarchy in a world of abundance suggests that consumers have become more selective in their purchasing behaviors. They have not moved down the pyramid because of the Great Recession—instead, they have sought out products, services, and experiences that combine elements of value that exist up and down the pyramid. The clear strategic insight from this is that every retailer and brand must think about creating value and connection to the consumer across the pyramid while placing increasing importance on the elements align with self-esteem and self-actualization.

A recent *Harvard Business Review* article demonstrates alignment with Maslow's hierarchy and different attributes at different levels. The authors identified thirty "elements of value"—

fundamental attributes in their most essential and discrete forms. These elements fall into four categories: functional, emotional, life-changing, and socially impactful. This is, of course, a close fit with how Maslow defined the levels of motivation.

As the authors describe,

> Throughout history, *self-actualization* has been out of reach for most consumers, who were focused on survival (even if they found fulfillment through spiritual or worldly pursuits). But anything that saved time, reduced effort, or reduced cost was prized. These patterns demonstrate that there are many ways to succeed by delivering various kinds of value. Amazon expanded functional excellence in a mass market, but also succeeds in connecting emotionally through convenience, speed and value. Apple excels on 11 elements in the pyramid, several of them high up, which allows the company to charge premium prices. TOMS excels on four elements, and one of them is *self-transcendence*, because the company gives away one pair of shoes to needy people for every pair bought by a customer.[12]

An increasing number of studies rooted in behavioral economics further illuminate the value people receive from activities, relationships, and purchases that reflect their high-order goals and motivations. Research describes the differences between the "defensive mode" and "discovery mode." People are constantly traveling between these two states, and while defensive mode is often frustrating and counterproductive, discovery mode feels much better because you're being rewarded with a sense of belonging, recognition, autonomy or purpose, or you are learning or experiencing something new. In fact, according to this research, people's need for a sense of social belonging goes all the way back to humans' days as tribes on the savannah—being part of a team was as essential to survival as food and water—and was in fact how people got these other necessities. Some of that importance still lingers: our brains still respond to signals of social acceptance, just as they do more basic rewards, like a delicious meal or a cool drink on a hot day.[13]

In fact, a lot of research finds that purchases that demonstrate accomplishment—either in terms of prestige or of achieving a goal, such as protecting the environment with a hybrid car—score the highest on both functional and emotional levels.[14]

One additional idea that we want to share here is that, while we talk about consumers, we must also increasingly think about the employees of retailers and consumer businesses in the same way. With so much fluidity in employment within retailers, they should increasingly view their consumers and employees as almost one and the same. The populist insurgency in politics in 2016 has started to creep into the language of consumer research—we hear people say, "I only want to shop at places where the employees treat me well, know what they are doing and seem happy." Clearly, the focus on standardizing tasks in the store, managing productivity, giving bonuses only for sales, and centralizing decision making has removed a lot of the human touch and active involvement of the in-store staff in creating a positive experience.

In fact, spending more on labor—to provide a better customer experience, but also a better employee experience—pays off. One study found that one standard deviation increase in store labor levels increased profit margins by 10 percent. Analysis of another retailer found that for every dollar increase in labor, a store saw sales go up $4 to $28. The reason for these increases was not only that good employees help reduce the incidence of items out of stock and increase upselling but also that they improve the customer experience through positive social interactions. The author points to retailers like Costco, Trader Joe's, and QuikTrip, all of which compete effectively on price while providing higher wages, promoting from within, and offering effective training. Customers get in and out of QuikTrip fast, thanks to merchandise set in the right place and employees trained to ring customers up quickly. Meanwhile, *Consumer Reports* ranked Trader Joe's as America's second-best supermarket after Wegmans—both have stellar staff who suggest products and recipes and truly engage customers.[15] Of course, the number of variables driving a retailer's long-term success are so great that in-store labor alone cannot drive success, but it is becoming an increasingly important part of the answer.

To return to our main argument, the supply and demand imbalance is the main driver of these psychological changes.

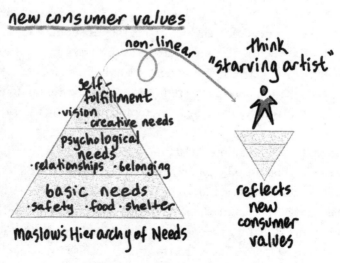

Exhibit 7.2. New Consumer Values

Consumers' values and behaviors have gone through a fundamental realignment, yet most retailers have not put commensurate effort into rethinking how to meet these needs. They have spent a lot of time on the technology component to provide online capabilities (usually without really thinking about what the consumer values) and relatively little to change the business model to meet the new consumer demands rooted in values.

In the next chapter, we discuss what we believe is the emerging transcendent value that all consumer-facing businesses must place at the center of their strategy: "Rational altruism."

CHAPTER 8

THE NEW CONSUMER VALUE
RATIONAL ALTRUISM

Maslow's hierarchy suggests that people seek emotional experiences that help them achieve personal fulfillment and strengthen their relationships, but what does that mean for what they desire as consumers? We know that their level of satisfaction and happiness associated with material purchases is diminishing and will continue to do so. So, what will they seek to consume instead? What are the new consumer values?

We recently conducted field research looking to understand consumers' evolving desires. The research first led us to a house on the outskirts of Denver owned by an individual we came to classify as a value shopper—someone with low income who was looking for bargains. She was her family's breadwinner because her husband had been unemployed since returning from military service overseas.

At one point in our conversation she remarked, "I want to buy things from retailers who seem to really understand my life." We probed what she meant by this. "Well, I have to cut coupons, look for bargains, and get in and out quickly because I have to get back to work, and I want them to respect and make it easy for me," she said. "It used to be more fun than it is today." She would be a prime candidate for online ordering and delivery if her budget was not so constrained.

Throughout our travels we heard a series of similar frustrations from customers who felt they were not understood. But they also felt that shopping was becoming increasingly soulless and functional, not enjoyable or emotional. When the big-box revolution started in the late 1980s, shoppers felt palpable excitement and visited stores with an expectation of awe and energy. The possibility of finding new products at unimaginably low prices in the vast selection offered was fun. The newness of these stores was highly stimulating, and their incredible value (in some cases every day) made them destinations for dreaming—a sense of what a complete material life might be like. And the store associates were energized and keen to show you what was available and new.

The same was true of the large grocery chains that expanded and rolled out stores full of almost every product you could imagine (even if they were cold inside with dauntingly tall aisles that were hard to see around). The expansion of malls was also fun, with the space filled by all the national chains in a bright, colorful environment that offered almost every small town, suburb or even city location an amazing selection of products previously unavailable, or unavailable in one place, not to mention a food court and restaurants to satisfy their hunger.

But that was then, this is now. The rapid expansion of chains and malls created a uniformity across the retail landscape that has drained consumers' energy and failed to provide a meaningful and fun escape from the everyday routines of life. The formula that was great at spreading product across the country was not great at evolving.

We heard these themes echoed across the country.

"The store is the same as it was five years ago but less fun."

"If they change the price, I would like to see the value that I got for it. I don't—they play games with me," another told us.

The issues covered everything from the frustration at poorly thought-out packaging to ridiculous interactions with automated call centers to poorly staffed restaurants looking to turn tables quickly or stores that offered limited service or places where customers assumed employees had been instructed to try to sell more instead of helping or just talking.

All these negative experiences are repeated in identical-looking malls and stores, with employees' behavior driven by time-and-motion studies of performing tasks, such as stocking inventory and changing prices, not by being actively engaged in creating an environment that takes consumers out of the ordinary.

Our observations are reinforced by others who have studied the US consumer. As the consumer branding expert Martin Lindstrom found, "Americans [are] in need of an escape, or reprieve from the sameness of their lives. A current of tedium and familiarity runs through every culture, but the uniformity of the American shopping landscape has drained away an element of unexpectedness." Or in the words of the Brazilian novelist Paulo Coelho, "If you think adventure is dangerous, try routine. It is lethal." In this context, Americans' obsession with smartphones makes sense: they give us a little of the much-needed stimulation our sterile daily environments lack.

If we had to sum up our interviews with one consumer's comment, it would be this: "It's like flying on all the other airlines and not Southwest. Other airlines charge funny prices, hidden fees and treat others way better than me, but on Southwest they know what it's like to be me and they get it. They are honest, straightforward and the employees have fun!" Even if you don't like the Southwest experience, it clearly works well for its customers. And the consumer made this comment before any airline passengers were punched in the face for not giving up their seat.

From the corporate side, we also heard the same opinions being expressed. The controversial CEO of T-Mobile put the issue nicely when he spoke about the wireless industry: "Customers [hated] being locked into contracts. They hated being gouged by extra fees for things that they didn't understand or couldn't fully control." The monthly fees hid the true costs of the phone, advertising was so dishonest about the level of coverage that the CEO said, "it became clear that the best way to succeed . . . was to do things as differently as possible . . . to do the complete opposite." He also expressed a sentiment that many others echoed: "Public attitudes have shifted about the rhetoric and candor we want and expect from our leaders. . . . People want authenticity from leaders, not canned phrases full of legalese." The same is true of the places we shop and the brands we buy.

That's what consumers told us, too. The topics ranged from service and engagement practices to organic foods, carbon footprint, water and power use, sustainability, nutritional integrity, ethical practices, and pastoral farming versus industrial farming—the list goes on and on. On the question of values, we've noticed an increase in both the number of people who say these issues are important and also the range of topics they discuss. These topics are indicative of an ongoing shift that is reaching the tipping point: from a world where value was determined by price divided by benefits multiplied by advertising dollars to a world where value is determined by price divided by benefits plus *values* multiplied by word of mouth (including social media or peer reviews).

All this culminates in consumers' wanting retailers and consumer companies to do three things. First, understand consumers' life circumstances, (relate to them) tell customers the truth and give them a sense of importance. Second, create an environment or service model that delivers products while being interesting, imaginative and engaging. Third, have an underlying connection to consumers' values.

Feel for Your Consumers

Consumers' expressed desire to be understood by the companies with which they must deal told us they were voicing something that did not seem to be reflected in the typical consumer strategy. The vast majority of such strategies go one of two ways. The first are big quantitative studies that segment the market into a series of reasonably sized (usually about the same size) cohorts based on subjects' answers to a series of psychographic questions—for example: Do you always wear the latest fashions? How important is quality to you? Studies like this can yield insights, but they also have clear limitations. For instance, the study typically limits to about five the number of segments any market can have. Yet, as we have pointed out, the market is increasingly fragmented— into many more than five segments. Additionally, the few questions used by most surveys to determine shoppers' cohorts are insufficient to reflect the many variations in respondents' thoughts and behaviors.

Finally, few questions ever really probe peoples' deeprooted values and needs or changing life circumstances. The real danger is that these quantitative analysts have an outsized influence and inflated status based on a false level of numerical precision.

Other common methodologies focus on understanding how

a consumer rates, ranks, or chooses a product, service, or shopping trip rather than a myriad of alternatives, almost as though the consumer was not present. For example, most of this consumer research is typically done in the context of an individual product or shopping occasion, not the totality of a consumer's life. Typical surveys ask people how often they buy a certain brand and what they think of it but almost nothing about how they use it or anything else about their life other than empty numbers like income and age. Even most visits to people's homes for research (typically called ethnographies) do not try to probe the household's total needs, family pressures, long-term goals and desires, fears, and recent life changes. Rather, they focus on specific aspects related to a certain product or shopping occasion. In doing this, they are missing a lot of what people need. Truly understanding these higher-level needs represents retailers' single biggest opportunity—and challenge—for the next decade and beyond.

You don't have to look far to see some of the shortcomings of traditional market research. Sure, the 2016 US presidential election was one of polling's biggest failures—the answer to a set of survey questions failed to detect that so many people's lives had changed so dramatically that old behaviors were no longer going to hold. Hillary Clinton's decision not to visit some midwestern states may have been based on this data—yet a visit to a few living rooms in those counties would have shattered the reliability of those survey results.

This is not the only case study; we can find many other examples closer to the retail and consumer world. A great example is a famous international consumer survey of ten thousand people conducted by the media company Universal McCann in 2007. It concluded overwhelmingly that consumers in affluent countries wouldn't want a product that combined in a single device a cell phone, music player, and camera. The iPhone had been announced but not yet released. Of course, just a year later facts rendered those study results ridiculous. Traditional market research has become even less reliable as consumers are increasingly influenced by new sources of information such as social media, whereas most market research measures consumers' past experience and knowledge—not how they will react to something now.

Consumers widely believe that companies don't understand them for many reasons, not only because consumers have shifted their priorities. Consumers have that impression because companies have been responding to other, often more immediate, pressures—those driven by financial targets. Yet this strategy of perpetual growth cannot work in the new world of excess supply in a highly fragmented and technology-driven market.

Similarly, the retail industry's newfound emphasis on big data all but ignores the lifestyle, economic situation or context of the consumer. Instead, it seeks patterns of purchasing behavior to try to predict what might be a good offer, promotion, or product to an empirically defined cohort of consumers (the segmentation we've been talking about). Many companies that are regarded as good examples of being customer-focused use data and algorithms to help increase conversion and basket size, even in the guise of creating a customized experience. You know this is happening when you see mindless email offering you a special deal on a product you have already purchased. The analysis conducted by newly formed analytic groups can be completely detached from the product and consumer—the conversation is all about the results of a test (Did their client sell more? At a higher margin?), the esoteric elasticities of price, or the rate of response to a new catalog. Within this world, the discussion often focuses on using the "irrational responses" of the consumer to drive purchases. The problem is a lack of understanding of the consumer's life.

Many retailers hope that technological breakthroughs like machine learning and artificial intelligence will enhance their ability to predict what consumers want to buy when they visit a brick-and-mortar store and to tailor their approach to the consumer. However, everyone has been a victim of repeated ads that Facebook thinks we want to see, and we have learned to tune them out. And most retailers do not have anything approaching Facebook-level data or the skills to mine it. Our research suggests that people will ultimately gravitate to places that treat them like individuals and will go online for fast, impersonal service. Today, this lack of connection and understanding by sales personnel appears to be why many shoppers find it so easy and compelling to order online.

Consumers' desire for emotional connection or understanding is starting to determine where they choose to shop. Research across nine diverse consumer categories shows that emotionally connected consumers spend 52 percent more than those who are "highly satisfied" but not fully emotionally engaged.[1] And this will only accelerate. In fact, to be a winner in retail or consumer goods twenty years from now, connecting with or understanding people's lives is the most important capability a company has to develop.

And once a company can do it, this capability will drive every aspect of product development, pricing, and selling. Value-driven retailing will turn the traditional business model upside down— a complete retail reset. It will not be easy to achieve because implementing it will often run counter to Wall Street's demands for short-term sales growth.

We kept looking for a way to better understand and explain the core idea at the heart of this emerging consumer desire. For that, we looked at the positive psychology movement, which is a natural extension of Maslow's philosophy.

We call the concept that emerged from this research "rational altruism." It is rational because it is linked to the fundamental economics of retail. That's right: it is critical to make sure all decisions fit within a clear profit motive. But it is also altruistic because it does not start from a profit motive but rather seeks to act in the interests of the consumer (both short and long term) without an ulterior motive. In other words, "the elimination of selfish desire" leads to "a life devoted to the well-being of others," as Auguste Comte, the founder of positivism, described altruism. However, we are not saying that companies should be giving to charity (though that could be part of the equation, for example, TOMS's donation of shoes to developing countries), not selling foods high in sugar (people love them) or forsaking healthy returns but that the source of that profit or growth has to come from a concern for the consumer above all else. Putting this concept into practice means being transparent about calories and ingredients (for food products), being clear on sourcing practices and ethics (for apparel from developing countries), or making it clear that an item is made in the United States so consumers can make informed choices. To use the example of T-Mobile again, that company saw what the consumer valued and disliked and how the current business model was designed for wireless carriers, not consumers. As a result, T-Mobile uprooted its sales pitches and practices to give consumers what they wanted.

Understanding Empathy and Its Power for Commerce

What consumers were telling us about their need to be understood led us to thinking about the importance of empathy for the customer, and this in turn led us to the work of Daniel Batson, author of *Altruism in Humans*. Batson has identified eight definitions of *empathy*, the last of which is feeling for another person who is suffering, also called empathic concern.

Empathic concern, he explained, means that one perceives another as in need and values the other's welfare.[2] That is, empathetic concern is more than just being aware of another person's internal state or projecting yourself into another's situation. Such simple definitions of empathy are often criticized as not helping people. The idea of empathetic concern is all about identifying people's true wants and needs and then taking action to provide them with compassionate assistance.

The benefits created by developing empathetic concern are many. The closer you can come to sharing someone's emotional state, the better you are at predicting their actions and behaviors. Empathy also provides the ability to more effectively collect insights and data about the business environment you have created. For example, empathetic interviewers can help companies gain insight into the lives and circumstances of their consumers—context that can help avoid costly and time-wasting ventures in product development, ill-conceived pricing strategies, or doomed-to-fail marketing strategies. Finally, empathy helps provide insight about how to be more effective and precise in communications. After all, when you know what something feels like and experience it directly, you can easily share it.

This level of empathic concern is, Batson argues, what creates an altruistic motivation to act and to help others. In other words, the goal is not to act out of a desire to further your own well-being but to direct all your attention to the other. This may seem like a high bar for retailers and companies, but with consumers continually searching for their higher selves, we believe this will determine who wins and who loses with the consumer.

But don't take just our word for it. The analytic consultant John Kim, winner of The World in 2016 forecasting competition who also predicted Brexit and Trump, said that his success was based on new information sources that enabled him to develop a deep sense of empathy for both sides of an issue.

There is a big difference between this approach and being motivated purely by the need to figure out how to sell more or make more profit, even if that economic goal includes trying to research product or shopping benefits that help the consumer. Few companies would ever state that achieving a level of "rational altruism" is a goal. We say this because we believe those that adopt this concept gain an incredible competitive advantage, because few companies are truly considering how to act in this way and consumers will reward those who do without even realizing why. It may be that for publicly traded companies the pressures of Wall Street might preclude such a public approach, but we believe that at the very least it must become part of the private discussion of strategy. What is your company's purpose in the eyes of the consumer? Why do you matter? Why will you survive the great shakeout?

As it stands, consumer research has no accepted measure for taking a consumer's life into consideration—most common metrics, such as net promoter score or likelihood to repurchase, are aimed at figuring out if the consumer understands the brand, not the other way around. Every company should consider and monitor its target consumers' answers to these key questions:

- Do you believe that we (retailer or brand) are genuinely interested in improving your life?
- Do we understand your life?
- Do you believe we have your interests at our core?

Patagonia was one of the early adopters of this approach with its 2011 campaign suggesting consumers shouldn't buy its products unless they really, really need them. Can you imagine the moment when the creative person at the advertising agency first suggested it?

As shown in Exhibit 8.1, Patagonia started to chart a path more focused on its products' ability to make a substantive contribution to people's lives and to the long-term environmental impact of its products. The ad detailed the environmental impact of a Patagonia jacket, informing consumers:

> The environmental cost of everything we make is astonishing. Consider the R2 Jacket. . . . To make it required 135 liters of water, enough to meet the daily needs (three glasses a day) of 45 people. Its journey from its origin as 60% recycled polyester to our Reno warehouse generated nearly 20 pounds of carbon dioxide, 24 times the weight of the finished product . . . Don't buy what you don't need. Think twice before you buy anything.

Patagonia took it one step further in 2016 and donated all its Black Friday sales—in-store and online—to environmentally minded organizations.[3] Patagonia also took its "don't buy new" ethos on the road, sending a reclaimed wood camper on a six-week, cross-country road trip powered by biodiesel to repair Patagonia products and sell used ones.

Clearly, pure growth is not Patagonia's objective. In fact, in 2013 the company stated on its website that "growth is a dead end." Elaborating further, Patagonia worried that even its green initiatives would not be enough to offset the growing demand for its products. Fear of meaningless growth goes back to the company's early days. Yvon Chouinard, a cofounder, remembers

Exhibit 8.1. Patagonia's 2011 "Don't Buy This Jacket" ad.
Source: Tim Nudd, "Ad of the Day: Patagonia," Adweek, November 28, 2011,
http://www.adweek.com/news/advertising-branding/ad-day-patagonia-136745.

a time in the late 1980s when the company grew too fast; when recession hit in 1991, Patagonia found itself overextended and on the verge of bankruptcy. The company had to lay off 20 percent of its workforce. "It was hard," Chouinard told *The New Yorker*. "I realized we were just growing for the sake of growing, which is bullshit."[4]

Patagonia is not alone. Lady Geek, a consulting firm, publishes a yearly Global Empathy Index and recently ranked companies like Tesla, Procter & Gamble, Apple, Walt Disney, and Audi in the top ten.[5] Interestingly, this index also hints at the growth benefits of being less focused on growth: the top ten companies increased their value more than twice as much as the bottom ten and generated 50 percent more earnings.

By offering this idea of rational altruism, we are suggesting that a company should make this idea a core part of its strategy. While we think the major focus of this work should be the consumer, the approach should be applied to all employees as well. And as these examples show, it pays off. By 2026 it will be fundamental.

So, our hypothesis is that consumers are going through a fundamental shift in their values and what they expect, want and think is right. We are not alone in our thinking on this topic. Peter Singer, the provocative philosopher, has written challengingly about the ethics of pursuing ever more consumption versus using the money to help millions of people worldwide who are facing life-threatening challenges. He is exploring the idea of effective altruism, a notion that is comparable to our thinking, even if his is more focused on global issues and not the new requirements of business. In his book *The Life That You Can Save*, he argues that people are morally wrong in not shifting their resources (expenditures) to agencies that are helping those around the world facing true crisis.

If even a small percentage of the population accepted his views, the impact on business would be immense, because people

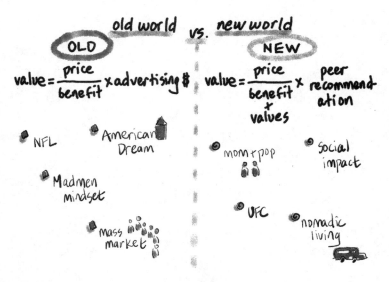

Exhibit 8.2. The Old World vs. the New World

would further reduce their material spending and restrict what they do spend to brands that reflect these values. His suggestions might be far-fetched for most of business today, but the same was said when he first wrote about animal rights in 1975 (in his book *Animal Liberation*). His ideas were integral to the animal liberation movement and today would be considered almost mainstream—and certainly no pet-minded consumer or business is untouched by this thinking today.

CHAPTER 9

THE FUTURE OF STORES

While our focus is on consumers' desires, we need to raise a topic we repeatedly heard from consumers: a desire for a shopping environment and/or service that is highly meaningful and appealing. But what does this mean from a practical perspective?

Stores are called stores because they store products. That's right—they were originally conceived as places to store inventory. From that beginning they've clearly evolved to offer much more. Stores can be educational, inspirational, convenient or fun places. A fashion store, for example, should always be linked to aspiration and transformation, as Martin Lindstrom suggests. A grocery store might be convenient and beautifully designed to aid easy, fun shopping.

Of course, it's not possible to provide one set of rules or ideas that applies to all types of stores (from Goodwill to Tiffany to Nike), but some themes or ideas based on emerging consumer needs will define stores' role in the future.

The key, we believe, is that they need to be either places of community or greatly entertaining, highly experiential centers.

If you are in the middle, as most retailers are today, you will lose customers.

Consumers will always be looking for highly engaging, entertaining places full of new items—new technology surrounded by fun restaurants. Constantly changing unique experiences and products will be worth the trip to the mall. We can already see this trend in the beautiful new malls that are being developed. But consumers will visit these only a limited number of times, making the number of locations for these centers relatively constrained. But we will see malls of the future—think *The Jetsons* or *Star Wars*—emerge.

However, to continue with our values-driven approach to retail, we see a gap in people's lives that is widening. That gap is in community. Traditional providers of community, from churches to social clubs, have been in decline for years now, as first chronicled by Robert Putnam in his 1995 essay, and later a book, *Bowling Alone.* Putnam details double-digit declines in volunteerism, a 15 percent drop in weekly churchgoing, union membership falling by more than half, and many other data points that show a lack of community and social interaction.[1] Another measure is that in 2016, 14.5 percent of American adults lived alone, the highest level in history, nearly double what it was in 1967 (7.6 percent), the first year the Census Bureau started collecting data.[2]

Even sports fans' attachment to teams is waning as fans become more involved in playing fantasy sports with people from all over the country. Maybe this is one of the reasons the National Football League saw such a big decline in viewership in 2016— the audience for *Monday Night Football* fell 24 percent, *Sunday Night Football* dropped 19 percent, and *Thursday Night Football* was down 18 percent, all from the year before.[3] The Super Bowl remains one of the few TV events that large numbers of Americans still watch; everywhere else, Americans have little shared national experience with media because TV shows—and the ways to watch them—are proliferating. For example, when *Seinfeld* premiered in the summer of 1994, it was the fourteenth-most-popular show in its time slot, yet it garnered the same number of viewers as the most popular show at any date and time in 2016, which coincidentally was *Sunday Night Football*.[4]

Retail and commerce have always been about connection and community, and today they have the opportunity to fill this void. But few stores do so effectively. Talking with people and having fun with employees, learning about new products, being recognized and known when you visit the store, feeling that you are doing something good (like buying local or organic produce), or being part of a group (fashion identifiers) by buying a product have all been central to retail. These are reasons why people love farmers' markets or artists' collectives.

The store itself should both be that community and offer it to the consumer. The trouble is that, today, the mass-market approach has tended to standardize and, in the quest for efficiency, eliminated staff and tried to automate. Anyone who has battled those self-checkout systems with a "store cop" roaming the machines has seen firsthand how connections, warmth, and community can be lost. But consumers are aching to be part of communities—as we discussed in chapter 7, the need to belong occupies a central spot in Maslow's hierarchy of needs—and retail offers that (or should).

One of the most common definitions of *community* comes from the social psychologists David McMillan and David Chavis. They described it in one sentence: "Sense of community is a feeling that members have of belonging, a feeling that members matter to one another and to the group, and a shared faith that members' needs will be met through their commitment to be together."[5]

In a world of superabundance this is something stores can provide and actually benefit from. And it's directly linked to the notion of empathetic concern or altruism, since it all starts from how to make consumers' lives better.

Later in the same article, McMillan and Chavis detail the four elements that typically create community:

- Membership: "feeling of belonging or sharing a sense of personal relatedness. Membership includes boundaries" to help determine what the community should stand for and who should belong, which helps members feel special and engenders trust.
- Influence: a sense of mattering. This is a two-way street—members should have influence over the community and vice versa.
- Fulfillment: members get what they need by joining a community.
- Emotional connections: storytelling is critical here—communities have to have a story, and members have to buy in to it.

We will return to these elements later, during our discussion of winning models, but suffice it to say that the store of the future will include a unique mix of these elements. But they are not isolated tactics—the right selection must come from a core idea of what type of community is being created. Increasingly, the representatives of this community will be the store manager and the staff. If they are not creating a high-energy community, the consumer will never feel it. Think of the energy at a farmers' market versus a typical supermarket—the difference is immediately apparent. But it shouldn't be. In the future it cannot be. Something we have heard from many retailers is that they cannot create that energy or excitement for many products. That's exactly the situation for detergent, paper towels and many other products the Internet will win. Subscribe-and-save will win these categories, period. (Sure, you can bundle a few of those purchases with a trip to the store, but we doubt many of these basic purchases will be worth the trip to even a "fun" store.) The Internet will also win basic and tested apparel. A lot of complicated analysis attempts to predict which parts of the store will be dominated by the Internet, and most of it is wrong. The answer is simple: for all standardized repeat purchases and non-tactile shopping trips (those with limited fun), the Internet and home delivery will win. Recognizing this early is key for the survival of a retailer.

But new tactile experiences, such as trying on tailored outfits, the warm smell of baking products, the lively banter of engaged employees, and places to hang out and meet friends are all things consumers will be craving, and as product proliferation increases

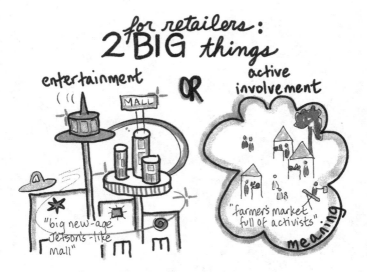

Exhibit 9.1. Two Big Things for Retailers

and prices fall, these elements will become even more important. And while technology is essential to creating these communities and that vision, it cannot replace the need for human connection and a values-based approach to retail.

In the next chapter we further test our theory that consumers will become increasingly values driven with a look at the next generation entering the marketplace right now—the generation of tech natives, Gen Z.

CHAPTER 10

GENERATION Z
AND THE FUTURE

If we are right that retail success will become increasingly correlated with values-driven organizations that at their heart develop an altruistic concern for and focus on creating fulfilling experiences, the implications for current retailers will be dramatic. To explore this idea further, we decided to look at the latest generation, Gen Z, to see whether this idea is reflected in its views and desires. We decided to explore what has influenced Gen Z, how this has shaped its values and how its members are already having an impact on the world.

A common argument against focusing on the young is that their opinions are often too fluid to interpret—that young people experiment and often change their positions. After all, people's political opinions do seem to change a lot as they get older and lose their youthful utopianism and optimism. To quote Winston Churchill, "If you are not a liberal at twenty, you have no heart. If you are not conservative at forty, you have no brain."

However, we believe that the experiences and attitudes of youth do have a long and lasting impact—on both the individual and society. There are a lot of reasons to believe that the

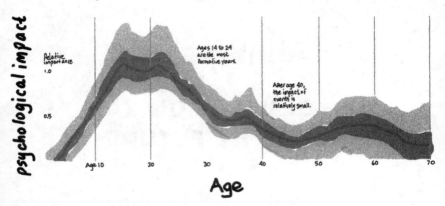

Exhibit 10.1. Formative Years
Events earlier in life play a greater role in shaping political beliefs.

impressions, opinions, and tastes formed when you are young have sticking power. For example, researchers are able to estimate when political preferences are formed and have found that events at age eighteen are about three times as powerful at shaping political attitudes as those at age forty. (See Exhibit 10.1.) What people experience, the attitudes that are formed, and the values that become important in their youth have great and lasting effects in their lives.[1]

This concept also seems to apply to the music that people have stuck in their head. For almost any age group, the songs that have stuck are those that were popular during their teenage years. The fashion, the brands, and even the foods that people like the most are typically from their youth—even your idealistic aspirations are most intensely formed during this period. It is one reason that newer confections find it hard to dislodge the most popular candies (e.g., Mars Bars, M&M's), established brands founded in the first half of the twentieth century when other classic brands started going national. Americans' tastes were set early in their lives, and they passed these preferences on to their children.

To demonstrate our point, we took a quick look back at the hippie movement of the 1960s. As some readers may remember, this era was dominated by the idealistic and often revolutionary values of the boomers, an enormous cohort of youth. The center of the emerging music, fashion, lifestyle, and philosophy scene at that time was San Francisco. A set of values and creative energy emerged in reaction to the dark years of the Cold War and the very real possibility of being drafted to fight the Vietnam War.

Hippie thinking made a mark on our culture that is still evident today. Legalizing marijuana has taken time (and is still being debated) but was a tenet of hippie culture—as were yoga, organic food, racial equality, and Tai Chi, to name only a few. Even as boomers got jobs and settled down, many retained their hippie mind-set. If anything, they continually looked for brands and companies that kept their idealism alive and bought those products even when they were poor. Maybe this link to the values and aspirations of the Sixties kept Apple alive through its dark years. Maybe this also helps explain why Apple is so loved: despite its size and power, its values are rooted in the boomers' coming of age and rebellion in the 1960s. In fact, Apple is just one of the biggest symbols of a Silicon Valley culture that celebrates abnormality, a culture that has its roots in the Summer of Love.[2]

The anti-establishment and anti-corporate vibe of the aging boomers lives on, and revival products like Dr. Martens and Converse capture this spirit. While it has taken time for these ideas to flow into the rest of society, they support our point that looking at Gen Z now will provide long-range insights into the consumer values of 2026. The experiences people born after 1996 are having right now will be three times more powerful and enduring than what they experience later in life.

Speaking of formative years, roughly five million people will turn eighteen each year between now and 2026. That means by 2026, there will be forty-nine million Gen Z adults, with another thirty-three million turning eighteen after that.

What are the driving forces influencing this generation right now? The first, and one of the most important, is the material abundance and weariness we have been discussing. Growing up in the shadow of the Great Recession and the income inequality it helped exacerbate, many Gen Zers have seen their parents grapple with rising consumer debt—which grew at a 5 percent compound annual growth rate from 2000 to 2016. So it's not surprising that 57 percent of Gen Zers we surveyed said they'd rather save money than spend it. The recession made Gen Zers realize that having many possessions can be a burden and can quickly vanish. At the heart of the desire to have access rather than ownership is this experience. Why own a car when you can borrow one? Why buy music when you can stream all you like? Why have a lot of things that require storage? Why not spend on experiences with friends instead?

Discussions with young GenZers reflect a high suspicion of consumerism. They don't appear to reject wealth—many said that they really want to be rich (who doesn't?)—but they don't want money so that they can buy more stuff. If they make a material purchase, they want it to be really special—"full of content" was the phrase they used most consistently.

Another clear trend among this group is that hanging out at the mall is much less common than for earlier generations. A recent survey of sixty-two hundred teens suggests that they increasingly prefer to shop online versus in a store, and the percentage of teens preferring to shop online has tripled in the last decade.[3] The Gen Zers we met also suggested that if you want to communicate with them, you have to go where they are—online, in the right communities with the right influencers, a relevant message or appropriate level of participation.

The combination of the ability to network and communicate with their friends on an almost constant basis negates the need for a central meeting place, and the lack of emphasis on buying things makes the mall even less important. This generation is always connected. They are mostly online within an hour of waking up. Seventy-five percent send a hundred texts per day, and texting is not even their medium of choice—Snapchat is. They report using five screens simultaneously and are vociferous in their creation and consumption of content. They love to see what is trending on YouTube, check out the latest photos and updates from their friends (fewer and fewer are from stores these days), and spend eighteen hours per day consuming media and nine hours on their screens.[4]

This generation believes that technology is providing them with the tools to navigate and shape the world. Their education is expansive and digital: they use these media to join, create or learn about a political movement (so don't be surprised by the creation of new social movements in record time, since the tools and means exist to create them), and their social lives flow through these devices. If you do not understand or know how to navigate this technology, your ability to be relevant will be significantly diminished.

Where does this time come from? Well, all other activities have lost out, but the biggest loser may well be shopping. After all, few trips to the store provide the fun to be had from visually engaging social media sites, the opportunity to watch a TED Talk, the ability to learn and finally meet other interesting influential bloggers or YouTube stars. In addition, streaming means there's no need to schedule.

The second big impact we found from our research is that

young people have been inundated with the specter of a dystopian society. Movies from *Harry Potter* to *The Hunger Games*
have created a vision of rising dark forces that want to control
society for a chosen few—the "pure bloods" or those in District 1.
These movies depict the use of technology, big data, and information to watch and control people as much as they show them
to be a source of liberation and creativity.

This cultural meme has coincided with the actual threat of
significant political turmoil and upheaval. From the brutal collapse of societies in the Middle East and the rise of global terror-
ism to the highly dramatic and unknown effect of the potential
dissolution of the European Union to the rise of more national-
istic political movements and the growing drumbeat of concern
about global warming—these have given Gen Z a worldview that
oscillates between fear and hope.

Our research found Gen Z expressing considerable anxiety
about the next decade: 47 percent believe the United States will
experience extreme effects of climate change, 42 percent said they
believe another economic collapse will occur, 50 percent believe
the United States will suffer a major terrorist attack, and 49 percent
say there will be war between major global powers. Nearly a third
said they believe the US government will mandate discrimination against minorities by 2016, whereas only 20 percent of other
age groups think this.[5]

Not surprisingly, this generation also lacks basic faith in many
of society's major public and private institutions. This manifests
itself in how Gen Zers behave online. Gen Z is much more focused on controlling the use of its online data than are millennials
and Gen Xers—our surveys show Gen Z is much more like
boomers and the silent generation in this regard—suggesting
that the amount of information we share openly online has al-

ready reached its peak. Gen Zers put only highly selective, managed information and personas online. Many have a different identity for each online platform and use them for different purposes, for example, Facebook for content they want their parents and grandparents to see and Snapchat for content for close friends. Gen Zers will uninstall tracking apps, are much savvier about encryption and its power to protect, much more likely to use apps that automatically delete their sent messages, and they provide personal information only if they perceive a direct benefit. For this reason, our research shows only 29 percent of Gen Z is willing to exchange personal information for loyalty points and rewards whereas 46 percent of millennials are willing to do this—loyalty programs don't resonate with Gen Z.

Another big challenge that big data faces is that future generations are going to be more skilled in how they share data and what true information they allow companies to have about them. The future of digital commerce is an interesting balance between security and privacy versus surveillance (by corporations and governments). It is fair to say that right now the Internet, from a privacy point of view, is broken, and near-constant reports of hacking, denial-of-service attacks and data breaches make tech-savvy consumers highly wary of sharing data. Our research finds that the critical ingredient for future success in the digital-retail world will be establishing a high level of trust. Without an altruistic set of values at their core, retailers will struggle to communicate or connect with future generations of consumers.

So, if this is the portrait of Gen Zers' anxieties, what about their hopes? Boomers came of age with the Vietnam War, the Cold War, and Watergate—all of which created great uncertainty and angst—and developed a new set of positive values. What events define Gen Z?

Any discussion of Gen Z's values has to start with diversity. As we've discussed, Gen Z is the first majority minority generation, with only 48 percent of Gen Z expected to identify as white by 2026.[6] Gen Zers are comfortable in environments with those of all colors, sexual orientations, and beliefs. People from diverse ethnic backgrounds now dominate popular culture—from Jay Z to Steph Curry to Ariana Grande to Lady Gaga. Sexual orientation and bathroom usage might be a big deal to older generations (particularly in certain parts of the United States), but for those growing up today, multiple role models from the LGBT community are leaders in retail, business, and music. Seventy-four percent of Gen Zers support equal rights for transgender people, and 80 percent supported legalizing same-sex marriage before the government did.[7] By 2026, these values are likely to be even more mainstream.

Another point at which Gen Z departs from earlier generation is the environment. While we did not find any big political movement lurking below the surface (but with the new connected technology that now could emerge in a flash) the environment was the most important topic to the Gen Zers we met. This generation often expresses the belief that they will be left to deal with the extreme effects of climate change.

Retailers and brands that begin today to recognize this anxiety in how they develop, source, and market products will be ahead of the pack. Levi's has already begun this journey with its Water Less process, which has saved more than two hundred million gallons of water in its manufacturing process since 2011, and its Waste Less jeans, which contain at least 20 percent post-consumer recycled content. About a quarter of all REI locations are powered by green energy, and the retailer plans to be a climate-neutral and zero-waste-to-landfill company by 2020 through cuts in emissions, use of green energy, and purchase of carbon offsets. And Nike has recycled more than twenty-three million pairs of shoes into more than three hundred sport surfaces while reducing its annual carbon dioxide emissions by more than 18 percent.[8]

The movements toward more natural foods, healthy living and sustainable development are part of this emphasis on sustainability, and these trends will not go away.

But what's most interesting is that, unlike earlier generations, Gen Z does not express a desire to create its own social movements. Unlike the teens and twentysomethings who organized and populated the antiwar demonstrations of the 1960s and 1970s, Gen Zers were content to join the movement of Bernie Sanders, a member of the silent generation, and were less likely to support Trump's anti-establishment movement. The Gen Z mind-set carries through to social media, where they are the group least likely to try to persuade others of their views (creating a movement) and instead look to create relationships and connect with existing ideas and groups.[9] Their activism shows up instead as an integral part of their daily activities. Fifty-two percent of Gen Zers we surveyed—compared with just 31 percent of boomers—believe public activism is the most important way to bring about change in the world.[10] Fifty-one percent of Gen Zers also believe that the social stance of brands is an important factor when they decide what to buy or boycott. And when they look for work, the third most important criterion is the company's impact on society.[11]

Finally, despite all the storm clouds Gen Zers see gathering on the horizon, they are optimistic about their future. Gen Zers believe they will be freer to live life on their own terms than earlier generations and that their lives will only get better, leading to a more satisfying and higher quality of life. They do believe that they will have to take more responsibility for that future than previous generations did. Perhaps as a result, they are more entrepreneurial and distrustful of corporations—nearly a quarter believe that they will be working for themselves—more than twice as many as in other generations. Part of that belief may be because they see large companies shrinking and creating fewer opportunities, but a large part is based on their desire to have more freedom.

They have heroes as well. The young activist Malala Yousafzai, Elon Musk, and Bill and Melinda Gates feature heavily. Gen Zers highly admire entrepreneurs, especially those who combine business success with social activism. Brands like Patagonia and TOMS will always have a following among these socially concerned consumers.

Seeing the impact of the Great Recession in a world of superabundance has made Gen Zers more frugal, less materialistic, less

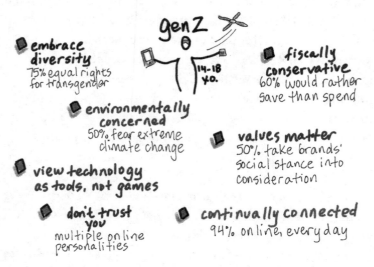

gen Z

embrace diversity
75% equal rights for transgender

14-18 y.o.

fiscally conservative
60% would rather save than spend

environmentally concerned
50% fear extreme climate change

values matter
50% take brands' social stance into consideration

view technology as tools, not games

don't trust you
multiple online personalities

continually connected
94% online, every day

Exhibit 10.2. Gen Z

accepting of debt, less brand-conscious, and more price-sensitive. They have a large concern for the future of the planet, but otherwise they do not have a consistent political viewpoint. If you want to sell them something, it needs to be special and imbued with meaning and authenticity. They seem likely to make fewer high-dollar purchases. In other words, the values-driven world we have been discussing as the next phase of retail is at the forefront of Gen Z's thinking. It will arrive.

So, what should retailers do about it? In the next several chapters we discuss the practical implications of this values-driven world for retailers, including the need for extreme fluidity and a new approach to brand building.

SECTION 3

WHAT WILL THE FUTURE LOOK LIKE?

CHAPTER 11

THE NEW RETAIL LANDSCAPE

The seismic shift is already having a dramatic impact on the retail world. Between now and 2027, the retail landscape will be radically restructured. The combination of product saturation and the power of the online model means that physical locations (and retailers dependent on those locations) are about to go through a major shake-up.

Phase 1: 2017–27
E-Commerce and Digitally Native Brands

The integrated distribution model, operating across multiple physical and digital platforms, will become the dominant distribution model of the future. Accordingly, pure e-commerce players such as Amazon and hundreds of other start-ups will continue to open physical stores.

The digital channel will continue to grow at a faster rate than the physical, but these will eventually reach a symbiotic balance—they will no longer be competing but instead will be sharing data and

U.S. Retail E-commerce by Product Category
(Percentage of e-commerce sales of total sales)

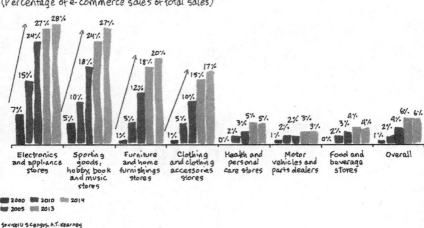

Electronics and appliance stores · Sporting goods, hobby, book and music stores · Furniture and home furnishings stores · Clothing and clothing accessories stores · Health and personal care stores · Motor vehicles and parts dealers · Food and beverage stores · Overall

■ 2000 ■ 2010 ■ 2014
■ 2005 ■ 2013

Sources: U.S Census, A.T. Kearney

Exhibit 11.1. U.S. Retail E-Commerce

products and both will be getting consumers what they want, when and where they want it. As Exhibit 11.1 shows, e-commerce sales in almost every category—especially electronics, sporting goods, books, music, furniture and clothing—have skyrocketed over time.

Malls and Shopping Centers

The United States now has thirteen hundred shopping centers and malls, and almost all are seeing thinning crowds, experiencing sameness, failing to make themselves accessible where and when consumers want to shop, and are peddling a ton of excess product at deep discounts. The future will bring a significant realignment, and only the strongest, and those ones capable of the greatest change, will survive. We believe more than half of all malls— roughly seven hundred—will go out of business because of their failure to offer a compelling shopping experience. The remaining six hundred will either become technologically driven urban destinations or adapt to serve the unique niches of their smaller, more suburban communities. The winners will become centers of great experiences. Which path they take will depend on investment, market dynamics, and the needs and wants of local consumers.

Many see technology as making malls less about shopping and more about entertainment. In these two hundred to three hundred technology-driven malls, cars or smartphones will have sensors that will lead drivers straight to an open parking space. The mall will know you have arrived and will immediately offer you deeply personalized suggestions for products based on purchase and browsing history; because the store of your preference already knows your size, it will have the right garments laid out for you to browse. While a small proportion of consumers will see this as an intrusion of their privacy, most others will happily hand over their data in exchange for a delightful, convenient experience—provided they trust the brand. If you buy these personalized products (seamlessly with your smartphone), they will be shipped to your home immediately so you have nothing to carry as you settle down for a nice designer coffee. Moving walkways and big digital screens showing personal messages from electronic concierges will bring the online world to you. Concepts for reinvented malls include all sorts of sports venues, dining facilities and retail space. The designs under consideration offer grandiose buildings that combine a futuristic *Star Trek* city vibe (high ceilings, domes and new age structures) with a nod to the bygone era of great architecture expressed at the World's Fairs. If the future of shopping depends on its entertainment value, it will occur in these settings.[1]

Another way the mall of the future may find success is by embracing progressive social and environmental values. This idea sees the mall as becoming a place that has a high mix of community usage, offering not just retail experiences but art galleries, places to recycle your old clothes, sites where artisanal products and food are made, a place where things are grown or made, and accommodates all modes of transportation (bike lanes, links to buses and trains—not just a focus on cars). The focus will be on green development with plenty of social centers for hanging out—the classic Starbucks-like third place between home and work. Of course technology will be everywhere, but the emphasis will be on human touch and community much more than space-age service levels. The mall will become a place that builds community, the element we have identified as missing in retail today.

Another two hundred to three hundred malls will change to appeal to their local communities. Oriental Mall in Atlanta, for example, was dying until it transformed itself to serve its increasingly Latino neighborhood. The mall, now called Plaza Fiesta, looks more like a traditional farmers' market or open-air community market found throughout Central and South America, with hundreds of small stalls selling everything from DVDs to candy to jewelry to makeup to tacos, along with a few larger tenants like Laredo Western Wear. The mall is also a cultural center, offering Latino-focused job fairs and celebration of Mexican Independence Day and Cinco de Mayo with music and carnival rides—even a pro-immigration rally. The mall is now thriving, meeting the needs of its new community—the area's Latino population grew 230 percent from 1990 to 2000.[2]

After they bought the struggling Oriental Mall, its new owners were in talks with Walmart and The Home Depot, planning to demolish the old mall and build a new, traditional one, until a look at the area's changing demographics and a trip to Mexico's open-air flea markets convinced them to change their minds. Other examples of ways in which malls might evolve to fit local needs include a mall in Florida or the Sun Belt with stores aimed at older adults with easily navigable, low-tech experiences, or malls catering to busy families with child care, a place to get car repairs done, or clothes washed while picking up a few things.

The remaining seven hundred shopping complexes will decline, as they will be seen as neither convenient nor experiential. The operators will seek new tenants (such as health care offices, gyms, baseball batting cages) but won't regain their retail identity. The future for these centers is bleak. As consumers drift away, the willingness to spend the resources to revive these centers dissipates, and with a few empty boarded-up buildings they may well start to resemble the dystopian future of *Blade Runner*. It will take a lot of creativity and imagination to find a second chance for these locations.

Mixed-use lifestyle centers and little villages are growing. They are built to resemble modern small town Main Streets but are built in urban areas. Stores, products, services, and entertainment will be tailored to local preferences. Mixed-use urban locations also will include residential units. Bay Street in Emeryville, near San Francisco, includes luxury apartments and condos atop a wide range of stores, all arranged around a central street with food carts, a movie theater and a central square. And The Boulevard in suburban St. Louis—a similar development—continues to grow and thrive despite being located directly across the street from a much larger traditional mall. The Boulevard is in the midst of a $78.9 million expansion that will almost double its retail and living spaces.[3]

Outlet centers will likely struggle as credible choices for the value-hunting consumer increase everywhere. The major off-price brands, particularly those of the TJX Companies (T.J. Maxx, Marshalls, Home Goods), will continue their explosive growth and will steal share from these centers as well as higher-end retailers.

Department Stores

As is already beginning to happen, department stores will evolve into flagship entertainment centers in major urban areas, with a reduced number of smaller stores in communities across the country. They will resemble showroom boutiques, tailored to local preferences.

The online and physical distribution process will be fully and seamlessly integrated across such enterprises. In addition to offering entertainment enhanced by technology and other experiences, the flagships will have a combination of third-party brands that will lease space to the flagship department store's strong private and exclusive brands. The flagship's strong private brands also will be available at small branded specialty boutiques.

No matter what, you will definitely see fewer department stores than today. The hope of the owners of these locations is that entertainment value, experiential content and service levels will be so great that they will make your trip worthwhile. But with all the new technology-induced fun most people have at home and everywhere else, they are not going to find themselves lacking things to do or places to buy products that will be delivered quickly. These department stores will have to reach a high bar to survive and flourish.

Branded Specialty Store Chains

The number of branded specialty store chains will become vastly smaller. The justification for having more than eight hundred locations is diminishing, and our argument suggests this decline will accelerate. Although it is a big driver, the Internet is not the only factor. Driving this change is the consumer's desire for more individualized product, something a large chain cannot easily provide. Plus, once a big retailer makes a mistake with a customer, tarnishing its brand, it is unlikely to achieve forgiveness, and repositioning an apparel brand now is extremely difficult. Furthermore, because of the supply-demand imbalance, the consumer has hundreds of equally compelling options, a key tap away or in a shop across the street.

Branded specialty store chains that survive will provide the same experiences and fully integrated omnichannel process (that is, they will make it possible for consumers to shop in stores, online, or by phone) as department stores, but will be especially focused on personalizing the omnibrand experience for the consumer. They will want to be cool above all else.

Just as Amazon must roll out small locally stocked physical stores with showrooms, Walmart will perfect its omnichannel model and leverage its forty-five hundred stores as both distribution centers and as places to shop. Using analytics, Walmart will maintain only the larger boxes that perform well. Instead, the company will develop smaller, locally curated stores in neighborhoods. Despite that model, dollar stores will continue to dominate, having already stolen a huge share of Walmart's business for several years. Walmart and Amazon will be fighting far into the future for the number one slot in value retailing.

Other big-box stores will continue to shrink their footprint and lose share because of their inability to create an intimate and differentiated experience.

Discounters and Clubs

The clubs, such as Costco, will have to follow Walmart's decision to offer omnichannel shopping, increasing their online presence and offering other consumer conveniences, including purchase online, pick up in store, and at-home delivery. If they fail to extend their reach in these ways, they too will fall victim to the convenience of less-expensive, online-only competitors for products that don't need to be tried on before buying them. All these big-box stores must eventually perfect rapid delivery (Instacart and Deliv represent early promise of the possibility), because consumers will be reluctant to drive to a big-box store, usually past several other grocery stores, and spend time parking and wandering around a gigantic space when they can get the same product delivered within minutes for the same price—or less.

Neighborhood Stores

Stores that are small, special, intimate, personal, social, and community-focused will win big, not least by being profitable. It's back to the future, to the time when local mom-and-pop owners were part of your life and knew everything about you with no need for analytics and algorithms. This model will become more popular and ultimately prevail.

For example, the Ainsworth Street Collective in Portland, Oregon, has a membership of more than fifty neighbors who meet to discuss issues related not just to their neighborhood but to the entire planet. Members of the collective have built a communal outdoor earthen oven, started a wholesale bulk food–purchasing program to reduce packaging and the need to drive to a store, and formed subgroups devoted to gardening, yoga, knitting, even fighting emissions from a nearby factory.[4]

But even big brands can tap into this kind of local energy. The key difference today is that data analytics and algorithms allow gigantic, multibillion-dollar enterprises to establish locally stocked niche stores and locally selected brands in neighborhoods across the country, including many different neighborhoods within major cities. A chain like Whole Foods, with many stores in New York City, will have different assortments in each. TJX, parent of T.J. Maxx and others, already has different stock and a different look and presentation in each of its neighborhoods, all chosen to satisfy local preferences. These differentiated stores might be only blocks away from each other.

Phase 2: 2027 and Beyond

If we put aside the absurd notion that anything twenty years out can be forecasted, we can nonetheless offer ideas of what retail life might look like based on the trends we see.

Stores

In twenty years, improvements in distribution will have largely eliminated the need to maintain huge inventories of goods that people purchase regularly. People will shop only in places that provide great entertainment or deep engagement and meaning for the consumer. Given the fluid nature of how we will live (our homes) and how and where we will work, many stores will be places that create community and provide a meaningful place to meet, be productive and hang out. Selling products will occur naturally in these environments.

Most stores will be little more than showrooms. There will of course always be fantastic places that display the latest trends and fashions and offer a great day of shopping with your friends. To survive, first-class malls boast cool technology and innovative retailers and products. Inside these malls the new draw will be large-scale entertainment vehicles that cannot be easily replicated at home.

But the only other shopping choices will be neighborhood stores and communities full of creative products, services and shows. These will look like a combination of farmers' markets, local boutiques, art shows, and perhaps even places for political and social discourse. Three-dimensional printing is likely to be available in every location.

All other stores will disappear. The distribution paradigm will have solved the economic challenges of e-commerce, and all the funky new delivery devices in their infancy today will be up and running, including self-driving cars and drones. Going to a store to purchase products that have low emotional engagement and high repurchase rates will be something we cannot imagine doing. Instead, big platform e-commerce sites will provide these products, but even they will have competition from a million new businesses.

By 2027, the word *store* will be archaic.

Peer-to-Peer Commerce

By 2027, the world of peer-to-peer commerce will be large enough to be operating at maximum efficiency. People will cooperate to build products. The technology will make possible easy connections, safe transactions, and highly secure and anonymous trading. That this is even remotely possible may sound crazy today. In 2013, 10 percent of all publicly traded companies accounted for 80 percent of all profits generated by these firms. Since 1980 the share of profits going to large corporations has increased by 30 percent.[5] The seismic shift we have outlined marks the start of reversing this relationship. By 2027, megacorporations' share of the consumer, retail and media/entertainment world will have eroded, shared instead by millions of small, disparate businesses. In many industries the advantage of scale is diminishing and may well disappear.

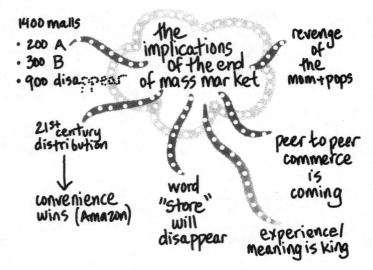

1400 malls
- 200 A
- 300 B
- 900 disappear

the implications of the end of mass market

revenge of the mom+pops

21st century distribution
↓
convenience wins (Amazon)

word "store" will disappear

peer to peer commerce is coming

experience/ meaning is king

Exhibit 11.2. Implications of the End of the Mass Market

Sites like OpenBazaar, a peer-to-peer trading network, may well feel like the next Amazon, except that they will not be platforms. The darknet may become one of the largest trading places as people seek security and anonymity. Large retailers or brands will dominate neither space—both of which will be full of small, cool, focused shops and brands.

In the next chapter we look at the principles that will define success in this new retail world.

SECTION 4

HOW TO WIN

1. **liquidity**
   - supply chain
   - organization
   - "frustrating frictions"
   - ex: spotify:
     "liquefy my music"

2. **platforming**
   - create commerce
   - leverage unused assets
     - relationship
     - data
     - space

3. **post-platform**

the new mindsets

4. **small is beautiful**
   - manage for cash
   - strategic descale

5. **branding**
   - values
     - raise self-esteem
   - innovative
     - small
       - not weird

Exhibit S4. The New Mindsets

CHAPTER 12

SMALL IS BEAUTIFUL

Price deflation, the end of mass markets and gargantuan retail corporations, and great market fragmentation are the central tenets of our thesis. This simply means retail is shifting to an infinite number of consumer niches served by an infinite array of focused brands. Whether the business is a department or grocery store or brand of makeup, our idea runs counter to the business models used by every mass-market retailer or brand. Yet if the executives looked at their own stores, they would find the data that supports our thesis. It's not difficult to find a mall where all the windows of a store are plastered with signs that say ENTIRE STORE 30% OFF—a tipoff to the problem of excess supply. Visit any big-box retailer and you'll have the same dull experience—the same mannequins wearing the same clothes, the same products stacked high in every aisle—a sign of a lack of creativity and the failure to connect with the consumer.

Standardization, efficiency, and economies of scale have brought mass retailers incredible success. Between 1996 and 2006—before the demographic, social and economic shifts started to have an impact—Best Buy's market value grew a crazy

2,260 percent, Sears saw 699 percent growth, and Target's value shot up 786 percent. Meanwhile, Macy's grew 402 percent and Nordstrom, Kohl's, and JCPenney saw growth of 264 percent, 42 percent, and 25 percent, respectively. But that business model is antiquated. The financial success of these companies already reflects an incredible decline in value from 2006 to 2016. Since then, Best Buy has seen a 46 percent drop in market value (but is fighting back), JCPenney experienced an 83 percent fall, Kohl's value has decreased 59 percent, Sears is worth 46 percent less, and Macy's, Nordstrom, and Target have seen drops of 46 percent, 21 percent, and 15 percent, respectively. Even Walmart, whose market value has grown 43 percent since 2006, can't come anywhere close to its 1996–2006 value growth of 320 percent. Meanwhile, Amazon's market value has grown 1,190 percent from 2006 to 2016.[1] Put quite simply, Wall Street believes mass retail formats can no longer grow in value. For these large retailers this poses two fundamental strategic choices: manage for cash, maybe into closure, or descale and potentially grow again in select niches.

Manage for Cash Flow

Surviving will clearly require such tactics as cutting costs, downsizing entire enterprises—including by closing stores and forming real estate investment trusts (REITs) to manage whatever real estate the corporation continues to own—as well as selling other assets, such as brands, and relicensing them to the retail operation.

The downsizing of Sears and Kmart under the leadership of the famed financier Eddie Lampert might be considered an exemplar of three potential moves: managing for cash flow or reducing the business so it either becomes a smaller, more fleet-footed entity or enters bankruptcy. Executives of Sears obviously would deny that their strategy is to manage for cash flow, but everything Sears has done is consistent with that approach—albeit with a Hail Mary approach to building an Internet business. The company has pulled assets out of the core, placing its valuable brands like DieHard and Maytag in a separate entity; put several hundred stores in REITs that the owners will control after Sears declares bankruptcy; and spun off Lands' End and ceased to invest in its Sears stores or people. Sears is now exploring options to sell its well-known Kenmore, Craftsman, and DieHard brands.

So Sears has shrunk as a business. As same-store sales and the number of stores declined, its revenue fell 8.8 percent in the second quarter of 2016, and its stock has fallen from a peak of $191.93 in 2007 to $8.79 in December 2016—and probably will have fallen even more by the time you are reading this book. Clearly, the viability of Sears remains a perennial question. Its recent cash infusion—and it's likely to receive another—was aimed at preventing a precipitous decline in confidence, but the goal is still to buy enough time to liberate capital. But no matter how much cash its owners reinject in Sears, it is unlikely to survive with its current business model because of the changes in retail markets that we have outlined. The market realities we have discussed—manifested in its many decaying, useless stores and consumers' perceptions of the Sears brand as outdated and irrelevant, and reinforced by the sell-off of its remaining marquee brands—while a rational response to the market challenges has fatally hobbled Sears.

Sears may provide an essential case study for other struggling department stores. The current dynamics suggest only a few department store chains will survive. If that is the case, how do you create economic value as you shrink? This is something that retail and consumer-facing businesses have never dealt with before.

When the Sears story ends, it will be interesting to see if Lampert made money by managing Sears for cash flow.

Another example comes from the highly acquisitive Brazilian firm 3G Capital, which has been behind some of the biggest mergers in the world: the marriage of Kraft and Heinz, Burger King's $11.4 billion takeover of Tim Hortons, and the birth of the beer giant Anheuser-Busch InBev, which was the result of a $52 billion buyout. It is clear that this approach understands the challenges of operating in a limited-demand environment and puts in place a process that immediately and aggressively restructures the costs of the business to better reflect current price and demand constraints. 3G Capital has taken the approach of massively cutting costs in each of the businesses it takes over; this typically involves widespread layoffs, smaller budgets, new levels of austerity, and a shift in corporate culture. For example, the InBev deal resulted in the elimination of fourteen hundred jobs at Anheuser-Busch, and six hundred Heinz employees lost their jobs after the merger—including eleven of the company's top twelve executives.[2]

So how will the excess capacity in retail and consumer-facing businesses be removed? It is a pervasive problem across the consumer industry. The overhead structures and economics of growing times are no longer applicable or sustainable. Cost structures must be radically reduced. Organizations must be streamlined. Now may even be the time for owners of profitable stores to shutter them, consolidate volume and move more sales online— the net result can be substantially positive from a cash-flow perspective. That's because customers of a profitable store may shift their business to another location that is closer to their homes or purchase online, allowing the retailer to keep the sale without the overhead. This is a radically different management philosophy. But as this seismic shift continues, cash flow is becoming king.

Whether you think financiers have taken on too much risk or have handled it too aggressively, the reality is that the forces we have identified make managing for cash flow a necessary survival strategy.

Strategic Shrinking

The second approach is to shrink more strategically in order to grow. Obviously, cost cutting is a critical component. Reducing costs will require great creativity. For example, should department stores hand over the management of parts of the stores to vendors? The approach of strategic shrinking requires the rethinking of basics, such as the optimal number of stores, store formats and an omnichannel strategy—that is, creating a compelling, integrated experience and providing for distribution no matter how, when or where the consumer wants to interact with your brand—that does not destroy short-term profits and has a clear long-term goal. Unfortunately, many retailers have no such vision.

What will the retailers who recognize the trends do? One obvious move is to combine—like QVC and HSN. Expect more mergers. Some will strategically downsize, fragmenting their models to serve the newly emerging consumer culture, those customers' divergent desires and the micro-communities they live in, as we described in earlier chapters. In short, the strategically downsized model will accommodate consumers' shifting desires. Said in another way, some will shrink into a niche and will sharply differentiate themselves from their competitors.

Among the retailers that are finding success by becoming more focused is the TJX Companies (Marshalls, T.J. Maxx, and Home Goods). TJX understood fragmenting markets and consumers' shifting interests early on, perhaps because it was an early beneficiary of excess demand. Ironically, the speed with which TJX continues to grow would seem to make it an outlier, not an example of our thesis. TJX's second quarter earnings report for 2016 showed $7.9 billion in revenue—7 percent more than the same period the year before and higher than its expectations. Same-store sales rose 4 percent during the same period, also easily beating estimates and the industry-wide average. Net income grew 5 percent over the same period in the previous year and still beat expectations. And this all happened while TJX added new stores.[3]

The fundamental driver of this growth is a value proposition that fits perfectly with a period of excess supply and price deflation. If initially this segment of the market was meant to be where people went to buy unsold goods, it has become a destination for consumers looking for the "treasure hunt" experience. And it's now where the entire retail market is moving. Another feature that gives off-price or closeout retailers an advantage is that they have always had a keen focus on overhead costs and minimizing investment. Their deal was clear: customers got great prices. The success of the model was so powerful that the level of investment in big information technology systems, loyalty programs or customer relationship management programs was not close to that of the more established retailers. Off-price overhead is more consistent with how the market is evolving and the new price level. One way for stores to survive is to sell at a price lower than the online world. This requires a much lower cost structure than most e-tailers have today.

TJX's success is also partly the result of its unique strategy—fragmenting its business to drive growth. Simply put, TJX analyzed each market, even neighborhoods, and customized the assortment of apparel, prices, and even the store layout and presentation, based on consumer preferences and each market's demographic profile. For example, the T.J. Maxx in Riverhead,

New York, which caters to a largely blue-collar community, is totally different from the T.J. Maxx twenty miles away in the tony Hamptons village of Bridgehampton, home of Wall Street multimillionaires.

Whole Foods is evolving in the same way. Its new 365 format offers more conventional produce—the assortment is only about 50 percent organic—and much of it is smaller or less perfect than what traditional Whole Foods stores offer. That helps the new format hit a lower price point and address a wider range of consumers. Even within its more than four hundred traditional stores, 15 to 30 percent of the goods in any given store is locally sourced. The retailer accomplishes this by fielding a team of "foragers" who develop relationships with and buy from more than sixty-five hundred local vendors nationwide.

Becoming smaller also means creating or acquiring products that serve distinct niches. Big food companies are rushing to add organic and localized brands to their portfolios to appeal to consumers' shifting desires. Kellogg's has owned Kashi for more than a decade, General Mills bought Annie's Homegrown in 2014, and Campbell acquired the organic baby food company Plum Organics in 2013 and started an organic soup line in 2015. Many traditional brands are also revamping their core products to make them healthier or to include more natural ingredients— General Mills cut the sugar content of Yoplait yogurt by 25 percent and is removing synthetic materials from its cereals; Kraft is doing the same with its classic macaroni and cheese and is removing sugar from genetically modified sources and artificial dyes from Jello. Even Mars is searching for natural colorants for its classic M&Ms.

Certainly, we believe that if huge department stores like Macy's, JCPenney, Kohl's and others will succeed in the future, they will have to break up their huge enterprises. They need to first close many of their underperforming stores, which is already under way—before this book went to press in 2017, Macy had announced it was closing 15 percent of its stores, Sears and Kmart had decided to shutter more stores, and some stores owned by CVS, The Limited, Aeropostale, American Eagle, Chico's, Finish Line, Men's Wearhouse, and The Children's Place also were closing their doors in 2017. The next step for large chains is to strategically downsize or fragment by reconfiguring their remaining stores in nonurban areas to match local community tastes and lifestyles.

We believe that department store chains must first remake their huge flagship stores in such major cities as New York, Chicago, San Francisco, Los Angeles, and Dallas as go-to destinations for entertainment, restaurants, fashion shows, and other events while redesigning the stores so that consumers do not feel they are shopping in a huge building with a lot of stuff but instead along streets of small boutiques that feel intimate, exclusive, and personalized.

And we believe the chains can achieve this only by combining their own private or exclusive brands with a selection of powerful brands (even competing brands) that the chains have invited to lease, staff, and run space in their stores. Selfridges of London is the exemplar of this model. In the United States, Walmart and Target continue to implement their small neighborhood store strategies. Although Walmart announced the closure of its small Walmart Express stores in January 2016, it's doubling down its Neighborhood Market format, which has almost seen hundred stores, most of them located between dense urban centers and Walmart's more rural full-size stores. Target, in contrast, has open its thirty-two smaller stores in densely populated urban areas.[4] One reason Target and Walmart adopted this strategy was to respond to the dollar stores, whose model was originally built on serving niches and many thousands of small blue-collar neighborhoods. The challenge still remains for these and others: How do you move to smaller stores with an overhead structure designed for economies of scale? What are the right organizational models for this new world, and is the large, centralized gatekeeper a sustainable function?

Many other big-box retailers have also been thinking small.

The Home Depot has operated urban stores since the 1990s, but many are still comparatively large at eighty to ninety thousand square feet (versus the average suburban Home Depot, which is 120,000 square feet). The Home Depot's early move into urban areas has helped it outperform Lowe's in same-store sales growth, with Lowe's playing catch-up in many cities and recently opening urban stores of about thirty thousand square feet.[5] These stores have avoided the immediate pressures of the massive shift to online and still offer a wide assortment of goods, a combination that has given them breathing room.

Office Depot's small stores are one of the rare bright spots in the retailer's performance. In 2016 the chain announced it would close three hundred full-size stores in the next three years but would open more of its "stores of the future" (at fifteen thousand square feet), bringing the number to twenty-four by the end of 2016 and to one hundred by the end of 2017.[6]

And many other retailers are pursuing the same strategy.

Major single-branded specialty chains like Urban Outfitters, The Gap, J.Crew, Victoria's Secret, Chico's, and many others, regardless of their current financial performance, are already in niche markets. However, all are cookie-cutter models with the same assortments, layouts and presentation. So, they too must localize each of their hundreds of stores—downsizing through fragmentation.

Yet everything from the overhead structure to sourcing is

based on economies of scale and standardization. To create this level of localization (and even personalization) characteristic of the smaller stores, these retailers will need to change the current approach of their factories, which is to maximize production runs, and shrink the time from creation to consumption. All this has to be done with fewer personnel in management.

We spoke with Michelle Lam, CEO of the online-only bra start-up True&Co., about the inherent conflict between mass production and personalization and what that conflict means for the future of her highly-customized company.

"The physical supply chain has little incentive to be innovative—it favors scale, uniformity and cost," Michelle said. "Most brands will share a product concept with the factory, and then, based on their own grading system, based on prior production runs, [the brands] make different variations from that. But are they right? Most often the customer does not get what they really want, especially in a world where the customer no longer wants the same thing."

Meanwhile, major wholesale apparel-sector players, such as VF Corporation and PVH, are creating their fragmentation efforts by acquiring niche bands like The North Face, Timberland and others at VF, and Tommy Hilfiger, Calvin Klein and others at PVH.

This approach naturally raises the question of whether a shared services model, with centralized but reduced overhead costs that are shared by different consumer-facing businesses, can work. This is being tried in different ways—Ascena Retail Group's acquisition of Ann Inc. was predicated on this approach. Others, including Procter & Gamble and Diageo, are doing this in different sectors.

The jury is still out on the efficacy of this approach. Bureaucratic central organizations may be too ponderous to respond nimbly to the demands of the marketplace (especially if information tech-nology is one of the main shared services, since it has to be nimble and entrepreneurial, often while supporting divergent goals by brand). The oft-repeated need for The Gap to spin off and sell each of its divisions to increase its responsiveness and value suggests that achieving sustained savings from shared services is difficult. Finally, as of this writing Amazon is testing small, locally curated book and grocery stores as well as mall pop-up stores designed to sell the Echo. We believe that, once tested, Amazon will roll these stores out across the country and even the world.

These Amazon stores are likely to be showrooms featuring localized merchandise based on consumer preferences in specific neighborhoods, as determined by mining Amazon's Pentagon-sized consumer data base. In fact, one former Walmart execu-tive acknowledged this scenario is one of Walmart's greatest fears. And, quite logically, it may have ignited the huge reposi-tioning that is now under way at Walmart, with the objective of competing with Amazon head-on.

The cultural challenge of managing this process of down-sizing is very real and difficult. Consumer-facing brands have al-ways been about the promise of growth and creating new things and experiences for the consumer. Now they face a new environ-ment in which they are under pressure to shrink and survive and change their internal roles. At the same time, the need for ener-gized employees, especially in stores, is even more acute.

Growth

If this story has a silver lining, it is that there has never been a better time to start and run a small business. Consumers are crying out for innovative products, experiences and services. They do not want or need to pay for the old gatekeeper functions like merchandise planning and allocation, which required economies of scale and provided large companies with a big advantage.

Today the emphasis is on small unique quantities of meaningful product, things ideally suited to a small business. From artisanal chocolate to coffee to t-shirts to locally produced denim, the opportunities abound. The prospect of starting with an effective digital strategy and then looking for partners or retail space to expand is highly appealing. Companies from Mack Weldon (men's underwear) to Casper (mattresses) are proving that point.

The only caveat: Make sure you don't think that you can scale easily. Scale should not be the goal. Achieve profitability (and sustain a nice creative lifestyle). If you do keep investing and losing money as you try to grow, sell as soon as you can. One great example of this is the Dollar Shave Club, whose founder sold the online-only razor seller to Unilever for $1 billion—or five times the company's sales—in mid-2016. Remember, the market is not rewarding scale.

For retailers the next steps for success are clear. Pick your niche. If you are massive, get rid of the mass by fragmenting into niches. Create differentiation and awesome experiences for each niche. As we discuss in the next chapter, this is critical to building a successful brand in today's changing consumer market.

CHAPTER 13

BECOMING A BRAND

We have discussed the concept of rational altruism as a reflection of what consumers will increasingly desire from the places they shop or the brands they buy. This concept captures the idea of truly understanding your consumers' lives, placing their holistic needs and values at the core of your strategy and creating an organization that embraces this values-driven mission. The embodiment of this approach is antithetical to seeing your customers as mere consumers—and in many ways it is antithetical to the traditional notion of consumerism. There is nothing wrong with consumption per se, but we see a radical shift in the motivation behind consumption and the level and way in which people will consume in the future. Building a brand that embodies this shift is critical.

Becoming a brand is critical. The data support that assertion. Analysis of the top ten most valuable brands (as captured by Millward Brown's annual BrandZ survey) shows that if they were a portfolio, they would have outperformed the Standard and Poor's 500 Index since 2007 by 75 percent and the world index by 400 percent.[1] During the next twenty years, the importance of brands is going to increase. That's right—don't believe anyone who suggests that brands are declining. After searching the web, gathering their peers' opinions and checking prices, consumers are going to still buy from brands. True brands, that is. Today, almost all products and retailers claim to be a brand, but few actually attain that status.

Brands and brand value are defined in many traditional ways: awareness, loyalty, purchase intent, net promoter score, emotional connections and more. All are arguably important, but for our discussion about the future building a brand has five key dimensions. A brand (both retailers and products) must

1. Have a clear set of values
2. Raise the consumer's self-esteem
3. Be innovative
4. Be relatively scarce
5. Have a consistent identity

Let's start with a discussion of values.

Have a Clear Set of Values

We have written at length about the emerging importance of values and Maslow's hierarchy of needs (with its link to self-esteem and self-actualization) so we need not revisit their importance.

But reflecting on what those values might look like is worthwhile. The spectrum is wide. The Ultimate Fighting Championship (UFC) represents a clear set of values: aggression, courage, and camaraderie—and profits. Spotify was quick to issue a playlist for Black Lives Matter, followed swiftly by attempts by other favorite millennial brands—Facebook and Google—to show they supported the movement. Lush and L'Oréal were active in the support of the refugees streaming into Europe in recent years. The issue of gay marriage provided opportunities for companies like Ben & Jerry's and American Airlines to provide vocal support. To paraphrase the opinions of the youth leader Amani Alkhat, editor in chief of *MuslimGirl*, the public will reward companies that pay more than lip service to values like diversity. Uber and Lyft provide other good examples—Uber has suffered some for the sexual harassment alleged by female employees, Google's lawsuit charging theft of trade secrets and intellectual property, and the company's use of an app to deceive city officials where its service was banned. Lyft has actively positioned itself as the socially responsible ride-sharing company.

But other brands' values become apparent in different ways. The southern food chain Bojangles clearly has as its core values simply providing great, high-quality comfort food. Hobby Lobby led the fight against the Obamacare requirement that businesses provide employees with coverage for birth control. After Donald Trump Jr. tweeted a comparison of refugees and Skittles, Wrigley responded: "Skittles are candy. Refugees are people. We don't feel it is an appropriate analogy." The candy maker felt the need to enter into the debate—despite its awareness that not everyone would applaud its response.

The point here is that consumers will have a heightened desire to spend their money with companies or on products that have a clear set of values or are actively articulating them.

Raise the Consumer's Self-Esteem

Branding has always been about raising the self-esteem of a product or store's fans. From making people part of exclusive clubs (think

Prada or Burberry) to making them feel part of a community (the great Coke ads with songs about teaching the world to sing) to marketing aspirational markers of the end of a great journey (like buying a Porsche . . . maybe) to sending secret signals to each other (think Fred Perry shirts) to making people feel good about what their purchases do for the family (environmental or organic brands) or for others (TOMS) or helping people develop identities by buying specialized products (craft beer, cold brew coffee, ten-dollar juices) in contrast to what they see as the products of the masses. In chapter 7 we described how the need for self-esteem drives the continual fragmentation in tastes and buying behaviors. It is central to the idea of a brand.

So the question that every brand must ask is, "Do my products, brand and experience really raise my customers' self-esteem?" For most, getting to yes is difficult. If they do not, surviving the coming wave of excess product will be a real challenge.

Be Innovative

New and innovative experiences keep customers coming back. This can derive from the product or the service itself or from the experience surrounding the purchase. Obviously, in fashion, increasingly small and increasingly rapid product cycles have proven to be a winner with an increasingly fickle consumer (think H&M and Zara). The innovation that supported this shift came from the supply chain and allowed for shorter and shorter product development cycles. Continuing to do this while minimizing the environmental impact (for example, the water and energy required to produce lots of disposable clothes—and to dispose of them) is likely to be a winning model in the long run. The first one to succeed will win.

Another key trend has been the consumer shift from merely

wanting stuff to demanding experiences. Innovation is critical here. In *The New Rules of Retail*, we listed many ways that experiences can be created or enhanced. Kevin Kelly, in his book *The Inevitable*, recently captured and nicely amplified these rules. He listed eight powerful ways that experiences, or what he calls "generatives," meaning "a quality or attribute that must be generated at the time of transaction," create value:

1. Immediacy: Eventually, you will be able to find a less-expensive version of whatever you're looking for, but being able to get it now carries value.
2. Personalization: A product customized for you is more valuable than a generic one.
3. Interpretation: Sometimes it's not just the product, it's someone showing you how to use it or telling you the story behind it.
4. Authenticity: Finding value in high-quality, "pure" items with a distinct point of view.
5. Accessibility: Being able to make use of a product anywhere, anytime, even if you don't own it in the traditional sense.
6. Embodiment: Just like you might pay hundreds of dollars to attend a concert that's streamed free online, certain in-person experiences cannot be matched on the web.
7. Patronage: Finding fulfillment in rewarding the creators of your favorite products.
8. Discoverability: Products have no value unless consumers can find them.[2]

As these generatives show, there are many ways to create value outside the product itself; many are wrapped around the experience of discovering, researching, buying and owning the product.

Innovation is already having a profound impact by providing experiences to the consumer in many ways (and will continue to do so). Many technological innovations appear quite gimmicky and unlikely to last (think automated fitting rooms, digital shelf edges—also call smart shelves—and location-based mobile alerts), but as the prices of products continue to drop, these generatives, or experiences, will become ever more important, especially in getting people to visit a store.

But innovation will be deeper and more extensive for both products and experiences. One of the best descriptions of a product that we have heard is that it's a "crystallization of our imagination."[3] Before any product is created, it's imagined. The retail and consumer goods industries offer an almost unparalleled opportunity for people to express their creative imagination. There is always the promise of what a product, service or experience—and ultimately a brand—can be. It must be a true reflection of both imagination and incredible knowledge. This is becoming evermore true.

In fact, the job of developing an experience must become one of the most important functions in every company. Today, product or experience development often is staffed by the newest members of the organization, and those who do a good job get promoted to management. It is no accident that Apple's success was driven by a CEO fixated on product development who surrounded himself with a small group of the brightest and most creative individuals he could find. Then he copied this practice in rolling out the Apple retail concept. This process is also evident at many other techcentric consumer brands. Many will say CEOs cannot spend their time developing experiences, but in the future, CEOs' future will depend on it. CEOs will have to spend more and more time on the process of generating new and better products and experiences, as well as the processes that build this creative force and imaginative capability into the organization.

It is impossible to describe all the innovative ways to improve various retailers or brands. But from creating a better shopping environment or delivery experience for the poorest members of a community to providing the one percent with the coolest new products measuring their biology or a mind-blowing technology-driven experience, innovation is crucial.

Don't Be Ubiquitous

Whatever wonderful elements are embodied in and created by the brand, they will run up against another requirement of brand building: they cannot be ubiquitous. Exclusivity has long been a mainstay of the fashion world, recently abandoned for the sake of growth and pursuit of mass markets. In chapter 4, on fragmentation, we laid out one of the major drivers of self-esteem: achieving social status by having unique identifiers or products or by being important to a particular group.

Future consumers (with abundant choice) will be looking for increasingly exclusive experiences and products, whether that is a cool new specially designed pair of jeans, a craft beer available only in a few locations, or a VIP meet-and-greet with their favorite author, designer, or creator in a select store. Whether you are rich or just getting by, your disposable dollars will be spent on things that are hard to find or replicate.

Of course, this also means that the days of pretending growth for the brand is infinite are over. Remember: small is beautiful.

Have a Consistent Identity

Finally, in building a brand, it is critical that you never do any-thing that is perceived as strange or in conflict with the core values of the brand. This may seem obvious, but the pursuit of growth has led retailers and brands to take a variety of ac-tions that confuse consumers and tarnish the brand's sense of authenticity.

One of our favorite examples of the risks here goes back to when the steakhouse Ponderosa tried to move upscale. The chain saw the increasing popularity of higher-priced and better-quality steaks and decided to move in that direction. Ponderosa elimi-nated its lower-priced steaks and offered a great value but more expensive alternative. The trouble was their core consumer could not afford the great value and deserted the chain, while its aspi-rational customers stilled viewed it as a purveyor of a product of lesser quality. The result was a clear defeat for the chain. Evolv-ing your offering (which is good) must be carefully balanced with staying true to your values—it is not easy.

JCPenney under Ron Johnson is perhaps the best example of a retailer that confused its consumers when it changed its pric-ing strategy and changed its merchandise in favor of new brands. The desire to rapidly overhaul the retailer and completely change its course was met with heavy losses and an open revolt by its traditional customers. Time will tell whether the brand can recoup, but it is courting the value-minded consumer with a renewed focus on promotions and its "Get Your Penney's Worth" advertising campaign. The retailer is also adding more products, like its partnership with the cosmetics chain Sephora, bringing back major appliances in a new showrooming manner and add-ing a new plus-size women's collection—all categories that con-sumers prefer to shop in-store, according to Marvin Ellison, the

CEO. JCPenney is also adding more private label products—more than eighteen thousand from more than two hundred designers. Such products make up more than 50 percent of Penney's sales.[4]

The customer confusion that can sometimes accompany brand repositioning can occur in subtler ways. For example, in rolling out "My Macy's," every store was heavily localized and made so different from other stores in different locations that many consumers found shopping at a Macy's other than their usual store to be strange and disorienting. A unique product assortment, different sizing, unusual brands, and pricing all led consumers to question exactly what the Macy's brand stood for.

Reebok is another example: over the years it has gone from being the apparel of choice of women to sponsoring the National Football League to Allen Iverson (the original bad boy of basketball) to now sponsoring the UFC and extreme sports like Cross-Fit. Time will tell if the latest positioning works or still feels like the brand is trying to find its true DNA.

Lands' End has also struggled to reinvent itself. As Becky Gebhardt, the chief marketing officer of Lands' End, told the crowd at a 2016 Shop.org conference, in its quest to turn itself into a "meaningful lifestyle brand" since being spun off from Sears in 2014, the company has gone after a younger, more fashionable consumer than its outdoorsy/sensible L.L.Bean-like roots might suggest. To reach this demographic, Lands' End rolled out slimmer-fitting designs and pop-up shops in trendy neighborhoods like Fifth Avenue in Midtown and SoHo in New York. But so far the turnaround has failed to pay off, with revenue in the second quarter of 2016 down 6 percent from the same quarter the year before and the resignation of the CEO who oversaw many of these changes.[5]

These examples show that if you act without a clear set of

values, or try to change too fast or too quickly, it is easy to become strange or unrecognizable. The ever-growing number of consumer niches means that every brand has to get closer and closer to its core consumer.

In the next chapter we explore another key concept central to surviving and thriving in the current climate: becoming liquid, which means flexibility. To evolve, brands will need the support of a responsive supply chain, to quickly and affordably get the right products to consumers.

CHAPTER 14

THE LIQUEFIED ORGANIZATION

Of all the concepts we cover, becoming liquid is paramount in achieving the state of mind required to run a modern retail operation. So, we're using it not simply to refer to the classic definition of liquidity of cash supply but more generally to describe something that can be quickly used or changed in almost any environment or can be rapidly moved to a new location or form. The notion of the liquid organization will become increasingly important as companies strive to become more innovative and to make sense of all the data they receive. The concept challenges traditional ideas about how companies work with other partners and the relationship they have with their employees. Everything will have to become more fluid and flexible.

Like many new ideas, the concept of becoming "liquid" is demonstrated most vividly in the digital space. I just liquefied my music collection by signing up for Spotify. Now every album I ever owned is available to me (and my family) wherever I am, on any device, in whatever order I want to play the songs—all instantaneously. In addition, music that matches the tastes of my collection is also now available to me, with a constant flow of suggestions and recommendations. Even my friends' suggestions are liquefied through a constant stream of digital missives.

The Liquid Supply Chain

Let's start with the idea of becoming liquid as it applies to the supply chain. The concept emerged from a dinner conversion we had with one of the leaders of a global sports brand's supply chain. The challenge that our thesis lays out for all megabrands is meeting the demands of a highly fragmented marketplace with stores everywhere (increasingly becoming showrooms), new distribution paradigms for store and online orders (such as same-day delivery), and what 3-D printing will mean for retail when it becomes an everyday reality. In other words, how do retailers manage small lots of exclusive product tailored to re-gional preferences that they must show to customers (providing a tactile, compelling experience) while also providing a highly con-venient delivery mechanism that efficiently manages inventory?

We realized as a result of the dinner discussion that the large, highly rigid supply chains of today are not going to work in this world. The big warehouses stockpiled with shirts, socks, foot-wear, and every other kind of item are a necessary evil but effectively support only the mass markets, which are in decline. Inventory has to become more like a just-in-time system—arriving in small quantities and stored for increasingly brief periods before almost instantaneous delivery to the end consumer. That inven-tory has to be available in increasingly tight spaces as a diverse crowd of people seeking their unique styles continues to flock to major cities.

So what does a liquid supply chain look like? Three main con-siderations cut across most industries:

It has no barriers. Today's supply chains struggle primarily because of a lack of communication between channels and long, complicated production processes. Without these barriers, the supply chain can support all points of sale equally well and adjust rapidly to new sources of demand. Eliminating barriers requires maintaining inventory in a way that works equally well for serving the in-store, online, and telephone customer and that makes no distinction between purchases in stores and online orders. It means goods can flow quickly and easily to the point of sale and requires short lead times for short production runs. The future will require a more flexible production approach than even those used by Zara, H&M, or other fast-fashion retailers. To pull this off, brands will need excess production capacity available locally (and will need to avoid stockpiling inventory). This will eliminate the time barrier for replenishment.

It is asset-light. This means small warehouses (perhaps old unused retail spaces) close to the market and fewer large distribution centers. It means using last-mile delivery without creating a huge fleet of vehicles or a hiring a team with big fixed costs— using the so-called gig economy instead. It means piggybacking on others' infrastructure and sharing assets. What it means most of all is not managing long production cycles by building enormous new warehouses or large factories that lock up capital. It means investing in digital data for the supply chain (more product accuracy, more use of data) and investing in 3-D printing—the ultimate long-term, personal, and local production capability. By 2026 expect to see a high percentage of all production located within your city.

It is highly fragmented. The future will bring fragmented supply chains that are not dominated by one point of production or supply. This is a natural outcome of both consumer demands and the process of fulfillment. The ability to cut supply chain costs will make smaller supply chains economical. These will be focused on serving a set customer need (for example, retro shoes produced and delivered to your house in an hour) that will differ by product, customer, and location. In the future, brands won't have one supply chain but lots of highly flexible, highly responsive, liquid ones.

Flexible Organizations

Fluidity also applies to the organizational structure of the future. Organizations today usually have a clear hierarchy and run under a command-and-control mind-set. Yet technology-driven centers like Silicon Valley clearly benefit from loose organizational structures that enable cross-collaboration of departments and enable people at all levels to be involved in decision making and to participate in innovation.

Google's organization is famously flat and collaborative, and it encourages employees to be creative and think outside their traditional roles—to the point of encouraging them to take time out of their workday to think of new ideas. Google's flexible work spaces embody this idea—taken to the extreme in the Google Garage hacker/maker/design space, nearly every piece of furniture is on wheels.[1]

More established companies also have made these organizational shifts. Perhaps one of the highest-profile cases of organizational change in retail was instituted at Zappos. The company adopted holocracy, a move from top-down management to a circles-and-links–based structure that empowered employees to work on what interests them. When Zappos implemented the system, 18 percent of the company's fifteen hundred employees took buyouts, and another 11 percent left without a severance package. Zappos learned that many employees craved the structure of defined roles and job titles. But Tony Hsieh, CEO of Zappos, didn't give up—he said the changes take time to sink in and that since adopting holocracy the company has flourished.[2] The company even offers holocracy training for other brands looking to make the switch. Time will tell if this model takes the concept of fluid organizations too far—but meeting the challenges of the retail shifts will require new Zappos-like experiments.

At Chewy.com, the online pet food store, the strategy of being a high-service, high-touch online provider has led to new levels of empowerment and decision making. For example, call center employees have complete latitude to decide what to do to delight the customer. The company tracks how long someone is on the phone and celebrates employees who have the longest calls serving the customer!

We are not saying that these early models have found the perfect solution, and, like many new ideas, they may fail. But the future will require a willingness to shatter old organizational structures in favor of a more fluid approach.

Such organizational transformations can occur outside retail too. Companies like Southwest Airlines and Yum! Brands give their employees autonomy to make decisions, especially those that create a stronger customer experience or help fix immediate problems. For example, at Pizza Hut, employees are empowered to make any decision that costs less than $15—the cost of a large pizza. So, if a customer complains about an order that is slow or incorrect, an employee has the power to correct it on the spot by offering a refund or freebies.

The next step for a liquid organization is to apply these new organizational structures to forge better relationships with external partners. Among the most commonly established are those between brands and their vendors, mills and suppliers, or wholesalers and the retailers that distribute their products. Research by A.T. Kearney, the management consulting company, shows that strong partnerships have resulted in "10% to 15% lift in topline performance, 40% to 60% faster new product launches and up to 20% decline in total inventory."[3] One of the many brands doing this is Maybelline, which relies on retail partners to distribute its products. Maybelline has an especially close partnership with Kroger, and their arrangement gives both the brand and the retail partner access to the same customer data in real time, which helps Maybelline stay on top of trends and accurately customize its assortments by store.[4]

The new retail environment also demands that historic competitors rethink their rivalries. In a world where fluidity between companies and jobs will become the new norm, fears of poaching staff and revealing product secrets may actually be holding companies back, because they will have shut themselves off from partners that could provide them with insights or data about their core consumer. Especially in an environment in which consumers' data are so critically important, sharing and collaborating may be the only way to get a complete picture of your consumer's wants and needs, which will help you to improve your products and experience. Let's say you have a shoe brand— wouldn't it be helpful to know about the new dress your customer just bought at a nearby retailer so you can send her a targeted offer for a perfectly matched pair of shoes?

The ability to move between jobs, functions and even companies is beneficial to innovation—and will be increasingly important. The ability to establish networks of collaborators is critical, yet most organizations are not set up to do this or even actively encourage it. The millennial generation of employees grew up with the technological tools that are increasingly central to the evolution of retail and consumer companies, yet the managers of these employees have the least familiarity with these tools. The digital revolution in marketing, innovation and data management will flourish only in organizations that become more mobile, more flexible and more decentralized. In other words, liquid.

Liquid Commerce

The concept of the liquid organization also applies to commerce. Removing frustration from commerce is clearly one of the big ideas driving the new age of retail. The goal of frictionless—that is, frustration-free—commerce is to have products, services and payments that flow easily, unimpeded and around, any barriers or, ideally, through a process without barriers. Achieving liquidity requires that organizations invest in making this natural flow of goods as easy and fast as possible.

Again, digital companies have an immense natural advantage in this arena. Uber is one example of an early company that showed the consumer what to expect in a frictionless world. Uber not only shows you where the car service is, where you're going, the likely cost and the music that you can play during the ride, but also allows you to do all this without having to go through a clunky payment process—unlike the classic yellow taxi that always seems to have a broken credit card reader. This is what we mean by a frictionless, or a truly flowing, liquid process.

Amazon is doing this with its one-click checkout and payment button, and Prime obviously has been perceived as a huge remover of friction. Amazon's Dash button is next. This gizmo from Amazon can be placed near an item in the pantry or refrigerator, and the consumer orders replacements simply by tapping the button. In the future, sensors will replace even the need to tap. Amazon Prime Air is another component. Amazon holds patents for drone deliveries to a consumer's current physical location rather than the stored shipping address, and its drones are capable of delivering packages weighing as much as five pounds within thirty minutes. And Amazon's patent for anticipatory shipping and a new algorithm could make it possible for the company to send shipments to customers before they even realize they need to order. Even more revolutionary is the company's recent announcement of the Amazon Go store (as of this writing, a single store in Seattle)—customers make selections throughout the store, which is equipped with smart shelves, and Amazon charges customers' Amazon accounts through an app as they leave—no need to add anything to a virtual shopping cart or stand in a checkout line.

Having smart assistants, technology such as wristbands at Disney theme parks, and smartphones will make commerce even easier to conduct and will further disrupt trips to the store. We are at the early stages of this journey.

The reality is that all consumers want to save as much time and effort as possible, at least for buying their regular supplies and probably for almost any purchase. That means changing the dynamic from the consumer as the agent who initiates a sale to the retailer who provides consumers with what they need when they need it or even before they realize they need it. This means that in the near-term more businesses will use subscription models, membership models, and voice-activated ordering tools, and eventually sensors at home, work, in the car, at school—anywhere—will alert retailers to send products and connect to other smart devices that collect data that allow retailers to anticipate their customers' needs. All this after consumers have entered their information or payment data only once.

The question is not whether every consumer wants access to these technologies and delivery methods (of course they do and will—why spend hours shuffling around dull supermarkets with large boxes of detergent or toilet paper if you can have it delivered?)

but when costs will be low enough to make delivery models economical and sustainable.

Grocery may already be at that point, and if grocery works, then every other retail sector works. The grocery category accounts for 30 percent of consumer spending—the consumer's single largest source of spending on products or goods. A variety of new players (Amazon, Google, Instacart, Fresh Direct, Blue Apron, and many more) and traditional players (Kroger, Shop-Rite, H-E-B Grocery, and others) have targeted the category for digital ordering and delivery.

The connected home is becoming a reality too, with affordable connected kitchen devices recently making an appearance in the marketplace. Macro trends are favoring e-commerce in grocery, with the repopulation of cities here and abroad, especially by tech-friendly millennials and Generation Zers, making possible denser and more cost-efficient delivery networks.

One example is Samsung's smart refrigerator, Family Hub. It has a 21.5-inch monitor and built-in cameras that monitor food levels. It offers the first-ever shopping app integrated in a fridge, allowing users to shop and purchase groceries directly from the display and have them delivered by FreshDirect and ShopRite. The fridge can also connect to and control all of Samsung's other smart appliances. Future versions will integrate Amazon Echo.

In the next ten years, it is not inconceivable that people will receive 50 percent of grocery supplies through online ordering or predictive frictionless commerce. E-commerce and predictive commerce will fundamentally redefine the role of the grocery store.

No sector is immune. Forty percent of all consumer spending will be digital by 2026, and 15 percent will be frictionless—this kind of purchase will grow at an annual rate of 24 percent between now and then. By 2026, apparel purchases could account for nearly 60 percent of digital purchases, with 20 percent or more provided in a frictionless manner. Purchases of housewares are likely to be 75 percent digital and 10 percent frictionless.[5]

Some retailers are already preparing for this world. For example, Walmart is testing technology that allows consumers to scan items with their smartphones as they put their groceries in their carts and then go through an expedited checkout process before leaving the store.

One area that will see major changes in this fluid world is payments. Physical money will start to become extinct. Smart payments will upend the financial services world and merchant relations and may ultimately determine where the transaction is made. The time for every consumer-facing business to embrace the notion of becoming fully liquid is now—even if the resulting changes are still years away.

In the next chapter we discuss the impact liquid organizations will have on distribution and explore how Amazon is already paving the way for a truly fluid distribution paradigm.

CHAPTER 15

AMAZON AND THE DISTRIBUTION CENTURY

Chapter 14 described the future of supply chains and how liquid, fluid, efficient, and nimbly responsive they must become to serve a fragmented and infinite number of discrete niches. We believe distribution will become perhaps the most critical link in the retail chain. The number of distribution points today can be as many as the total population of Earth. Without exaggeration, with a future of infinite numbers of discrete market niches, we will see an infinite number of discrete and liquid value chains that will be creating value closer to the end consumer's home and will be liquidly and rapidly distributing the value, literally seeing the product travel its last mile in a matter of minutes.

Distribution's Standard-bearer: Amazon

The phrase "the last mile" refers to delivery to the consumer of the item ordered, either online or off. It's all about the speed of distribution and delivery, and now it also includes returns. Amazon initiated and has steadily improved its value chain, continually shortening delivery times—delivering some items within an hour.

Indeed, Amazon is turning the last mile into a hundred-yard dash. Again, Amazon leads the way. In fact, the force of Amazon's millions of users, who have learned to expect their purchases to arrive ever faster, has driven all retail sectors to follow suit, adding enormous costs, a necessary evil for a more rapid, responsive and fluid value chain.

Amazon's distribution system has evolved to the point that it can sort through millions of goods and billions of SKUs to organize them into packages sent to locations near the buyers' ZIP Codes for delivery over the last mile at low cost. Amazon's new act is building its own delivery fleet of airplanes, trucks and vans—and, yes, drones.

In 2013, the Fulfillment by Amazon (FBA) service (which stores, packs, and ships for the brands and retailers selling on its site) got a shot of steroids. The company's strategy wizards developed a project named Dragon Boat, designed to aggressively expand Amazon's global fulfillment capabilities. It came up with a global delivery network that controls the flow of goods from factories in China and India all the way to customers' doorsteps in New York, Atlanta, and London.

And the company didn't stop with Dragon Boat. It became the impetus for a venture called Global Supply Chain by Amazon. Envision Amazon as the hub of the logistics and distribution industries that does without not only shippers like FedEx, UPS, and DHL but also the thousands of middlemen that handle the paperwork and cargo associated with transnational trade. In leaked internal documents, Amazon described a "revolutionary system that will automate the entire international supply chain and eliminate much of the legacy waste associated with document handling and freight booking."[1]

Amazon's plan is to buy space on planes, trucks, and ships at reduced rates, based on the massive amount of inventory consolidated in shipping hubs in manufacturing nations like China, India, and others. Essentially, Amazon is bypassing all the brokers who were in the middle, cutting out those costs as well. Acquiring the space at lower wholesale rates also allows small merchants to participate. So, merchants in China, for example, will tap on their smartphones to order Amazon trucks to pick up products from their factories. Once the shipments reach their distribution ports, Amazon's delivery system kicks in again for speedy delivery. Amazon is describing it as "one click-ship for seamless international trade and shipping."

The leaked internal documents said, "Sellers will no longer book with DHL, UPS, or Fedex but will book directly with Amazon. The ease and transparency of this disintermediation [elimination of middlemen] will be revolutionary and sellers will flock to FBA given the competitive pricing."

Amazon also has Alibaba, its massive Chinese competitor, within its crosshairs, because they are fighting for dominance of the cross-border, international e-commerce markets. AliResearch (Alibaba's research company) expects the total value of this international commerce to reach $1 trillion by 2020, serving nine hundred million shoppers.[2]

While Amazon is moving into the fashion and branded apparel business, the grocery business, maybe the furniture and large appliance business with showroom stores, publishing (of all types), and hundreds of others with no apparent boundaries—testing, learning, and eventually intending to steal share from the very clients that pay Amazon to trade on its site—the company is quietly partnering with third-party shipping carriers to further build its global distribution enterprise. Once Amazon has mastered the shipping model and has achieved economies of scale, it is expected to kick these third-party vendors out and run its business exclusively. Talk about vertical integration and superior value-chain control!

Another example of Amazon's Pac-Man approach to gobbling up markets is its aggressive position in cloud services. This vital back-office service started quietly as Amazon developed it internally. Then it quickly expanded. Now the cloud is Amazon's fastest-growing and most profitable business.

Colin Sebastian, an analyst at Robert W. Baird & Co., an international financial services firm, said of Global Supply Chain by Amazon, "This is classic Amazon fashion." He said the global logistics operation could become a $400 billion business for Amazon. "They take baby steps along a long path, which allows some companies that could be disrupted to remain in a sense of denial. Amazon rarely takes one big step forward that shocks the market."[3]

So, the dirty little secret is that Amazon is not a marketplace. It's angling to become a nation-state and a highly developed one at that. What will its next target be? Manufacturing all the goods Amazon sells? After all, owning and controlling all the delivery systems is just one step short of acquiring and owning the production, which would give Amazon a totally integrated value chain. That's one hell of a vertically integrated company.

Today, another value chain function; tomorrow, the world.

CHAPTER 16

PLATFORMING

Although you may not have heard of the word *platforming*, you should have, because it will soon be central to every strategy for consumer-facing businesses. The idea is that every retailer or consumer-facing business should consider itself a platform.

Our definition of *platform* is quite broad. We see a platform as analogous to the stage in a theater. On any given stage, all sorts of different plays, musicals, improvised shows and even conversation with or participation from the audience occurs. A business often defines itself narrowly, like a particular play that is performed on stage again and again. The play is the main asset, and the ability to deviate from its script is difficult or totally precluded. The audience's involvement is passive. That mind-set worked in a world that required standardization and efficiency. But it also missed the many hidden and unused assets created by the theater company while putting on the play. In fact, the broadest definition of a platform here would open every space in the theater to new uses, For example, as active members (even creators) of the production, theatergoers would be able to communicate with each other, the cast, and the playwrights and ultimately collaborate to build things previously unimagined.

We see a business as a platform or stage (or theater company) that has the ability to create any number of new modes of interacting, transacting, providing new experiences, developing new products or services, creating new partnerships, leasing assets to others to build upon—the list goes on—all by creatively using their entire collection of assets, talents and resources in imaginative ways. Leadership's job at all levels is to develop ways to create new opportunities by looking at the business as a platform that engages its consumers in creative ways. One idea that is central to developing a platform is allowing (or actually investing in and creating) the means for people to interact and use your platform without your being the interface or in the middle. Few businesses achieve this, but it should always be the goal. In the physical world this problem is often difficult to envision, but it must be part of the new approach to strategy.

The easiest way to explain part of our concept is by using the digital world, so let's start with Apple. Apple can be considered a platform. It wants to provide a stage for its consumers to use to create their own productions—and experiences. Consider the iPhone as a platform. On this device, developers can build their own apps to create a whole new business that is integral to making the iPhone useful. Uber built its business on Apple and Google, both platform businesses. Venmo and Square are revolutionizing payments by building on Apple and Google's platforms. Instagram and Snapchat wouldn't exist without Apple and Google. Many more examples exist.

But the iPhone platform is also great for movies, music, creating and sharing photo albums, providing instantaneous updates on people's lives, shopping, working, and much more. Blackberry lost its commanding position because it never offered itself effectively as a platform but only as the best email device. Adopting the mind-set that your business is a platform does not tell you where your business will go, because that may well be defined by people outside leadership—your employees and customers—but it creates the opportunity for new thinking.

When most people refer to platform businesses, they typically think only of a series of technology, information-sharing or entertainment businesses. Uber created a platform for ride sharing and food delivery; Airbnb for room sharing; Google for collecting and sharing information; Netflix for content development and delivery; Facebook for sharing news, both personal and political. WeChat in China is attempting to put as many apps as possible on one platform. Its goal is to use the simple messaging platform to provide a complete suite of services for the mobile consumer.

The hard part is finding examples of platforms that are being developed in existing established retail and consumer businesses, especially any that have made a significant economic impact. Most fail to think about creating user connectivity and building relationships across the platform. This conceptual blockage must be removed.

However, we think that regarding a business as a platform is an incredibly valuable and necessary tool for evolving all retail models. As we have stated, stores as a point of delivery are losing market share and will continue to do so, and focusing only on the product will drive value down. The model has to evolve, and thinking about your business as a platform is the best means for achieving this.

So how should you start to think about your business as a platform? The first step is to look at all the assets, relationships, experiences, and processes embedded in the business. These could be customer data, space in a retail storage room, psychological rewards that customers realize when visiting the store or buying the product (this may well be the most important), experiences a store provides or could provide, visits a website receives, supplier relationships, assets that others own that you wish you could use—the list is endless. Cataloging all these is the starting point for understanding the strength of the platform.

The next step is to determine the capacity or ability of these assets to create new and exciting opportunities. The potential for the business to evolve typically depends on whether a series of conditions exists. In the book *Platform Revolution,* Geoffrey G. Parker and Marshall W. Van Alstyne suggest several ways to think about the concept of platforms.

A platform opportunity is likely to exist if these (or some of these) conditions are present:

* Underused assets that could benefit others
* High information content
* New ways to use your assets to connect buyers and sellers
* Ability to add information, fun or experiences to the asset to increase its relevance
* Opportunities to take advantage of existing patterns of behavior by adding new information, transactions or content
* A highly fragmented market structure
* Presence of the network (the number of users increases the value)[1]

Finally, how can you provide employees, customers and suppliers or just plain outsiders with more access to your assets? Simply providing the connections, technology, data or space may create ways for the business to evolve in unforeseen ways.

Let's explore these ideas through a few examples from the perspective of a retailer or consumer brand.

Every retail store typically has unused space—for example, the storeroom or square footage that your business cannot use for anything. Is it possible to put all this space on an app and make it available for others? Could these be places where others store their inventory to meet short lead-time deliveries? Most big-box and department stores increasingly have ample space that is often poorly used. Looking at the business as a platform makes it easier to see that this space is something that could be shared or used by outsiders in potentially unconventional ways.

Department and big-box stores are already exploring leasing space to outsiders for stand-alone shops. And Waffle House uses its storage rooms for drop-off points for the Roadie app, which provides cross-county deliveries. This is but one example of a growing trend.

Another example of the platform model in action centers on data. Many retailers have the opportunity to collect and use data or information. We have mentioned the push by Nike and Under Armour into the collection of fitness data. These new apps have incredible amounts of health and activity data to build upon.

Most retailers have a lot of transaction data that is hard to use because of both its inaccuracies and the incomplete picture of consumer purchasing it provides. However, this is an area that is underused. Apps could be developed to give employees access to data that would enable them to explore ideas or trends that today are the sole purview of centralized analytics groups. The increase in usage might foster new ways to collect more accurate data, generate more insights or create a new business. There may be a lot of hidden trends and ideas that remain untapped.

A platform mind-set makes getting the data into employees' hands a priority. Who knows where it might lead? The development of Amazon's cloud business was a direct result of the Amazon's being forced to access data and communicate through an internal network system. The method of accessing the information led to a new business idea.

Few retailers and brands have explored the opportunity to connect their existing or new suppliers with their customers. This has been a big missed opportunity. Retailers' need for more unique product to make their sites and stores attractive, the challenge for new suppliers of reaching the consumer, and the consumer's desire for niche brands make establishing these new relationships seem obvious. The retailer would not even have to hold inventory, just take a transaction fee.

The barriers to connecting businesses' customer and suppliers have been a reluctance to lose control of the customer transaction and a lingering attachment to the traditional store-based fulfillment model. In niche markets, such as pet supplies, health foods, and arts and crafts, retailers with great brand awareness should explore the idea of creating a new transaction platform. After writing the software, they might even be able to hand the content and products sold over to the community. Why don't large apparel stores or brands create sites that allow people to buy new items and sell their old clothes, even from other brands? This idea is also one that could benefit from the network effect.

Another example that is worth highlighting is the new role the store will play in a highly competitive world. The store will have to become a platform for experiences. We see the store as a place that has to become a center for consumer experiences. The only key point we need to make here is that by thinking about the business as a platform, how you create that experience is likely to be very different than if you consider the store to be a relatively fixed, internally controlled asset.

Best Buy provides a great example of sharing its platform

with several other powerful branded platforms in an attempt to build Best Buys as a gathering spot for the fans of these great brands, thus gaining a much larger consumer base. Samsung, Apple, Microsoft, Sony, HP, Pacific Kitchen, Verizon, and AT&T are some of the branded platforms now leasing space from Best Buy.

For an example of the synergy that both Best Buy and each of these brands appreciates, consider an Apple loyalist who lives across the street from a Best Buy outlet, whereas the nearest Apple Store is twenty minutes across town. The loyalist will go to Best Buy to purchase an Apple product and while there might browse and purchase other items to which the Apple fan would not have been exposed at the Apple Store across town. Likewise, a Best Buy loyalist who purchases one of its products also browses the Apple shop-in-shop and purchases an Apple product. So it is a synergy: both Best Buy and Apple get a fundamentally new customer and revenues.

A win beyond this synergy is that neither company has to make huge capital investments in opening more of its own locations. And the shop-in-shops can set up almost overnight in however many of Best Buy's one thousand platform locations they arranged to use.

Additionally, and of great significance, Best Buy is able to guarantee it will meet its revenue goals by making a leasing deal with each of these brands that achieves those goals. The lease is calculated on the minimum sales per square foot that Best Buy wants to achieve, which is paid whether the brand's sales reach that goal or not. And if the brand performs above the minimum, the lease is likely to specify a bonus for Best Buy.

Another example is Macy's, which now hosts both Best Buy and Apple, along with Ralph Lauren, Sunglass Hut, Burberry, Lush, Finish Line, Destination Maternity, and others. While Macy's as a whole continues to struggle, a victim of excess supply and the vicious cycle of discounting, its new CEO, Jeff Gennette, clearly sees these types of partnerships as a bright spot. He announced in early 2017 that Macy's will be adding more LensCrafters shop-in-shops and is considering remodeling a section of its San Francisco flagship as an area that hosts luxury brands.[2] So, while Macy's and other department stores are still evolving as branded social/community platforms, they are simultaneously pursuing this synergistic distribution strategy. Most of these brands have their own stores but also choose to use the Macy's platform as another access point for their own consumers and to gain sales from Macy's traffic. And, instead of eschewing brands that are competitors of Macy's, combining forces creates a stronger synergy for both.

Macy's acquired another branded platform to provide synergy when it paid $210 million for the Bluemercury spa and beauty chain. While this acquisition was a brilliant tactical move for all the reasons detailed elsewhere (not the least of which is a new source of revenue and growth with sixty Bluemercury stores in eighteen states), it also provides a stronger and much larger strategic message about the future, not only for Macy's but for the entire industry. Bluemercury can also be considered a potential social community, and Macy's will be expanding Bluemercury shops across its platform.[3]

And a few blocks away, Nordstrom's community platform plays host to J.Crew, Madewell, Top Shop, Brooks Brothers, Bonobos, Beyoncé's Ivy Park activewear, the Charlotte Tilbury beauty brand, Shoes of Prey, and HauteLook, some of which Nordstrom has acquired and some of which represent exclusive partnerships. This clearly indicates that Nordstrom understands the epic transformation that the old-line department stores must make. And this strategic imperative ushers in the destruction of the traditional retail/wholesale process and structure.

When asked in a *Women's Wear Daily* interview about the Macy's deal and whether it meant J.Crew was moving to a wholesale business model, then CEO Mickey Drexler replied, "It doesn't at all suggest wholesaling." If we were to complete Drexler's thought, we would say that he understands distribution in the twenty-first century, and he envisions placing his brands on many distribution platforms that are compatible with the consumer positioning of his brands and that give those brands access to new consumer traffic.

And oddly enough, despite the bad press about its execution, Ron Johnson's strategy for JCPenney was onto something. He saw the company as a platform for providing a breadth of new experiences for the consumer—one that was not going to be centrally controlled. He envisioned allowing others to use the space to build their experiences and turning JCPenney into something more like a small city than a department store, complete with boulevards of small shops—with not a single JCPenney private label among them—arranged around a central square where shoppers could grab a meal, see a show or take a class.

His vision is not dead—in many ways Marvin Ellison has taken a similar approach, forming creative partnership with suppliers to use the JCPenney platform as a showroom and to become more experiential. One of the biggest success stories of JCPenney is its partnership with Sephora. In 2010, JC Penney had only 155 Sephora shop-in-shops, although it had more than eleven hundred stores, but by the end of 2015 it had 518 Sephora locations, even as JCPenney closed stores.[4] The partnership is a win-win for both brands, bringing new customers and a sense of prestige to JCPenney while helping Sephora expand more quickly and less expensively than it could on its own. JCPenney has also brought back major appliances. Time will tell whether JCPenney or any of these other retailers can move faster than the supply-demand imbalance and other disruptive trends—but thinking about themselves as platforms clearly offers a path to success.

The final example of thinking of a business as a platform addresses the sharing of underused back-office functions. Large companies will need to grow by acquiring niche brands to serve niche markets. Managing them with a set of capabilities that already exists and is tested but underused is another way to take advantage of existing assets. This has been VF's strategy for many years. For example, when VF purchased Timberland in 2011, VF's back-office functions helped the new acquisition grow. "Having access to VF's platforms and resources has been an incredible advantage for Timberland," Timberland president Stuart Whitney said. "Whether it's deep consumer insights work, access to tools like Life Cycle Analysis or materials innovations, we simply did not have the resources five years ago that VF can offer us today." Whitney said that with less time spent on back-office and operational functions, Timberland has more time to spend on its "passion points," such as sustainability. That will allow Timberland to provide valuable insights to other green-minded VF brands like The North Face.[5]

Should many of the small denim companies, all of which are struggling to remain relevant, merge so they can consolidate their back-office functions? Is there a need for a company that does nothing but provide all the support functions for small brands or retailers?

Ascena takes a similar approach with its Shared Services Group. For example, when Ascena acquired Ann Inc. in 2015, the company identified $150 million in savings by tapping under-used back-office functions to handle sourcing and procurement, distribution and logistics for both companies.[6] But the path to glory is hard and risky.

The challenge with this type of platforming is that too often the search for synergies in too many areas compromises the needs of the individual business. If information technology, sourcing, and product development are left untouched, this approach can work. If not, it can make the time to market too slow, the compromises too great to satisfy the consumer and the reporting too arduous. Nonetheless, the platforming mind-set requires consideration of this option.

The idea of being more than just a retailer or brand can be difficult for many to wrap their heads around. But in reality they already are. In the minds of their consumers, brands stand for more than just their stores, websites or products. Platforming allows brands to uncover and exploit these hidden opportunities and engage consumers, employees and even competitors in the process.

After Platforming

It is, alas, not enough to think of your business or brand as a platform. Distributed computing (computers located in different places but working on a common task) and all that entails are already ushering in the post-platform world. More and more, the ability to connect, communicate and transact without a large-scale intermediary will become the norm. In chapter 11 we mentioned OpenBazaar, which was the first post-platform network to be established, and it's too soon to predict its potential impact on the world of commerce. But there are other approaches.

Let's look at designing a new product. Individuals form a network design team. The group quickly sets up a contract to split the royalties (again through shared ledgers—block chains) in different parts of the world and design software to manufacture the new product. The team never meets face-to-face. They manufacture their product on a 3-D printer. The designers then showcase their product on the latest, coolest social media site that targets their "tribe"—people likely to want it. The product is a hit, and people immediately request the software for their own 3-D printers. They send the software to the buyers, who pay with Bitcoin. The product is made in a few thousand locations around the world with no platform, no centralized product development team, no distribution, and no stores. Some buyers add their own features and resell the software creating a layered, textured, and original product. New products will come into being much as collaborators in different countries have been coming up with new music forms (reggaeton is the new music emerging from the cultural mixing of artists in Latin America—or called "neoperreo" the way the music is listened to and created virtually across borders by shared artists).

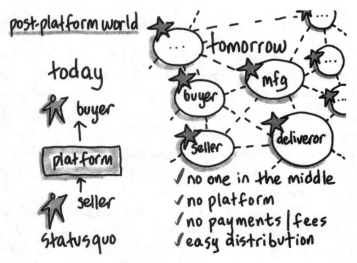

Exhibit 16.1. The Post-Platform World

The ability of peer-to-peer commerce to pick up trends, react to events and make products that are truly individualized is enormous. By 2026, we should expect to see real impact from this phenomenon.

In the next chapter we put together all the idea we have discussed to offer what we believe are the key ingredients for success.

SECTION 5

VIEWS FROM THE TOP

CHAPTER 17

MAKING CHANGE PRACTICAL

The time for change has never been more urgent or needed for retail and consumer-facing businesses. But the ability to create and execute a new vison requires a new way of thinking. Here are potential ways to move forward after you have thrown away your existing strategic plans.

1. Confront reality. The purpose of this book is to share a vision of the future that is both radical and grounded in emerging trends. Few organizations have understood or accepted the seismic shift. Answering three questions is critical:

* Which parts of the seismic shift apply to your business?
* What are the consequences of these shifts for you?
* How long do you have before they arrive?

2. Adopt rational altruism. It is obvious but worth stating that the discipline of the market will not disappear. Having a good purpose is not enough, but without it you have no path to success. The sheer volume of options available to consumers and their evolving relationship to materialism means products or services will suffer if they do not articulate their purpose with a strong underlying set of identifiable core values. After reuniting with your company's purpose—or finding a new one—your brands need to define why their customers need them and identify what else your platform can bring to the consumer.

3. Create the culture for change. Creative change can occur only when there is a high level of organizational trust. If people can trust, they can be playful and then access their creativity. The challenge for leaders is to create the environment that fosters this trust, and eventually creativity, as the old profit model disappears. We are reminded of Peter Drucker's four steps for effective change: awareness, understanding, commitment, and then action. We cannot provide every detail for every store at every step, but we can emphasize the importance of the first building block: awareness. Without this perspective, leading an organization on this journey is almost impossible. Accepting the reality of the seismic shift is the necessary first step to build organizational commitment to the hard and necessary changes to follow. Failing to see the enormity of the shift will lead to piecemeal actions and the false hope that next season will see a return to normal.

4. Leverage the power of the seven Cs. Even with a clear set of values, businesses face an enormous challenge. We believe that in ten years every successful consumer-facing platform will have seven supporting pillars. In fact, all seven will be necessary for survival alone. Those who want to win big will need to excel at all seven. To make them easy to remember, we begin all with the letter C. You need to evaluate every strategy according to how effectively it addresses each element.

Community
Customization
Connectivity
Convenience
Content
Curation and choice
Control

Community

Community is one of those concepts all businesses seek to harness but only a few understand. You might think of it in terms of the idea of the commons, which was popular before the industrial revolution. A commons was a space—often used by people to graze their animals—that belonged to everybody or nobody. The community owned the resource, and everyone could use it. Although it was public space, each person had a stake in it.

A contemporary example is Wikipedia, an asset created, owned, and shared by the community. Other examples include Twitter, which in its early days was a community where people wrote their own apps and developed things like the hashtag. Data.gov, a project of the Technology Transformation Service of the US General Services Administration, is an attempt to encourage technological development by making information in the US government's data banks open to all. Wikileaks (whatever it has become today) was born of the idea that the community owned the right to have access, use and share the information that was collected by their governments.

The values that underpin this concept of community are experimentation, collaboration, freedom of thought, and freedom of information. They walk the walk by creating open and extensible repositories so that people can use and remix its resources as they see fit. At the extreme, the makers of the community give everything it can away for free or as an in-kind trade, in the hope that others will join the commons with new great innovations, ideas or artistic creativity. Communities are not transactional businesses but may need to be supported indirectly by all kinds of community contributions. That is the biggest problem for a true community: how to generate profits (hence the struggles of Twitter and Wikipedia).

But to return to businesses and communities, the first step for a business in building a community is recognizing that the responsibility for owning and developing that community belongs to its members. After setting the course of the community, the companies probably will have to cede control. Another way of putting it is that they will lose control, whether they like it or not. The core part of any strategy is how best to help create a community, exploit the network effect and still be relevant as a business. Even in the post-platform world, characterized by peer-to-peer interactions with no central node in the physical world, consumers still will have an intense desire for community. The future digital world will have communities, even if they are not centered on corporate transactional platforms.

This concept has already been instrumental in turning around declining real-world businesses. One example, as we have mentioned, is the Plaza Fiesta in Atlanta.

There are many places where people go for community. One growing trend is exercise communities. Soulcycle, a chain of cycling communities, has attracted hundreds of thousands of followers to pay $35 for a challenging forty-five-minute workout that taps into people's desires to be entertained, be the best, and be part of something bigger than themselves. It's the draw of being in a club of fit, attractive people—instructors routinely ask their classes yoga-esque questions like "What makes you beautiful?" as the class cycles away in the dark, music pumping, custom Jonathan Adler candles burning (and for sale in the lobby). This is only one of the many cultlike training activities that have exploded and will continue to explode in the next decade. Yoga has already led the way. Personal training will continue to grow for social reasons as much as the focused training.

Interestingly enough, the actions of VF, an established apparel company, might be showing the way through one of its brands, Vans. In London it literally turns its Vans store, located under Waterloo Bridge, over to its customers, who organize events, skateboard, and connect. In the future one question may well be "Who owns your store?"

Social network communities on Facebook, Instagram, Snapchat and others are thriving. In fact, they continue to gobble up commercial advertising dollars (with Facebook in the lead), stealing from traditional media, because these community members share similar interests and are likely to ask their neighbors' opinions and even pass along great reviews, which could go viral. Facebook's advertising revenue grew 51 percent in the fourth quarter of 2016, compared with the fourth quarter of 2015, although at a slower rate, to $8.81 billion.[1]

The important lesson for everyone who is developing a digital strategy: You cannot own the content, and you have to quickly hand over the keys to your community. If consumers do not feel a sense of ownership and control, they are not going to show up—no matter how much you spend on sleek, corporate content development. The idea of the shared commons is still the point—you can still sell on it in ten years, but you should not try to control it. This is how the network effect may work for these businesses.

New communities are being formed on the Internet almost daily, among the thousands already out there. You can find a community for almost any human interest or need. Reddit is a community of millions of micro-communities devoted to everything from the late Billy Mays of Oxiclean fame to birds Photoshopped to have arms, to old ladies posing with pies. Communities also exist for people who like to chew ice, men who want to discuss caring for their long hair, and basically anything else you could think of.

Apple provides a terrific example of a gathering community. Selling stuff in a store is never mentioned in Angela Ahrendts's vision for Apple's retail business, which she runs as its senior vice president. Her vision of the brand is that it should be a living, breathing, human gathering place, a community whose DNA matches each of its discrete communities and that it should look for ways to add value to those communities. Apple has the sincere desire to build a community by creating a gathering place, or a town center, where everyone is welcome. It offers educational sessions, workshops and product demonstrations. Today, 64 percent of its in-store employees are focused on service, answering questions, and educating customers.

You might not define the Amazon platform as a community per se. But we believe that the growing millions of Amazon users will need to feel they are part of a community. Today much of Amazon's sense of community is rooted in the social aspect of sharing reviews of products, but that is not very powerful. How can Amazon build even more community? What data does Amazon want to share with universities or just plain consumers to play and experiment with? Right now, the growth and competitive pressure around closed systems are too great to see the formation of such a community. In ten years it will start to occur.

Legacy consumer-facing businesses, even those with well-known brand names, such as Macy's, Walmart, Target, JCPenney,

The Gap, Coach, Kroger, Procter & Gamble, and many others are finding it difficult to build a community feeling on their platforms, and this will continue to be the case.

Many of these legacy businesses have identified their loyal core customers and are able to provide special amenities, including exclusive parties, fashion shows, and celebrity events, all of which do begin to feel like a member-exclusive community. However, even coming close to the types of new-world community models that we mentioned earlier will be a long, arduous task.

All consumer-facing businesses must shape their platforms into communities to the degree possible, and the community must offer all the things people like about communities: friendship, common interests, a role in shaping it, trust, a warm, pleasant and exciting environment with lots of fun things to do and experiences. The closer a business can get to matching this description, the more it is likely to gain acceptance as a community and the more that community's energy is likely to go viral. When that happens, people will flock to the community (platform) faster than they did to Groupon's daily deals when they started. This community of consumers will not leave. And they will not care only about price. They will buy more. And they will want to come back often.

Customization

Customization refers to creating a unique tailored product or experience for each customer. *Personalization* or personal commerce are the current buzzwords, so we will use them and customization interchangeably.

The CEO and founder of Enjoy, Ron Johnson, who was also the architect of Apple's famous "genius bar" (and formerly served as CEO of JCPenney), has said that consumer-facing businesses have gone through three stages: the store; e-commerce and mobile commerce; and now personal commerce, the current stage. Briefly, Johnson's Enjoy.com, which sells technology, has an expert deliver whatever you ordered online, wherever and whenever you want it delivered, and the expert then provides an hour-long tutorial on the product's use and benefits. Essentially, Enjoy delivers the "genius bar" to you.

Why is personal commerce coming of age for consumer-facing businesses? The short answer is because it can, thanks to technology and big data. The long answer is that consumers have raised the bar on what they want, as we have pointed out. Personalization will be about knowing the details of your customers' lives and how you fit.

Personalization will be most prominent in the digital world because of the ability of the newly emerging apps or assistants (or whatever else) to collect data through voice and video conversations, emails, chat, purchasing history, text-messaging systems, and even notepads and to-do lists. The potential exists to use data that describe the user's preferences, activities, physical experiences and even desires to drive commerce. From all this data businesses will not only figure out what users want but will teach them how to find products or services better, how to make the most of them and provide new ideas the consumer had not even thought about. They will even shape what we want to do.

With artificial intelligence and learning algorithms, these apps and sites will gradually become more and more personalized. They will speak the consumer's language and know the consumer's attitudes. They will help offer customers solutions and products that best suit their needs, and they will offer tutorials about how people can improve their lives or live a healthier lifestyle.

If this is where business heading, where should you start today? The first step in achieving customization is defining each consumer's distinct lifestyle and behavioral patterns, likes and dislikes and the physical, social and mental communities in which they participate, as well as all other relevant personal information. This information (currently called big data—but it must include more than just bytes of data), will help to determine which consumers will permit you to enter their lives, what they want, where they want it, and when.

This is accomplished over time by tracking their lifestyle patterns at each of their thousands of browsing and transactional points of contact, both online and physically. This is the first and easiest stage of aggregating information. The next two stages are progressively more complex: determining which data points are most relevant and how to use those data points. The last is the toughest and most important.

Gathering this information is obviously much quicker and easier on the Internet; it also goes deeper into behavioral and life-style patterns than did earlier efforts to collect data through re-search and information gleaned from credit card and/or the check-out process in stores. With this data and technology retail-ers can also respond in real time.

Using a simple example, Amazon—or any Internet retailer—quickly learns whether I'm a regular, heavy, or light shopper; what I browse; and what I purchase intermittently or on a regular basis. Let's say mystery novels are something I buy a lot of reg-ularly, along with lightbulbs. Using algorithms and machine learning, Amazon will send emails suggesting new releases of mystery books, timed to arrive ahead of my usual purchasing cycle. Because Amazon has perfected predictive analytics, it will deliver lightbulbs just before I need them, when even I didn't know I would need them.

A popular anecdote is about a guy who arrives at home and finds a package on his porch from Amazon with a lightbulb in it. He scratches his head because he had not ordered it, but an hour later a lightbulb goes out in his kitchen.

On a scale of one to ten, legacy retailers and brands are perhaps at level 2, beginning the process of learning which consumers will permit them into their lives, enabling those retailers and brands to learn precisely what their customers desire (goods, services, experiences), and then being able to deliver it where, when and how those consumers demand. Amazon is probably at level 6.

When we once asked a top-level executive of a major department store what was at the top of his priority list, he responded without hesitation: "I would like to find someone with about ten PhDs in data analytics."

Subscription commerce will be one of the game changers for on-demand personalization. Birchbox is an early example of personal commerce. It uses algorithms and expert curation to address specific beauty-related issues of individual customers and then sends monthly beauty boxes on subscription that the customer can decide to keep part or all of, returning any products they don't want. Based on "try, learn, buy," personalization becomes the winning sales proposition. The economics of these businesses today remains a challenge, but with sustained price deflation this will be solved when value shifts from just the product to this new level of intimacy and service.

The same trend is evident in grocery, where start-ups like PlateJoy, Fuel, and Sunfare provide personalized meal plans and grocery delivery based on users' health goals, dietary needs, and preferences.

While Amazon and other e-commerce examples reflect what it's possible to do in personalizing their relationships with individual consumers, the complexity and difficulty of achieving such individual relationships is enormous for physical big-box department and discount stores, supermarkets and other large formats. However, as they perfect their own online data-gathering capabilities, at the very least they will more easily identify customers, personally connect with them and customize their product, service and experiential offerings.

The complexity that large stores encounter in building a personalization strategy was very much on the mind of Macy's CEO, Jeff Gennette, who said that it's difficult enough to determine which personal data to use and how to use it. But the incredible challenge for an enterprise as big as Macy's is how to integrate whatever strategy you come up with so that it informs not only the four huge functions of merchandising, marketing, store operations and the supply chain but also its hundreds of stores.

We expect that Macy's, along with many other huge platforms, may be able to bring their online personalization to a level close to that of Amazon. However, to narrow personalization to an individual or a "universe of one" in their physical operations will be next to impossible for legacy bricks-and-mortar retailers, because of traditional lack of communication or information sharing between channels, a massive inventory of aging stores, and the cost of technology necessary to bring online levels of personalization to life in stores. They also must fragment their business by tailoring marketing, merchandising, stores, and supply chain for a particular cohort or community of customers. Already, Macy's is personalizing much of its marketing (targeting groups of like-minded consumers) and has been localizing each of its hundreds of stores to its community's preferences. While execution of this strategy may be bumpy, Macy's should nevertheless continue to perfect it.

VF Corporation, a $13 billion portfolio of brands such as The North Face, Vans, and Timberland, is another example of decentralization, demassification, and fragmentation, and it is moving toward community-level personalization. VF's strategic model has been in place since the 1980s. All the shared functions, such as sourcing, finance and human relation, are centralized, taking advantage of speed, efficiency and productivity, while each of its powerful brands is decentralized and autonomous in all functions that touch and connect with the consumer. So, The North Face, for example, controls its brand's personal relationship with its communities, both online and off. And, its core The North Face Athlete Team works alongside the company's research and development teams to come up with new products as well as performance-enhancing fabrics, such as those used in its lightweight mountain climbing jackets, which are resistant to high-altitude conditions. This is a form of personalization for each and every one of its core performance-minded athletes. The North Face also is perfecting the use of beacon technologies to personalize the store experience, connecting with a loyal consumer's app even before that customer enters the store, by texting a note that lures the customer into the store with a promotional deal. And once that customer is in the store, employees cross sell and up-sell goods the store knows that customer likes.

The problem today is that personalization is too often seen purely as a means of gaining additional sales. That is not true personalization based on understanding a customer's entire life circumstances (or even close to it). This must become central to the strategy.

Retailers and brands are increasingly realizing the significance of the personal customer relationship in which they are engaged and the responsibility it carries. Invasion of privacy usually comes up in any conversation about personalization. Hitting the right note between intrusion and a welcome call is difficult. For example, Target's use of big data to figure out when customers are pregnant and offer them discounts on baby products was often so sophisticated that Target knew a consumer was pregnant before she or her family did. But such examples aside, the prevailing opinion is that if there is a value, and customers see it, they will be happy to use the product and talk to the brand or retailer, if, of course, consumers have allowed them to enter their lives.

Connectivity

Connectivity used to be a one-way street. Consumers went to the store or supermarket when they needed something. In the golden age of marketing and advertising (1950–80), consumer-facing businesses did try to use advertising to entice consumers to buy their products or services. But today connectivity is a 24/7 immersive process.

It is, as we have said, no longer a one-way street. Consumers are producers and vice versa, consumers don't need to go through a platform to connect with other consumers and even peer-to-peer trade will occur through connections that no one controls and ultimately will even know about.

Connectivity today, or connecting with those consumers who have allowed select branded platforms into their lives, is a proactive, reactive, and repetitive process. And connectivity is not just between commercial platforms and consumers— it's about the integration and connection of consumers' entire lives through artificial intelligence (AI) and the Internet of Things (IoT).

Be Proactive

The first step in establishing a platform is for the business to proactively reach out to engage consumers who have expressed interest in participating in the platform's community (again, obtained through data analytics). The business should gather information about when, how and where its customers want to be engaged, even if only by receiving regular messages about the community's activities, innovations, and areas of interest to those consumers.

But this will evolve, because as we have stated throughout the book, any one company's ability to control consumers or keep them interested in its content will surely wane. The next evolution of your business means being proactive in developing program interfaces that allow your consumers to connect with you in whatever manner suits them. What resources should you allow your consumers to use without your being present? In the post-platform world connectivity will bypass even this question, but if you are proactive in looking for connectivity, you have an opportunity to stay relevant.

Be Reactive

The platform must be accessible wherever and whenever consumers want to use it and must be instantaneously responsive both online and off. The most important link in the value chain is the sales associate or customer service rep. You need to ensure that they have expertise about your business and products, know how to use game-playing techniques to engage consumers, have the use of an iPad or other device that lists inventory and its location, all platform content and personal information about the platform's community members. If your customer service personnel have these tools, they become the last and most important point in the purchase chain.

Be Repetitive

Essentially, the platform's entire process must be fluid, frictionless and never ending.

A (Shopping) Day in the Lives of . . .

The best and easiest way to explain the connections between commerce and life is to observe a day, including shopping, in the life of a young couple of the future. This example illustrates ultimate connectivity through the use of AI, machine learning, augmented and virtual reality, big data, IoT, interactive touchscreen devices, iBeacon technology, digital pay, robotics, apps, permission-based marketing, and more.

Jackson and Sophia wake up and begin to get ready for work. Their Alexa-like assistants give them personalized suggestions about what to wear that day based on the weather and the clothes in their closets. Sophia's phone knows she has a big meeting with her boss that day, so it suggests a more formal outfit, while Jackson's phone suggests incorporating a new sweater he received in his weekly customized clothing shipment the day before. The couple gets clothing delivered weekly by subscription, with the selections based on their upcoming activities, weather, and style preferences. They don't feel the need to buy clothing that will last for longer than one or two uses.

They head to the kitchen to make breakfast. Fortunately, their refrigerator had sensed earlier that week that they were running out of milk and ordered more. It's sitting right outside their front door, packed in dry ice. The refrigerator also gives Sophia a healthy smoothie recipe that uses only the ingredients currently available in her kitchen.

They hail a self-driving car to take them to work. In the car they watch the news on a screen, and when Jackson sees his favorite band will be in town that night, he instantly buys tickets by scanning the ad with his phone. An app automatically makes dinner reservations at two spots near the concert hall—one Jackson loves and one he would probably like based on his preferences—and schedules another pickup by a self-driving car.

The next day, the couple heads to Tahoe for some skiing. They're renting their apartment out for the weekend through a website, and they are renting someone else's home in Tahoe. They order another self-driving car for the journey, and it arrives already loaded with all the gear they will need, rented for the weekend from a local sporting goods store. Once they get to Tahoe, Sophia realizes she forgot her contact lens solution. A drone delivers it within thirty minutes, and Sophia doesn't even have to tell the drone where she is.

On the slopes the next day, Jackson notices the ski jacket worn by a man in the lift line. He takes a picture of it—hands free, from his ski goggles—to show Sophia. As he's walking into the ski lodge later, he gets a push notification that the jacket is on sale a few steps away. In one click he buys it, and it will have been delivered to his rented Tahoe apartment by the time he gets back.

Convenience

As we've said, time is the new luxury. Again, with more of almost everything in life that any human being would ever need or even want, the real challenge for all platforms is to gain quicker and easier access *to* consumers and to provide quicker and easier access *for* consumers. This also requires a frictionless and fluid value chain, as described in chapter 11.

Convenience used to be a store across the street or ordering something from a catalog while lying on the couch in the living room. However, having to wait for its delivery two weeks later wasn't so convenient.

Convenience today is to use a mobile device to browse wherever you are, select, then click once to purchase, and then receive your purchase within the hour, wherever you want to receive it. Of course, Amazon once again is way ahead of every other platform. All other consumer-facing platforms are racing to catch up, both online and off. We believe Amazon will continue to innovate conveniences internationally and as far into the future as we can see. This is good and bad news for everybody else. The good news is all other platforms can copy Amazon's innovations (we hope). The bad news is Amazon is likely to leave the rest of the field in the dust for years to come.

Convenience is Echo's Alexa telling you it's time for your car to have another lube job without your having to actually keep track. Convenience is Stitch Fix's sending, on a cycle you chose, a new and personally curated box of fashion items for you to pick from and return at no cost. It's Lyft's picking you up in minutes wherever you are and charging your credit card without your having to pull it out of your wallet. Convenience is Instacart's shopping and delivery of groceries to your front door, or Tesco's subway station wall images of the entire grocery store in South Korea, where commuters can scan the bar codes of the groceries they want, which will be delivered to their home by the time they get there.

It's tapping an Amazon Tide Dash Button on your washing machine when the machine, through its connection to the Internet of Things, tells you that you need to reorder. Sometime soon the machine itself will inform Amazon.

Convenience is opening your Macy's app, informing your personal stylist that you need a party outfit for the evening and, upon arriving at Macy's an hour later, the stylist has picked six outfits she knows you will love, having gotten to know you through Macy's personal data. By downloading all six to Macy's virtual fashion mirror, you can see which outfit looks best.

Convenience is also about fragmenting the enormous physical platforms like Walmart, Target, Macy's, Best Buy, The Home Depot, and many others. They need to have smaller, customized neighborhood social gathering places that are stocked for local tastes.

And, while Amazon is so far the leader in convenience, the big-box stores and retailers understand enough to know they will need to accelerate their rollout of physical platforms in all categories, a few of which they are now testing.

Content

During the twentieth century, all consumer-facing businesses' mantra for success was that product was everything. If you had a great product and a great brand, you would win. Today, product is just the price of entry—as we have said, there has not been enough focus on creating "crystals of imagination" that truly differentiate the leading brands. Even great new products do not win the day by themselves and not for long. Consumers expect great new products all the time, and on sale to boot.

The content of any consumer-facing platform in this new world, both online and off, includes all the perceived and real benefits expected of both the host brand and any other branded platforms with which the host may be sharing its platform. It includes the community environment (real or perceived) that consumers expect, along with fun, entertaining, educational and interactive experiences.

Content also includes customization, community, connectivity, convenience, and even choice and curation. So all the examples we mentioned while discussing those first four Cs are relevant here.

Beyond the content *on* the platform, content must emanate *from* the platform, reaching out to and connecting with the branded platform's community of consumers wherever they are. This is called content marketing. The sneaker purveyor Vans, for example, creates videos that star professional skateboarders like Kyle Walker, who starts off chatting with a couple of skateboarder pals about the sneaker's new performance-enhancing features, then performs a wild ride over impossible obstacles. It's both hysterically funny and thrilling at the same time.

The point here is that young sports-active consumers (skateboarders or not), will seek those videos out because they gain "value" by learning from Walker's cool moves on the board, and getting a few laughs out of it as well. Even if they don't seek them out, they will likely come across them as their friends share them on social media. And if they're watching the video on Vans site, a purchase is just a tap away.

Samsung created a content-marketing platform in Manhattan's Meatpacking District in the spring of 2016. It is a quintessential social community, a go-to destination that provides cocreated experiences (those created by brands and consumers working together) and a fountain of knowledge. It's a huge, multistory digital playground and cultural epicenter. An auditorium for concerts or films, an art gallery featuring rotating digital installations, a multitude of Samsung monitors and tablets, a connected living room displaying how the smart home works, cooking demonstrations and classes, and a café are all part of this enormous co-created experience. This is not a store. It's a gathering place that happens to have all of Samsung's products, as well as a product-servicing station that replicate Apple's Genius Bar. This content-marketing platform was designed around eight passion points: art, music, entertainment, sports, wellness, cooking, technology, and fashion. Every section of the building focuses on these topics.

HSN is a branded online and TV social community platform that streams content marketing 24/7 with demonstrations of the use of special products that can be ordered on the spot. Watch a cooking class featuring Wolfgang Puck, learn a lot, and order any number of featured products. They are merging with QVC to navigate the broader trends in retail's seismic shift.

Another great example is the start-up men's clothing brand Chubbies. The online-only brand invests heavily in content, especially social media. Much of its content is generated by customers: snapshots of customers wearing its products with funny captions—the brand gets more than a thousand a week. But Chubbies' biggest content success may be its videos. Like the customer photos, the videos never try to sell products; instead they show video game racing, men's synchronized swimming, huge water slides, and drinking games on rope swings—customers having fun and doing crazy things all while wearing Chubbies' shorts and swimsuits. Videos like these routinely rack up five to seven million views a week.[2]

Other examples of content marketing are numerous. In fact, many luxury-branded fashion platforms have replaced their catalogs with luxury lifestyle magazines and blogs that educate and entertain, complete with beautiful images of elegant people wearing the platform's offerings.

Curation and Choice

We are combining curation and choice here because the curation of goods, services and experiences is totally driven by the objective of providing the perfect Goldilocks choice of not too much and not too little.

Curation, when used correctly and in the context of our thesis, means creating, editing, and managing relevant collections, indirectly including experiences. It also includes knowledge and information that delights consumers, saves them time, and makes them feel that real thought has gone into how this will improve their life. All this must match the branded platform's social community desires and the brand's DNA. The curator, guided by big data, also strengthens connectivity and content.

In recognizing the enormous scope of this function, you might conclude that branded platforms of the future should have a chief curation officer.

The Goldilocks balance is driven by the objective of presenting the best curated selection to the consumer. As we again reflect on a future with an infinite number of discrete market niches served by an infinite number of discrete brands and branded platforms, this also translates to the choices that any given platform offers. As the psychologist Barry Schwartz pointed out in his book *The Paradox of Choice*, if consumers have too much of a selection to choose from, they become frustrated and anxious and may even be turned off.[3] This thesis also supports the importance of good curation.

Many online subscription services, some of which we explored earlier in this chapter (Stitch Fix, Birchbox), are great curators based on personal preferences. Personal stylists in many luxury and department stores are excellent curators and use personal data to help customers make easier choices. TJX, as we have mentioned, is an ubercurator, curating different platform experiences and assortments, customized for local communities.

Trader Joe's also shows how to curate at a less personal level. The grocer usually only offers one or two versions of any given product—only about four thousand SKUs versus fifty thousand for the average grocery store.[4] Yet this limited selection is acceptable to the wide range of consumers who walk through the door, many of whom probably are grateful because fewer choices make for a faster shopping trip.

Control

The issue of control is a paradox. At first glance it may look like a no-brainer: to successfully accomplish and to deliver all the Cs we explored earlier, a branded platform must have total or near-total control over its entire value chain, from creation to consumption.

But the notion of control starts to break down as the retail world becomes more fragmented, as it needs to engage with and encourage its consumers' active participation, including ownership of content by consumers, and as capabilities for peer-to-peer commerce emerge. In 2026, you will have less control of all this. So maybe the answer is take control now to survive, while you determine what and how to stay relevant when control is no longer desirable or possible. In a world of 3-D printing, even the ability to control design and production is likely to slip away.

In chapter 14, we described today's imperative: a liquid, fluid, rapidly responsive and fragmented value-chain process to serve the infinite number of discrete market niches of the future, both online and off. Just as it is imperative to create a frictionless shopping experience for consumers, so too it is imperative to create a frictionless value chain.

Tight collaborations with outside entities that are more skilled, efficient and effective at a particular function must control functions in the value chain that the branded platform does not own. Technology, information transparency, and globalization make all functions in the value chain capable of finding expertise anywhere in the world.

While we predict the growth of many smaller chains and more localized creation and production, large commoditized or specialized products produced at scale and the retailers that sell them, such as Apple and Walmart, will still be part of the retail scene and will drive the continual pursuit of low-cost or specialized production sources around the globe.

However, while some such functions in the value chain will be shared, the entity that originates, owns or creates the brand platform must control it or at least relentlessly pursue control. For example, Foxconn Technology Group is a Taiwanese multinational electronics manufacturing company that produced products under contract to Apple, Amazon, Nintendo, PlayStation, and others. Yet each of those brands oversees a tightly controlled collaboration to make sure Foxconn closely adheres to the brand's attributes, imaging and general positioning.

VF Corporation also outsources two-thirds of its manufacturing to low-cost Asian, Central American, and African countries. To maintain control over those collaborations, VF uses a program it calls the Third Way. The program brings VF's deep manufacturing knowledge and specialized equipment into external factories—along with VF's consistency, quality and cost controls, which is essential when you're making 1.3 million diverse products, from apparel and footwear to sleeping bags and luggage, every day.[5]

As VF's CEO, Eric Wiseman, told us, this helps keep costs down as labor costs rise. "A lot of the sourced factories that we use . . . have historically thrown labor at their problems because labor was so cheap," he said. "Now that labor's becoming so much more expensive, we've been able to help control our costs by taking some of our factory engineering skills and process skills to those factories so that they can get the kind of labor efficiency that we have in ours. In our factories in Mexico, for example, where we make a lot of our mass-channel jeans, the reason we have those factories is we can't buy those products cheaper anywhere in the world—we've tried. But those factories are so fine-tuned that they produce goods at a lower price than any factory in any place in the world, and that's why they're part of the family."

Most important is that brands must control those parts of the chain that directly touch the consumer. After all, continuous innovation emanates from tracking and responding to consumers' ever-changing desires, so the dominant brand must control origination, development and marketing. And it must also control

Exhibit 17.1. The Winning Model

distribution and the so-called last mile to gain quicker and easier access *to* consumers and to provide quicker and easier access *for* consumers, geographically and strategically, on all relevant distribution platforms (the term we coined for this in our previous book, *The New Rules of Retail*, is *preemptive distribution*).

And finally, control of point-of-sale is perhaps most essential of all, as it allows the brand to create the emotionally connecting experience we have found to be so critical. Apple, Amazon, Starbucks and Disney are examples of brands that may share control of various functions of their value chains; however, they exercise dominant control over all functions that touch the consumer: creation, innovation, marketing, distribution, and point-of-sale.

CHAPTER 18

INDUSTRY IDEAS

Lest you worry that the core changes and principles identified in this book are merely theoretical, we'll move now to examples of retail leaders from across the industry who are grappling with the changing landscape and confronting the forces we've identified.

"An Online Brand Figuring Out Offline"

Andy Dunn, CEO and Founder, Bonobos

Any discussion of the future of retailing would be incomplete without including Bonobos, the visionary online-to-brick-and-mortar menswear brand recently acquired by Walmart.

Founded by Andy Dunn, its CEO, in 2007, the company grew steadily online before opening its first Guide Shop (called shops instead of stores because they don't carry massive amounts of stock—something that can suck up 60 percent of store associates' time) in 2011. These shops are so far from traditional stores that they don't carry any merchandise for sale, just samples. Consumers can then complete their purchase online. Bonobos has since partnered with Nordstrom to create more traditional retail shop-in-shops, but Dunn said he has no plans to stop innovating. We discussed his vision for the future of Bonobos and the retail industry as a whole.

Leading the Charge

When Dunn started Bonobos in 2007, he had no idea e-commerce would disrupt traditional retailing as quickly as it has.

"If you had told me then that within a decade we would see the emerging meltdown of the traditional way of doing retail, that within a decade we would prove to be so prescient that traditional players would have trouble existing, I would have told you guys that it was ahead of schedule," he said. "From a vertical retail perspective, like The Gap brands, or The Limited brands, the existing store structure you have built to support the brand is too big. So with the decline in foot traffic you have to both condense your fleet and change your footprint. We will see those retailers come under significant threat. They have [put] too much of their vertical orientation into bricks and mortar."

He said he also didn't originally envision Bonobos as having a brick-and-mortar presence. But the brand has twenty-one Guide Shops and plans to have thirty-four by the end of 2017.

"We were wrong in thinking that we would be online only," he said. "What we discovered is there is a future in offline. Now we know you need to be an online brand figuring out offline, not an offline brand figuring out online. We want to be small, experiential [and have] high intimacy, high customer service. By 2026 I think the physical store will be massive for us. We'll have hundreds of Guide Shops without physical inventory, just people and samples."

He talked about the importance of choosing the name Guide Shops. "We didn't want to use the term *store*, because it connotes 'storage,' which is not what we're doing," he said. "Three challenges that make retail stores hard are leases, people and stock. The last one is the most capital intensive and make[s] the other two hard. You can focus on the human beings when you take inventory out. When you think about stores, and the staff, usually they're playing around with the stock, and they have marginal attention for the customer."

Bonobos went a different route with its partnership with Nordstrom—full inventory. Dunn said this move was designed to help the company achieve economies of scale quickly.

"We looked at our [profit-and-loss statement] and decided it will take time to scale the Guide Shops, so if we want to have national ubiquity, who actually gets it?" he said. "We decided that Nordstrom was the obvious partner to build the brand and deliver the service offering. We're the Number One chino and short at Nordstrom and have been able to build the brand quickly with them and drive consumer awareness, and [we] are able to drive the customer base to the online business. But you want to make sure the power is shared. The wholesale model is good, but you don't want 80 percent of your business in wholesale."

Dunn says Bonobos is just one of many of what he has dubbed digitally native vertical brands (DNVB). Their ranks include retailers like Everlane, Pinrose, Casper and Dollar Shave Club.

"I've invested in fifteen of these brands, and literally thousands are starting, the biggest of which are hitting $100 million, many of which are $20 [to] $50 million," Dunn said. "Those DNVBs, together with Amazon, will be taking a huge amount of retail share."

Winning in Offline Retail

Despite this huge growth in DNVBs and other online-only retailers, Dunn doesn't think what he calls offline retail will go away entirely.

"I don't think we're trending to[ward] 90 percent e-commerce, 10 percent offline retail—I think we're trending to fifty-fifty, excluding perishables," he said. "That's because we're accelerating the pace of technical investment into these categories at a ridiculous rate. In 2007 we were the only DNVB. Today there are about five per day starting around the country."

So what will set the winning 50 percent apart from the losing 50 percent? Dunn said it starts with a core offering that you can transition to a new channel mix that is more appropriate for 2026 and beyond.

"It takes a core offering that you're able to evolve toward the new channel mix," he said. "You've got to identify which pieces of your real estate portfolio make sense. For those that don't, you need to negotiate your way out. Not everyone will be able to share-shift out of hundreds of doors. Those that can't make that shift, because they're too dependent on it, or don't have a reason for being outside the channel, will probably go bankrupt. Is it a channel-led business or a product-led business? Or is it a service-led business?"

Dunn believes strong brands will be in the best position to make this transition.

"Brands are slow to build and slow to die because human beings form trust and have a loyalty to them," he said. "It takes a decade to build a great brand, and you're just getting started. I fear not for brands that have good direct-to-consumer DNA, like L.L.Bean and Patagonia, or for brands that have good store build-out like Kate Spade—there's a possibility for those types of brands to evolve."

When it comes to DNVBs, brand is even more important—it has to be strong enough to transcend product and channel.

"The DNVB brand is increasingly an experience, a bundle of good product and service at the same time," Dunn said. "We can own the relationship with the consumer. I think it's too commoditized to just compete on the clothing. If you add the service, then you can be loved by the consumer. When you vertically integrate the two things together, that's what makes the DNVBs so powerful."

In his mind, all these changes signal one of the biggest transitions in retail history, one that will push aside any retailers who fail to see it coming.

"We're in a hundred-year change to businesses' being built and brands' being built using smartphones and the Internet as their primary source of engagement," he said. "We spent the last hundred years organizing retail around the automobile. We'll spend the next hundred years reurbanizing, using the smartphone."

Playing with the Future
Dave Brandon, CEO, Toys"R"Us

Many CEOs dream of a world with less Wall Street pressure. Dave Brandon, CEO of Toys"R"Us, came on board at the request of Bain Capital and KKR in 2015 to help improve the retailer's performance with an eye to eventually taking it public, as Brandon did with Domino's Pizza, then a Bain holding, in 2007. That was in the middle of his eleven-year stint as CEO.

So far, Brandon's turnaround plan at Toys"R"Us seems to be working. After posting a 2.3 percent drop in same-store sales in 2015, the company's first quarter of 2016 showed tentative signs of growth, with same-store sales growing 0.9 percent globally and 0.1 percent domestically.

Brandon told us what he's learned from a career of turnarounds and what he sees for the retail industry's future.

Rough Waters Ahead

Brandon was clear-eyed about the challenges traditional brick-and-mortar retailers face now and in the future.

"I see three big issues: retailers—and consumers—are fixed on promotional activity like it's a drug," he said. "No one will pay full price anymore, and promotion has become a crutch for retailers and it's killing margins. At the same time retailers are struggling with foot traffic. And millennials—and likely the generation after them—are not as brand conscious as their parents."

To Brandon what these troubles mean is clear.

"There'll likely be a brick-and-mortar shake-out sooner rather than later," he said. "The winning stores will have to get more efficient in sales per square foot. The ones that don't will cease to exist."

The Store Situation

Speaking of stores, what separates the good from the bad?

"Stores are an incredible advantage if used correctly," Brandon said. "Our online sales are stronger in neighborhoods with a physical store, and stores can help expand distribution through buy online, pick up in store and ship from store, and make returns easier."

Brandon also said that stores can provide a powerful consumer touch point and connection point, especially if they're used to engage consumers. One example: a Toys"R"Us event in October 2016 that invited children to build a Lego structure in stores that they got to take home.

"Winning stores will be experience driven, like Dick's Sporting Goods," he said. "They'll offer a high level of customer service that can't be matched online. For example, customers will always buy baby and child safety items, like cribs, high chairs and car seats, from stores, so they can test them out, learn about them, make sure they're right."

In fact, baby items account for 38 percent of the chain's sales.

Product and inventory decisions are more important differentiators than ever. During the 2015 holiday season, Toys"R"Us attempted to differentiate itself with exclusive *Star Wars* merchandise and tried to avoid being out of stock by stuffing shelves to the max with merchandise, especially items that an in-house algorithm said would be most popular.

Brandon said being omnichannel brings its own inventory and supply chain challenges.

"The key to omnichannel success is managing supply chain issues," he said. "Planning is everything—planning and allocation have to sit inside the supply chain because they're so incredibly linked. Otherwise, you'll have lots of financial planning problems."

Store locations and size s also are critical, of course. Brandon joined Toys"R"Us just as the company was getting ready to shutter two iconic locations—the FAO Schwarz and Toys"R"Us flagships in Manhattan. Although the decisions were made before Brandon joined the company, he agrees with them—despite strong sales and lots of foot traffic, high rents and expenses meant the stores cost the company $22 million a year.

He said the company is looking for another location in Manhattan, but that it probably will be smaller, perhaps eight thousand to twelve thousand square feet, patterned after the urban models that have served the company well in China.

"Retailers will have to do three things to have a winning real estate strategy in the future," Brandon said. "First, they'll have to downsize and lease smaller stores. Second, they'll have to make sure the location is right given their target audience.

And if both of those two things are right, then they can activate the store, do some event marketing around it to engage people."

Looking for Leaders

As any good CEO knows, leadership is one of the critical challenges facing retailers now and in the future.

"I think one of the hardest roles to fill well is the chief digital officer," Brandon said. "It's hard to find someone with the right skills."

But acknowledging the importance of this position is half the battle. As Brandon and many other retail leaders know, digital is reshaping the future of retail, and the only traditional retailers who will win in this new environment are those that reshape their organizations to fit an omnichannel world and use their stores as a competitive advantage.

A Discounter's Dreams

David Campisi, CEO, Big Lots

The off-price channel is one of the fastest-growing segments of the retail industry, and Big Lots has recently emerged as a turnaround success story in this hot market. One of the big reasons behind this newfound success is David Campisi, the CEO.

As of the first quarter of 2016, same-store sales rose for two years after ten consecutive quarters of declines, and net income improved in 2015 after four years of decreases.

Campisi joined Big Lots as CEO in 2013, following a stint as chair and CEO of RYU (Respect Your Universe) Apparel, a publicly traded clothing and equipment brand that caters to the "urban athlete." Before that, he served as chair, CEO, and president of the Sports Authority, after holding senior merchandising positions there and at Kohl's, Fred Meyer Stores and May Department Stores.

Campisi credits Big Lots's turnaround to some of the same key principles he believes traditional retailers will need to succeed in 2026 and beyond: an intense focus on the core customer and employees.

Doing It for Jennifer

Throughout the organization Campisi has cultivated a laser focus on Big Lots's core consumer: a woman he calls Jennifer. According to Big Lots's annual reports, Jennifer is one of the most common names in the Big Lots loyalty program and serves as a stand-in for the company's core consumer. Every report and earnings call mentions Jennifer dozens of times, and "What would Jennifer want?" has become the central question asked by employees at every level in every part of the organization.

"Our rallying call at Big Lots is the consumer," Brandon said. "Everything we do, we do for Jennifer. For example, serving her better requires breaking down silos—IT is critically involved in merchandising and marketing, so why don't they all report into the same person? We changed that to better serve Jennifer."

This customer-first mentality means Jennifer's definition changes over time to accommodate the company's shifting core consumer base.

"Retailers have to start understanding their new consumer and figuring out what millennial purchasing decisions look like," Campisi said. "Our research shows that our customers spend the most with us when they're in their forties, so by the time millennials hit that point, we need to know how best to serve them and create that relationship so they come to us."

Campisi mentioned the added importance of making sure everything the company does provides a return on investment (ROI).

"Testing and learning is the most important thing any organization can do today," he said. "You always have to try new things, but make sure they have an ROI. E-commerce is one example—everyone's still trying to figure out how to make it profitable. Or iBeacons that transmit customers' location data—the ROI is there in bigger stores but not smaller ones."

So what does this brave new world mean for stores? Campisi is optimistic about the future—for some of them.

"Stores as a concept won't cease to exist—some stores will remain critical for the consumer," he said. "But winning stores have to first find their reason for being, their critical role in the world. There's too much sameness now. That means they have to stop trying to be all things to all people. Next, they need to regain leadership. We started calling store managers 'store leaders'—even little things like that make a difference."

Leadership Lessons

Rebranding store managers as store leaders reveals a powerful part of Campisi's strategy for 2026 and beyond: inspiring and empowering employees.

"The key to success today and in the future is all about leadership," he said. "In 2026 those that win will have found the ability to develop leadership models that are both new and build upon time-tested principles."

One new approach Campisi strongly advocates: building cross-functional teams and breaking silos.

"To succeed, you need the four C's: you need to be curious [and] have courage, confidence, and consistency," he said. "I've worked hard to embody these values at Big Lots and inspire them in my teams."

Campisi has dozens of emails from current employees extolling the value of working with him and for Big Lots. And this, he said, is one of his proudest achievements at the company.

As critical as company leadership and culture already are in attracting and retaining talent, they will become more important going forward. By 2050 millennials will be 50 percent of the US workforce, and they value qualities like inspirational leadership more than older generations, according to an IBM study.[1]

Millennials are reshaping the industry from the inside and outside, and Campisi is ready to meet the challenge—knowing what they want and figuring out how to get it to them.

Outplaying the Long Tail

David Jaffe, CEO, Ascena Retail Group

Here's one of the retail industry's biggest current conundrums: Even though new data science and technology allow retailers to customize and personalize their products and market to the individual consumer, should they?

David Jaffe, CEO of Ascena Retail Group, has some strong opinions about the quantified retail model. Jaffe has been CEO of Ascena since 2002 and held several senior roles with the company before that.

Personalization

Jaffe sees an end to the growth of small brands that cater to increasingly finite groups of consumers. The alternative? Customization on a larger scale. "As the market gets smaller and smaller, these smaller Internet companies are going to have a tough time finding enough people to sell to," he said. "So I think it's going to be about customization. Take something simple like sneakers. You have the same last and components, but you change the color and add stickers and zippers and laces. Eddie Bauer sent me a holiday card with a coupon for a custom lightweight down jacket. I came home and gave it to my son, who said, 'Cool!' He clicks on it, and it asks you which of twenty zipper colors you want or a lining and other details. Pretty basic. Imagine if they took it further and asked if you want pockets or a hood or asked if you want it waist length or longer?"

While the allure of customization clearly is strong, Jaffe cautions retailers to make sure it's cost effective. "How do you make it work for your brand?" Jaffe asked. "It's really interesting to talk about this stuff, but at the end of the day customization is going to be small, because it's expensive. If we give our supplier an order for under 100,000 units, they make a face. Although the factories are trying to restructure themselves to be more agile, so they can do smaller lots more efficiently. Maybe people are willing to pay more for customization. But some of the personalization is about marketing, where you're talking to the customer in a way that is unique to them."

Customization

In addition to individual customization, Jaffe and the Ascena brands are working to offer more variety at a higher level, hoping to increase turns and traffic. This strategy borrows from the fast-fashion playbook; fast-fashion leaders like Zara draw consumers into the store an average of seventeen times a year versus four times for the average retailer.

"Instead of having a stack of thirty-six blue polo shirts like

Old Navy, I'd rather have eight, and then the next week have sky blue or stripes," Jaffe said. "That helps that customer have a unique outfit. Old Navy will have limited numbers of styles, narrow and deep. When you think about Maurice's, they're in small markets. Our strategy is to go an inch deep and a mile wide so you didn't see yourself coming and going on Main Street in small markets. We're helping the customer customize their outfits."

Jaffe admires companies like Stitch Fix that have achieved this type of curation and customization outside the store. Stitch Fix uses an algorithm—and the eighty data scientists on its payroll—to help select products to ship to its customers.

"If you get it and you like it, you forget that it's full price—it's like someone sent you a present and took the time to put together an outfit for you," Jaffe said.

Jaffe thinks this "inch deep and mile wide" approach will catch on across the industry. "I think stores are going to be smaller and have broader offerings," he said. "A couple of years ago Staples cut their stores in half and doubled their SKUs. Now they don't have to stock inventory. Customers come in to look at things, then go online and order. It's almost like a catalog show-room. Like the Bonobos model."

Return on Investment

Jaffe says the ultimate consideration for any of these merchandising decisions, especially those resting on new technologies, is whether they'll deliver ROI. "We're developing something called Linebusters. At very busy times you can avoid the lines and check out using your mobile device," he said. "If I can have one fewer checkout location and have more people on the floor doing other things, that's a good return on investment. We're working to incorporate 'buy online, pick up in store' and 'buy online, reserve in store.' We're also offering Apple Pay. It's nifty, although no one's busting down our door asking for it. But we're ready. We have one foot in the old world and one in the new world."

When it comes to implementing these changes, Jaffe thinks the industry's current leadership is up to the task.

"I think the people in leadership are pretty smart," he said. "None of those people ten to fifteen years ago knew anything about the Internet. My point is [that] if you've got strong, smart leaders, they can learn new tricks. Each generation has a new twist. This generation's thing was the Internet. What's the next generation's new thing? Three-D augmented reality selling?" Ultimately, real or virtual, if a change produces no significant ROI, it has no real future for any retailer.

Volatility: The New Stability

Harvey Kanter, Chair, CEO and President of Blue Nile

When industry insiders toss around names of interesting, innovative retailers and brands that make a meaningful splash in the current environment, Blue Nile is inevitably one of them.

The online diamond retailer, which recently moved into bricks mortar, is run by Harvey Kanter, its chair, CEO and president. Kanter is also on the board of Potbelly Sandwich Works, formerly served as CEO of Moosejaw Mountaineering, and also held senior leadership roles at Michaels, Aaron Brothers, and Eddie Bauer.

Only Change Endures

Throughout his career Kanter has noticed one thing: constant change is the new normal. "The conversation in my mind is about choice and volatility," he said. "Those sound like different things, but in my mind they're one and the same. Volatility is almost predictable in the world today. Volatility is the new stability."

For consumers this volatile environment is contributing to significant behavior changes, especially among younger consumers. "Consumers are living volatility every day," Kanter said. "The stock market is volatile, and they're living through that. There is some level of instability in general everywhere, and the millennial customer is affected by that. In their world it's so much more important to live for the moment and in the moment, as opposed to for the future. They travel a lot more than I did and they have a lot more experiences. They're living in a world of volatility, so what do you create a business around? Is it higher quality? Fewer things? Experiences? There's a reason why cheap and cheerful goods are at one end and high quality on the other, with the middle going away."

At Blue Nile, catering to these changed and changing consumers means giving them more choice—so long as they have an easy way to navigate their diamond options. Founded in 1999 as a web-only company to provide education about purchasing a diamond while also reducing costs with minimal overhead, the company is now opening stores. These stores are designed to make the purchasing process interactive and informative. Consumers pick several settings with cubic zirconia and compare and contrast them with the assistance of a consultant who helps them purchase the ring—and real diamond—online.

"Consumers want more choice and want to navigate on their own, choosing how they buy things, on what device and what they spend their money on," Kanter said. "At Blue Nile we have a store, but we don't have diamonds in the store. We facilitate getting the stones to [consumers] directly after giving them the ability to navigate the range of choices. It's a broader way of giving them the independence to choose."

These model stores are a relatively new development. As an online retailer, Blue Nile experimented with a tiny shop-in-shop in Nordstrom's store at the Roosevelt Field mall on Long Island and hit more than $1 million in sales. It then opened its first store in the Roosevelt Field mall on June 5, 2015, and recently opened four more in Tysons Corner, Virginia; Portland, Oregon; Garden City, New York; and White Plains, New York, based on its initial success.

"Our research told us that 75 percent of consumers decide where to buy a diamond engagement ring based on recommendations from friends and family," he said. "It also told us they wouldn't buy a diamond online because they can't see, touch and feel. We believe that fewer than 10 percent of all engagement rings are bought online. We think we have 50 percent of that online business. But how do we move the offline customer online?"

Part of the reason for Blue Nile's initial store success is that the in-store experience doesn't feel much like being in a store at all. In fact, the company doesn't even call it a store—Blue Nile calls it a webroom. The model fuses an online experience, which is intuitive for millennials, with an in-store environment. Blue Nile's first store was also intimate—270 square feet of selling space—with only five or six staff members at any given moment.

"If you think about a webroom, it's the penultimate iteration of a digital experience, because you're actually transacting on an iPad or laptop with the help of a diamond jewelry consultant in the store," Kanter said. "It's a very robust digital interaction. There's a video wall that creates live feeds of Facebook and other social media so you can post pictures. Zero cash is taken in the building. The consumer interaction is all digitally driven. If you order your product by four in the afternoon, in many cases you can have it delivered to your door by 10:30 the next morning."

Leading Change

When it comes to surviving the current retail environment at Blue Nile and any other retail or consumer company, Kanter says it's all about leadership. "The single greatest challenge in business is leadership," he said. "Talent is one thing, but to mobilize people, impassion people, make decisions, take risks, be comfortable with failure—those are all embedded in effective leadership. It's really a balancing act, because you don't want to create an organization where you have to tell people what to do all the time. I believe there's a vacuum of leadership on a broad scale."

Kanter says the dearth of leadership makes it hard for companies to make the tough decisions necessary to thrive. But in an environment in which the only constant is change and volatility is the new stability, great leaders will be even more prized and will separate winning retailers from those that quickly become obsolete.

Is Bigger Better?

Ken Hicks, former CEO, Foot Locker

Conventional wisdom in the retail industry today says that smaller stores are better—they better fit into fast-growing urban environments and are more easily navigated by time-crunched consumers.

But Ken Hicks, former CEO of Foot Locker, challenges that notion. Hicks, who retired in late 2014 after overseeing impressive sales-per-square-foot and revenue growth at the footwear retailer, also served in a leadership position at JCPenney.

In Transition

To Hicks, being in the midst of transition is nothing new for the retail industry. "Everyone talks about the industry in transition, but it's always been in transition," he said. "First it was mom-and-pops, and then it was department stores, then specialty, then discounter, then big box. We've gone through a number of transitions, and people always worry that the new thing is going to kill everything that preceded it. Malls were going to kill mom-and-pops; big boxes were going to kill the mall. Retail is an industry of continual transition. We're in a business that constantly evolves and reinvents itself. It's not like we've never seen this before. We've seen it and managed through it multiple times. Each time you think your whole business is going to go away."

So how will retailers manage through this latest transition? Hicks says they should start by dropping stores. "That culling hasn't happened to the degree that it should," he said. "The first thing I did when I got to Foot Locker was to close six hundred stores. It was tough medicine but it positioned the company for future growth. From the time I got there to the time I left, we had fewer stores every year (with the exception of the first year) but more square footage."

Spatial Concepts

Less with more? Hicks advocates for fewer but bigger stores to enhance the customer experience. "We were making bigger, more powerful stores," he said. "The worst thing you can do is give a retailer too much space. The second worst thing you can do is give them not enough space. We wanted to make Foot Locker an exciting place to shop. So we needed a bigger footprint. We were adding more categories and things like House of Hoops, Under Armour shops, and the A-Zone for Adidas."

Of course sometimes too much space is also a problem. "JCPenney has the opposite problem," he said. "They've got too much space. So the tendency is to fill it up, and sometimes you do that with not-good stuff."

For Hicks, the key to answering the square footage question is using space to develop an inviting experience and tell a story. "In our new format we put the hottest shoes in the vitrines, near the BACK TO SCHOOL sign," he said. "Everyone knew it was back to school [time]. I don't have a chance to sell somebody who doesn't cross the threshold. So kids who were in the mall would walk by the store and see the hottest shoe, then come into the store."

Experience-Minded Generations

Speaking of kids, Hicks also challenges the idea that millennials are disloyal or indifferent to brands. "They're loyal to an idea, and if Nike is the right idea, they're loyal to that," Hicks said.

The secret is getting millennials—or any other customer—to buy in to the brand idea. To help a brand tell its story often requires paring back inventory and upping space. "When I took over Foot Locker, it was a wall of shoes eight or nine rows high from the front to the back of the store," Hicks said. "How do I know what's important? How do I know what's new? If you go to our new format stores, we've pared back the number of shoes on the wall. We have shadow boxes where we put the key shoes. We'd show collateral around it, put in games in the kids' stores, we'd engage them. We made a pyramid with the kids' shoes so they could pick them up and even climb the fixture. I wanted a customer to go into House of Hoops and feel like Michael Jordan. And it worked. We took our sales-per-square foot from $300 to over $600."

Healthy Competition

This type of experience and a focus on service also helps Foot Locker avoid having to compete on price with other retailers racing to the bottom. "We offer a service," Hicks said. "We'll measure your foot. You have to be competitive, but you don't have to be the lowest-priced option."

In fact, Hicks doesn't see his brand partners as competitors even when they open their own stores next door. "Wherever Nike opened a store in a mall we were in, our sales went up," he said. "We had a better assortment, including shoes Nike made just for us. And the average age of the Nike store customer is north of thirty-five. Ours is south of twenty-five, a customer who buys more sneakers."

Hicks said that JCPenney started to run into trouble when it moved away from its core customer niche and competed with other retailers in noncore areas. "Penney's used to mean a lot more," he said. "Arizona and St. John's Bay was a billion-dollar business. We worked hard to make them brands. But we knew our limitations. At Penney the buyer in our juniors' and young men's departments said, 'We really need to step up our sexiness, because we're losing to Abercrombie.' But I told him, 'We're the second-largest young men's retailer. We don't sell to anyone over sixteen. We don't sell for Saturday night. We sell for Monday through Friday at school.' We weren't trying to be Abercrombie. When Penney did, they got into trouble. What are you going to do in a big department store? You're going to make it darkly lit and have a model-type guy standing around with his shirt off?"

The Talent Gap

Hicks thinks the industry will continue to struggle because of a lack of innovative leaders. He believes young talent is not being given the chance to develop. "One of the problems is young leaders not getting the opportunity," he said. "Leadership is a learned skill. More people are becoming leaders later in their careers so they're not as proficient at it as they need to be. Leadership is critical to a company. When I told the board I was leaving, they said, 'No, you can't leave, things are good.' I said, 'That's why I want to leave—I want to hand the keys to Dick Johnson when the engine's running and there's gas in the car.'"

The Modern-Day Agora

Mike Gould, Former CEO and Chair, Bloomingdale's

It's easy to feel pessimistic about the state of today's brick-and-mortar retailers, or at least cautious about their future. But Michael Gould is an optimist and thinks stores will be just fine.

Gould, who was CEO and chair of Bloomingdale's for more than twenty years, sees modern stores as an extension of a social tradition that dates to the days of the agora. "I'm a believer that shopping and retail have survived since the time of the Greeks," he said. "People have been going to city centers because it's a social interaction, not just to buy and sell goods."

So in Gould's mind, stores aren't going anywhere anytime soon, so long as they give people that social, sensory connection. "In 2026 stores need to be a social interaction," he said. "Maybe Amazon and others will be able to figure out how to get people to touch and smell product over the screen and to talk to customers. Otherwise, you need to go to a store. Going into a store, I deal with all the senses. Touch, sight, sound, smell, feel, and human interaction. Our lives are about human interaction. We want connections."

Gould also said stores should focus on making consumers feel special and recognized, pointing out that his favorite restaurant in all of New York City is a diner where the staff knows him by name. Successful retailers also need to entertain, educate and involve their customers in the experience to create that all-essential human interaction.

When it comes to department stores specifically, this concept shouldn't be new. In fact, the first department stores, back in the 1800s, were all about entertainment and experience. "How did most department stores start? "Hudson's Bay was a trading post," he said. "Filene's and Lazarus were the peddler's wagons that became fixed places, then became a hut, then grew into a family store, and then they added a restaurant and Christmas displays."

According to Gould, many modern stores have lost this personal focus. He said department stores today are not struggling with low traffic but with converting that traffic into sales. "I hear about how traffic is soft, yet to me it's astounding how much traffic there is in department stores today compared to the little shops on Lexington [Avenue] in New York," he said. "How do we get more out of that traffic? If you put a food hall in the lower level of the mall or the store, how do you get them to come upstairs? They like the brand for food, so how do you invite them to experience the rest of the store?"

According to Gould, retailers who can answer those questions—especially with experiential solutions—will in the best position to succeed in 2026.

Let Me Entertain You

Mindy Grossman, former CEO, HSN
(now CEO, Weight Watchers)

Today's retail industry is obsessed with the idea of beating the competition, which they define as other retailers and purely e-commerce start-ups. But that is a narrow view. Your competition is not necessarily a retailer. Consumer brands are now competing with every other interaction customers have—and in every way they can spend their time and money. And on top of that, the line between sales and brand engagement is blurring.

Mindy Grossman, CEO of HSN, is a visionary and is racing ahead of the curve by betting on being a content provider as well as a retailer. Grossman has been the CEO of HSN since 2008 and serves on the US Commerce Department's Digital Economy Board of Advisors. She has also held leadership roles at Tommy Hilfiger, Ralph Lauren, and Nike. She's also the chair of the National Retail Federation.

Overstored

Grossman is opinionated about today's retailers who have too much inventory and too many stores. She believes they have only themselves to blame. "People have left the needle in their arm for too long," she says. "Retailers have their regular business and their outlet business, so they're becoming commoditized and ubiquitous. And the consumer's not stupid. The apparel business has become overinventoried, with brands available in too many competitive venues."

However, Grossman doesn't think stores should go away. In fact, she said HSN is venturing into the physical world, opening stores with its Ballard Designs and Frontgate brands. But her model is modern. She embraces mobile as a shopping tool to help make the stores successful.

"It all has to start from a mobile point of view," she said. "You have to be platform agnostic and audience-centric, and you have to be where the consumer is. And the consumer will decide when, where and how they want to transact. You'd be foolish to think that the percentage of digital commerce isn't going to increase and the role the store will play is going to change. I think we're 'over–real estated' and overstored."

In Competition

Why do retailers have to be everywhere? Because their competitors are. And Grossman doesn't view other retailers as the only competitors—she's thinking bigger.

"We used to think that our competition was vertical, but today our competition is the last experience a consumer had," she said. "If someone just took a ride with Uber, they're comparing you to the Uber experience, not their last shopping experience. I think of media and entertainment as competition, because it's competing for customers' time and where they're spending their money."

Content as Play

Enter the retailer-entertainer. Grossman and HSN have embraced this philosophy wholeheartedly. "We say we want to engage, educate, inspire and entertain," she said. "We're doing that through content. The reason our electronics business is so strong is we can show what the connected home is and how it works. We can show customers the ecosystem of a product and create digital content wherever and whenever they want to interface with it."

This idea of content creation extends beyond educational

content in support of selling a specific product. Content promotes the HSN brand before consumers ever decide to put a product in their cart. "We have a business with Wendy Williams," Grossman said. "She and her husband have a [nationally syndicated talk] show. This is not a typical TV separation of church and state. She has WendyWilliams.com, and we said, 'Why can't we also have our products there?' So we're running another commerce network off our platform. We also have the arrangement with Univision—created by Univision and powered by HSN. We do live streaming on Facebook. We're on the Samsung LG app. We do all our video distribution; we're on Roku, Tivo, Hulu and Apple TV. We now have three channels on Roku."

The Visionary Gap

When it comes to the challenge of actually implementing these ideas—and dreaming up the next big ones—Grossman wonders whether retailers will be able to find leaders who are up to the task. "There are 5.8 million unfilled [retail] jobs right now, and we don't have the talent to fill them," she said. This problem is not unique to the retail industry. Grossman mentioned that, for example, Lockheed Martin wouldn't be able to fill all its data scientist positions even if it hired every single graduate in the field every year.

So what makes a good leader in Grossman's eyes? "Leaders need to be brave, resilient, agile, and curious," she said. "I don't care what era you live in: you need leadership that can inspire, communicate a vision, and be able to execute. On top of that you need to have agility, ability to take strategic risks, and relentless curiosity. I don't think the maniacal need for agility has ever been more necessary. And the true idea of how to be a digital company—you've really got to change your culture and be more entrepreneurial. You have to be able to move and to have a structured environment in which to learn. You have to allow risk in your culture. People need to test and, if they're going to fail, to fail fast and as cheaply as possible."

The fail fast, fail at low cost mentality sounds as if it's straight from a start-up. Given some of Grossman's digital- and mobile-first, content-heavy ideas, it's no surprise she believes the retailer of the future will look a little more like a lifestyle publication than a big box.

Ongoing Transformation
Eric Wiseman, former CEO, VF Corporation

"Businesses that have thrived over time are generally great at changing," said Eric Wiseman, CEO of VF Corporation. "The companies that have experience in transforming and changing who they are have a pretty good foundation to help them survive the next transformation."

This sounds great in theory, and it's easier said than done. Wiseman, head of one of the industry's most consistently innovative companies, walked us through his vision of the future and how VF is working to address it.

Wiseman has held leadership roles within VF for more than twenty years and serves on the boards of directors of Lowe's, CIGNA, and the Retail Industry Leaders Association.

Anticipating Change

Be prepared. With any big transformation, the first step is recognizing and understanding it. That's why VF kicked off an internal initiative called "The Future of Shopping" in early 2015.

"Every six months we've gotten together with the operators of our biggest brands to update them on what we see as the big trends coming at us, recognizing we're probably wrong because trends are so fickle and move quickly. When we started this exercise, our aim was to have a 2020 plan," Wiseman said. "We recognized that a 2020 plan needed to have a point of view of what the world will look like by then."

The future is, of course, hard to anticipate, but continually staying on top of the trends is a way to avoid having to catch up to the future. And if you take a cross-disciplinary look at the trends and connect the dots, you have a shot at staying ahead of the most critical shifts. One of the biggest predictions that emerged from VF's initiative now seems all too obvious. "The upshot of all of this is the consumer is in total control now, and if you give them a fantastic experience, they will love you," Wiseman said.

He knows experience is more than how people interact with your products online or in a store: It's also how they experience and think about your brand systemically. And it's how your employees experience your brand's ethos. To that end, VF has made significant investments in corporate social responsibility and sustainable sourcing.

"In Bangladesh we're sending medical wagons into impoverished villages that don't have access to medicine," Wiseman said. "We feel if we have a factory there, and even if we only use 20 percent of that factory, then the people there and their families have the right to medical care. We dig wells in communities where they don't have wells. We're doing more of these things because—why wouldn't we?"

Staying Alive

It goes without saying that the level of competition on today's playing field is not only fierce but requires new skill sets and mind-sets to ensure leaders are both facile and visionary. VF has established a matrix of competitive strategies to help it thrive in the global marketplace.

1. Test and keep testing.

Wiseman says the company's growth owes in part to a willingness to try new things. "Nine years ago we did $7 million in e-commerce globally—now we're doing $700 million," he said. "I was at VF when people said, 'We're not going to open retail stores; we're going to be the best wholesaler that big-box retail has ever had.' Boy, am I glad we did open retail stores. We now have fifteen hundred stores around the world. Doing that just takes the mentality of being thoughtful and flexible and testing. Companies that are constantly looking forward and exploring, not just sitting at their desks looking at reports of last week's comp[arable] store sales, are going to be victorious."

2. Encourage out-of-the-box and out-of-the-company thinking.

Being curious and open is a key to not getting stuck inside your own ideas. Wiseman encourages VF's leaders to look outside the company for new ideas—their external research and observations are considered in their annual performance reviews. "If you structure a company that has the right balance of wisdom and experience with new voices, it will be okay. Then you have to make sure that your experienced leaders regularly expose themselves to new experiences," he said.

3. Be agile.

Wiseman points to the recent "Damn Daniel" YouTube videos featuring Daniel and his white Vans sneakers as a pop-cultural moment that produced immense benefits for VF. "It went viral on YouTube, got thirty million views, they went on *Ellen DeGeneres* the same week, then our social media people got wind of it, and the home page of the Vans website was all white Vans," Wiseman said. "On *Ellen* this kid was given a lifetime supply of Vans. We were able to move quickly on that." Capturing the moment, mobilizing quickly and taking advantage of a crowdsourced fan base—where existing fans of the brand helped recruit others by sharing viral content—was priceless in terms of media, marketing and PR costs.

4. Create urbanized stores.

Since the early 2000s, population growth in the fifty biggest cities in the United States has been three times higher than in the rest of the country. We estimate that people in these urban areas also earn 20 percent more than their rural counterparts. Wiseman says capturing this growing, increasingly affluent population requires a different in-store experience. "We did a pop-up Eastpak store in London last year and put everything in the store *but* product to sell," he said. "You could see product on the wall, and you were never more than three feet away from an iPad. You could order it and get it delivered the next day. The model was a small store with simplified shopping options for urban populations. What do we do with megacities? We're looking at a case where every neighborhood is different, so maybe smaller stores custom created for a local neighborhood is the future."

5. Find your niche.

Wiseman thinks trying to be the next Amazon or competing on speed or price alone is futile. "If what you want is quick order fulfillment, then Amazon pretty much has that buttoned up," he said. "What they don't have is a combination of fulfillment and experience. So if you can get your Timberland boots in two days plus the bonus that once you're there online, you have a great storytelling experience to understand what's gone into making them, the sustainability back story, and what they're worn for, isn't that a better pathway to tomorrow?"

6. Think globally.

VF is making big investments in emerging markets like China, even though the majority of consumers there can't afford its brands—yet. "We're working really hard on how technology will enable the growing middle class in China and how we can engage them in our brands," Wiseman said. "The big income bubble that will move the needle with discretionary income really hasn't happened yet, but it's going to happen in the next five to ten years. That's the blessing of rising labor rates in China. Those folks are becoming middle-class consumers. Our goal is to get them to aspire to buy our brands today, even though they can't afford them, and then remain relevant to them so that when they can afford it, they buy it."

7. Create a community.

Wiseman says developing a great experience is about so much more than product, it's about building an entire community where people can interact. This is the thinking behind House of Vans, a new store concept built in five old railway tunnels under London's Waterloo train station. "Since the brand is all about youth culture and creative expression, we put in an artists' gallery where artists can come and create art, hang it and sell it," Wiseman said. "Apparel art is appropriate too, so there are CAD machines where you can design and screenprint a t-shirt. One of the tunnels has been repurposed as a movie theater where films are shown. Another is a brew pub for beer and burgers. Two were transformed into London's only indoor skate park. The walls are arched like bowls, so you can skate up into them. The last tunnel is a performance space for eight hundred to nine hundred people [that is] ready for bands to plug and play. The Foo Fighters came and played a free concert because they liked what we were doing for the youth of the city."

Transformation can sound scary to executives if they aren't open and don't get it. Wiseman and his team at VF are redefining leadership, creativity and innovation to stay relevant and valuable in today's warp-speed culture. Looking at business through a cross-disciplinary lens and understanding the value of running an organization holistically is what leaders need to do today to be successful. Wiseman has taken VF to a whole new level, transforming it day by day.

Using Big Data to Empower Small Decisions

Michelle Lam, CEO, True&Co. (now part of PVH)

Perhaps the most talked-about concept in modern retailing is big data. Every brand is enchanted with the idea of using analytics to improve its understanding of its consumers and drive smarter decision making for all aspects of its business.

One of the leaders in this space is True&Co., which is using big data to tackle one of the most personal—and often frustrating—processes: buying a bra. True&Co. operates mostly online, although after the success of its Try-on Truck tour, it has also started a series of offline initiatives, such as a print catalog and Try-on Tent pop-ups. On its site, users can take a detailed quiz to help them find the right bra—and more than five million women have. An algorithm, which changes constantly as more women take the quiz, helps guide customers to the right product and helps inform future new product development.

We talked with Michelle Lam, the CEO, who founded

True&Co. after cofounding the Operating Group at Bain Capital Ventures, where she was also an investment principal and led deals for companies like LinkedIn. Before that, she had successful stints at Microsoft, Boston Consulting Group, and PricewaterhouseCoopers about using data to transform processes—and the retail industry.

Start-up Success Factors

Lam is convinced that the reason for the rapid growth of innovative start-ups like True&Co. is the huge gap between what consumers really want and the products currently available to them. One of the big reasons for this is that the production system has flourished by reducing costs and driving efficiencies through standardization—but hasn't accounted for evolving and diversifying customer needs.

"The physical supply chain has little incentive to be innovative; it favors scale, uniformity and cost," Lam said. "Most brands will share a product concept with the factory, and then, based on their own grading system, based on prior production runs, [the factory makes] different variations from that. But are they right? Most often the customer does not get what they really want, especially in a world where the customer no longer wants the same thing. For millennials, the standard look that was popularized by [the] Victoria's Secret push-up bra is no longer that popular. This generation has moved on. And we've found that for two-thirds of all women, the traditional bra cups that favor the full round breast shape does not work because their bodies are different."

Instead, Lam said, successful innovation in consumer products and apparel centers on four key dimensions: making simple product improvements across at least one critical dimension, compelling unit economics, attractive category characteristics, and ability to redesign the supply chain.

And Lam is doing all of that. True&Co.'s business model is predicated on using analytics to not only identify what its consumers want but also bake those insights into the product development process to ensure the brand can offer products to match its consumers' needs.

"Data is granular, production is mass," Lam said. "It's critical to get the supply chain involved early on to delay the commoditization process as long as possible and make sure that you have as much flexibility as possible. If you make a custom product, you can make sure it is the best one for the customer—as you make products for larger groups of customers, compromises start to build up. There can be too many operational compromises that stop you [from] getting the product the customer wants. The factory will want to control the fabric, they will want to manage the complexity of the manufacturing process, and they will want to control order sizes and volumes. In the end, the customer does not get what they want. The solution is working collaboratively with partners in the supply chain to ease these restrictions and for True&Co., since we collect extensive feedback data from our customers as part of our business model, to examine this data to spot production errors by the factory."

According to Lam, the goal for start-ups is to create customer value on at least one highly differentiated attribute and build the business from there. For True&Co., that starting point was the consumer quiz, which helps match products and consumers and vice versa—and it's why True&Co.'s return rate is 50 percent below the industry average. The quiz, which has since been borrowed by the likes of Amazon and Victoria's Secret, was developed in Lam's living room.

"I bought five hundred bras and invited as many women as I could find to take a pen-and paper quiz and to try on bras, while I did all the bra math based on their quiz answers," Lam said.

"With their feedback, I was able to find out what kind of questions women wanted to be asked—mainly the issues that they felt were important to communicate about their bodies—and this became True&Co.'s fit quiz."

But doing something like that is only the first step toward meeting the challenge. The next hurdle is growing the business. An initial wave of early adopters and digital channels make it easy to spread the word, so achieving critical mass isn't the hard part. The hard part is attracting the next wave of customers. The other lesson that lots of start-ups have learned is that early adopters are not their core customers—success in cities like San Francisco and New York does not translate quickly or easily to success in other cities.

As Lam says, it's important to be in a category that has structurally attractive characteristics.

"Lingerie works well, because it has a high initial order value, loyal customers and the ability to use the data to help the customer get a better product," she said. "Our goal is to have 65 percent private label unique product that is exactly matching the customer's preferences and the rest are brands that we know we can sell and meet the customer's needs."

Strong category dynamics are work in favor of businesses like Casper, which serves a category (mattresses) with an even higher initial order value and high customer frustration with the traditional purchasing cycle of not being able to try a mattress at home for a period of time. For many other start-ups, the concept of giving the customer lifetime value has driven fund-raising and valuations, but no start-up is certain its customers will return in three to five years. Many digitally native vertical brands are opening stores to get more customers, not least because the cost of getting new customers from digital channels like Google and Facebook is reaching new, unsustainable heights.

Inevitably, this produces an "innovation gap": How can small companies grow and how can large companies attract new ideas, business models and talent?

According to Lam, there is an opportunity for large companies to partner with the new wave of start-ups in meeting customers' increasing demands for personalization and reaching more customers faster.

"We are understanding customers' needs—we are designing new supply chain and go-to-market models to deliver new products," she said. "The future should be about how we can also leverage assets that already exist."

We have no doubt that as True&Co. continues to grow, Lam will continue to use new tools like advanced analytics to remake old systems like the traditional supply chain—and produce benefits not only for customers but the industry as a whole by showing what re-envisioning the industry, starting with the consumer, can make possible.

Building a Disruptive Brand in the Digital Age

Jeremy Liew, Partner, Lightspeed Venture Partners

Every retailer has heard time and time again that a million start-ups are coming for its business and its customers. But knowing which ones will succeed and which ones will sputter is another matter—and figuring that out can help companies of all ages, shapes and sizes see what it takes to build a winning brand in the digital age.

Jeremy Liew, a partner at Lightspeed Venture Partners, knows a thing or two about the art and science of building a successful start-up. He has been with the firm since 2006 and invests primarily in consumer-facing mobile and online companies. Before taking on his current role, he held several leadership positions at AOL and Netscape, where he helped to define the early days of the Internet.

Challenges Facing Start-ups

Our interview began with a discussion of the competitive challenges today's start-ups face.

"A start-up should never win against an incumbent," Liew said. "They have no scale, no brand and no distribution when they start. The odds are enormous. But the thing a start-up has is speed and the ability to react quickly. But speed only matters when the environment is changing."

Of course, the retail environment is definitely changing, making this a prime time for start-ups to challenge traditional competitors. Consumer demands are evolving and growing day by day, making speed and agility an incredible advantage for start-ups.

"There are changes [in the business climate] when you can really get traction as a start-up," he said. "The first is if there is a big shift in consumer preferences. A great example is the move to organics. A concern like Jessica Alba's The Honest Company can grow fast in this environment. Her authentic activity in the area with the relationships she had already built enabled her to rapidly grow a brand that was seen as distinct from the large CPG [consumer packaged goods] companies that do not have credibility."

Alba cofounded The Honest Company in 2011 after her frustrating experience of looking for nontoxic products during her pregnancy—and that experience gave her instant credibility. The company has tapped into parents' concerns about classic, chemical-laden cleaning and personal care products for babies, and its focus has fueled impressive sales growth—from $10 million its first year to a $1.7 billion valuation in 2015. Today 75 percent of the company's revenue still comes from online sales (although its products are sold in boutiques, Target, Costco and more), and much of that is from monthly purchases of bundles of diapers and wipes.

According to Liew, this authenticity is critical because it helps avoid commoditization.

"You have to avoid competing against Amazon at all costs," he said. "Amazon is a ruthless competitor who will win. Competing in a space with multiple brands on convenience and price is a losing strategy."

Changes in the Air

As we continued to discuss his thesis that changing environments create opportunities for start-ups to exploit, Liew helped us identify a few other shifts that are reshaping retail.

First, he discussed changing distribution patterns, using as an example Stella & Dot, an online jewelry brand that debuted during the Great Recession. It allows consumers and fans of its brand to host trunk shows and jewelry parties or to work from home as brand stylists, bringing authenticity and social connection to the brand.

"Stella & Dot took advantage of multilevel marketing. . . . People wanted to work in that way [during the recession] and also people wanted to buy," he noted. "That is getting squeezed out now, but distribution changes offer opportunities for start-ups to exploit."

According to Liew, another big change that start-ups can exploit is a sudden shift in customer acquisition costs.

"This happened, for example, when Facebook was in its early stages—traditional marketing missed it and the access to customers was mispriced," he said. "So companies like Groupon, Gilt Groupe and gaming companies were all able to get [economies of] scale very cost effectively. That has disappeared now as incumbents dominate."

Speaking of Facebook, Liew said different online marketing channels can create different opportunities, depending on the brand and category.

"The reason you would go on Facebook was because it was a fun place and so all new and fun things grew there," he said. "Getting customers on Google was different because they went with intent—they were searching for a specific thing. So in this environment start-ups like Lending Tree, Expedia and insurance products all grew—[these are all] considered purchases [that are usually thought about in advance]. Now things have changed again, and there is more of a 'social organic' way to acquire customers, that is, for example, Instagram that has more about a mission, a cause."

For an example of this new approach to customer acquisition and generating positive brand awareness, Liew points to Dove's body image campaign, which included a series of truly viral videos celebrating real women of all shapes and sizes—not models—that created instant relatability and emotional connection.

Given all these constant changes, what does Liew see as the future of the consumer start-up space—and what does that mean for the old guard?

"All start-ups now realize you must be omnichannel," he said. "Brands must have vertical integration. Digitally native brands are good, because you find out what works or not quickly. Those that use data are good, like Stitch Fix. You have to use new social channels to get traction, but an authentic personality like Gwyneth Paltrow can lead a business quickly—as long as it's part of her brand. In building a brand, you must know what you stand for and what you don't."

Change: The One Constant in Retail

Jerry Storch, CEO, Hudson's Bay Company

For Jerry Storch, changes in the retail world don't mean the sky is falling. In fact, Storch said radical change has always been a part of retail reality, and while the retail environment today brings its own unique challenges, the ingredients for success haven't changed as much as many fear.

Storch is certainly in a position to analyze long-term changes in the industry. He's the CEO of Hudson's Bay Company, where he oversees Hudson's Bay, Lord & Taylor, Saks Fifth Avenue, Saks OFF 5TH, Home Outfitters, and HBC Digital. Storch has had a storied career in the industry, including a stint as chair and CEO of Toys"R"Us and serving as vice chair of, and in many other senior roles at, Target.

Through all that experience Storch said the one constant was change.

"We won't be saying that in 2015 the world changed," he said. "The world is changing, but it's changing every year—it didn't just change at that one moment."

But today's retail environment has new forces to reckon with, such as omnichannel. He says many retailers take far too narrow a view of omnichannel.

"The retail model will evolve into a multifaceted model—it won't be all one way or the other," he said. "People are way too focused on a few omnichannel levers, but there are a hundred different variations, depending on where the customer is, what and where the product is, where the customer wants it received, at least a hundred different paths. It provides a broad range of possible options."

This way of thinking informs Storch's opinion of Internet

retailers—that they don't have inherent competitive advantages that mean they'll be at the top of retailing in 2026.

"There's no Internet-only advantage," he said. "If Amazon—which by the way has the only chance of winning in the Internet-only world—wins, it won't be because they're experts at shipping to people's homes. It's because they're really good at customer intimacy. They still operate a very expensive supply chain. They have so many [distribution centers], they might as well be operating stores."

Instead, Storch thinks one thing Internet retailers share with every other retailer, regardless of channel, is the challenge of providing stellar customer experiences. And that's one way retailing hasn't changed over time.

"If you have the vision of staying fresh and exciting—it's always been about experience over things," he said. "That's nothing new. Nobody wants to sit home in their undershorts and shop online. That's a nerdy view of the world. They want to go out and do things, but it has to be worth it."

Applying the logic that experience trumps everything to brick-and-mortar retailing should result in stores that are incredibly profitable, he said. Compelling experiences can save even department stores, which he is working to do with Hudson's Bay.

"When we went to Canada, we were told, 'People don't like department stores anymore,'" he said. "I had looked at Hudson's Bay, and some of the stores were real junkers. Richard Baker [Hudson's Bay Executive Chairman] and his team started to invest some capital, and the stores have been doing better every month—in good times and bad. It turns out that people don't dislike department stores: they dislike bad department stores. They want good ones. They're more than happy to come when there's something to see and do, and experiences. That's nothing new. People have always liked department stores."

Of course, the revitalization of consumer interest in Hudson's Bay requires investment to give older stores a badly needed facelift and implement technological improvements. Storch said this investment is essential to winning.

"We announced in our earnings call that we are spending $750 to $850 million in capital to renovate stores," he said. "That's a huge amount of money for our company, but we're taking buildings that were neglected and making them fantastic. Second, we are investing in technology. We're putting in fulfillment that is better than anyone's. People are scared of not spending the money, so they guarantee their own failure."

Looking to the future, Storch knows the one constant of retailing—change—won't be going away anytime soon. Yet he's less concerned than many industry insiders about the impact of millennials.

"I read that millennials are responsible for the change in shopping behavior in the last six months—that's a big bunch of hooey," he said. "Millennials aren't responsible for the change. Their age range is eighteen to thirty-four. Suddenly they all changed? Something changed in our business last year [2015], and it wasn't because of millennials. Our business changed too, so something happened to the thirty-five- to fifty-five-year-olds too."

Millennials, after all, are the nation's biggest age demographic, so treating them as one homogenous group is too narrow-minded. Storch understands that many characteristics associated with millennials, such as a distrust of large brands and a preference for experiences over stuff, are actually larger societal changes.

But regardless of which demographic groups are driving the change, it's guaranteed to continue. And from Storch's perspective, those who focus on creating a truly special customer experience will be in the best position to succeed, no matter what the future brings.

The Future of Luxury

Karen Katz, CEO, Neiman Marcus

One of the most talked-about sectors in the retail industry is luxury—some insiders have recently started casting doubt on its future, saying consumers are becoming less brand loyal and less obsessed with stuff.

But Karen Katz, the CEO of Neiman Marcus, is confident her company and her industry will survive nicely. Before taking the reins at Neiman Marcus, she served as the executive vice president of marketing, strategy and business development there, as well as in many other leadership roles.

Katz talked with us about the future of the luxury industry, the tremendous change facing all corners of retail and how to structure the organization of the future.

Change Artist

Unlike some of the other veteran leaders we've interviewed, Katz believes retail is in the midst of a truly revolutionary transition—one that will last for many years.

"There is almost chaos in the industry because of the amount of transformation that needs to take place, plus the anticipated changes for the future, which are still unknown at this point," Katz said. "It's all happening at such a rapid pace that it's also a challenge and an opportunity . . . to get a leadership team that can think three-dimensionally about those changes. The three dimensions are customer, product and engagement today, what to look for in the near term and what is all that going to look like ten years from now? We need to keep one hand on the steering wheel focused on today and tomorrow, but we also have to keep an eye on the future, concentrating on what we are learning today that could be applicable ten years from today."

Despite this dizzying change, Katz is confident Neiman Marcus—and other retailers—can find their way by keeping their eyes fixed on their core consumer.

"If you start with the customer and think about the ways she feels about service, pricing and experience and then figure out how we deliver that in a way that is technologically sound, digitally easy and really delivers on the service component, that's what our customer expects," she said.

Looking Ahead in Luxury

Katz mentioned several significant changes shaping the luxury industry, starting with what she calls "the phenomenon of athleisure."

"I think there continues to be the push towards [a] much more casual lifestyle, even from those customers that buy the best of the best," she said. "I think we have just scratched the surface of this casual luxury and it will continue to grow. Just for example, we're selling men's sneakers at crazy prices. We're in the first or second inning of luxury casual."

Another big change: how to grapple with millennials, whom many industry insiders believe are not brand loyal and don't value stuff as much as their parents. Katz disagrees with this generalization.

"For people who sell luxury and the experience of luxury, it's still not clear what Gen Y and Gen Z are going to need because they are not yet in their powerful earning years," she said. "There's been a lot of analysis [of] whether they only want experiences or things, and in my mind it's going to be an equal amount of both. Now she may want a different luxury buying experience than her mother's. So that story will really play itself out in 2026 when they are at the height of their careers. We are watching all this very carefully, and we do know from the data we have that Gen X is acting very similarly to baby boomers in the way they shop, although they are more digitally focused."

Stores

When it comes to stores, Katz is also less pessimistic than some others in the industry, provided stores change to better integrate with the digital experience and provide better service.

"I would not count stores out," she said. "We have 70 percent of our business in brick-and-mortar and we are believers that stores are going to make a difference. But I do believe they need to be reinvented. They are going to need a more social interactive quality with more emphasis on the service experience in the store."

Neiman Marcus has forty-two stores, and Katz said she thinks the US market is overstored in general and that many stores are too big—especially department stores.

"If you make stores smaller and inject a few things that give them more intimacy and soul, I think people will want to come to a store for an experience," she said. "You can walk lots of the big department stores, and so many of them feel so big, so soul-less, with way too much product. At Neiman Marcus we have small stores. We offer good experiences with restaurants and spas. We put a champagne bar in the shoe department of the Beverly Hills store. We want people to enjoy themselves while they are shopping. We have a world-class art collection on display. We have memory mirrors—you stand in front of the mirror, and it takes a 360-degree video of all the different outfits you try on that you can share with your friends, so it's a very social activity. It all adds to the 'OMG, you thought of me!' factor."

Like the memory mirror, digitally connected experiences will be critical to any in-store initiative, she said.

"Digital has become an integral part of the store shopping experience," she said. "A large percentage of our customers do research online first and then come in to the store. Or they're receiving information from our sales associates, who are all powered up with iPhones and our internally developed sales associate apps. Or [customers] are receiving texts and emails from our sales associates with product suggestions based on what they have bought in the past."

According to Katz, this level of personalized experience is essential to continuing to deliver on Neiman Marcus's brand promise—high-quality service and personal relationships—in the digital age.

And in the future, she said, Neiman Marcus plans to take this idea to the next level.

"We're not selling commodities, we're selling emotion," Katz said. "So we're thinking about how to satisfy emotional needs via data analytics. There are so many ways you can become ubiquitous in your customers' lives. Imagine this, based on the permission you give us to be in your life: your alarm goes off on your iPhone, and the first thing you get is a text message suggesting what to wear that day from Ken Downing, our fashion director, who is so well known with our customers. How can we do this? We have access to the weather in your ZIP Code and access to your calendar so we know what your day looks like. And we have a pretty good idea of what you've bought at Neiman Marcus. That level of personalization is not that far off. Customers trust Neiman Marcus, and they want us to help them get dressed every day. They want to know what's appropriate, how to wear things, what goes with what. It's just a matter of time before they allow us to truly be part of their lives."

An Omnichannel Organization

Katz believes one big contributor to Neiman Marcus's success is the organization's structure, which is customer-focused above all else.

"Our head of e-commerce leads every touch point for the customer in store and online," she said. "We work to have this perfect connection between everything digital and everything in the store. Now no one is territorial because they all share one purpose. We look at customer spend[ing] from a 360-degreee perspective, from what we buy across channels to evaluating inventory. We have a head of customer experience to provide a channel-agnostic ultimate customer experience."

Neiman Marcus has made these organizational decisions because Katz believes that much of the company's business is digital first, and that will only continue to grow.

"I believe that the starting point for our customers is our site," she said. "Mobile sites have to be really strong because that's where she starts with our brand. We hope it excites her to engage with the product or bring her into the store if she lives in one of our markets."

Innovating for Everyone

Marvin Ellison, CEO, JCPenney

Any conversation about the present and future of retail has to include Marvin Ellison, the man in charge of the latest remake of JCPenney. Ellison joined JCPenney in 2014 as president and CEO-designee, and became CEO in August 2015. This was after twelve years at The Home Depot, most recently as executive vice president for the company's more than two thousand stores.

Before that, he spent fifteen years working his way up from associate at Target.

Ellison has helped turn the company around from the depths of the Ron Johnson era.

He clearly learned some things along the way about private label brands, customer targeting and the future of the physical store.

Going Private

Ellison said consumers are now focused on two things more than ever: convenience and value. This is understandable, because adults employed full time reported working an average of forty-seven hours a week, an increase of ninety minutes from 2006, according to Gallup.[2]

"The price transparency that exists online has made every consumer even more conscious of value and making sure they get the best value," Ellison said. "And there is the whole convenience factor: Everyone is time starved. We're connected to our businesses, friends, family and social networks twenty-four hours, seven days a week. So we want to get things done in ways that are most convenient for our lifestyles."

With these guiding principles—value and convenience—in mind, the big task left is to figure out what they mean to target consumers. Ellison said the definition of *value* varies, of course. For most younger consumers value is about style and price, but the story is different for millennial moms.

"Her kids grow so fast, it's about fit and price, not about quality," he said. "But if she's buying for herself, she wants things to be durable and last and not have to always invest in new things. So *value* is different to each consumer and retailers need to understand the uniqueness of these consumers to be sure they're going to market in the proper way."

This value pressure has driven Ellison and JCPenney to put a renewed emphasis on private label brands. Ellison saw some of JCPenney's toughest competitors—Zara, H&M, Uniqlo, and Mango—exemplifying the benefits of private label. Then he looked at JCPenney's own data and found that, online, JCPenney's private label brands got more five-star ratings than its national brands.

"I remember a lot of retailers talking about how they are increasing their penetration of national brands," he said. "And how these brands are going to be growing e-commerce business and driving profits. Now, I'm not a mathematician, but none of that adds up. Increasing your national brand penetration in the age of online price transparency, you walk in the face the enormous pressure from these sophisticated pure-play e-commerce retailers with their pricing engines and ability to change prices. So for me, it was a pretty simple equation. If you're going to go with national brands in an aggressive way to grow e-commerce, you'll have a lower gross margin because you have to compete on price. But if you go with private brands that are highly rated, it's the best of both worlds because with the lower cost structure of bringing private brands to market, you can still be competitive on price without having the pressure to perform against the sophisticated e-commerce companies competing on price scraping."

Targeting Customers

Ellison said one of his biggest realizations was that JCPenney has two different consumer types and can cater to both successfully.

"We have . . . an emerging customer and a current customer," he said. "Our current customers are rather mature white females with grown children who do not live in the house. Our emerging customer is a millennial mom in her early thirties with, on average, two kids—and she works."

These two customer types have different brand and buying preferences, of course, and are also swayed by different marketing and media, an idea Ellison brought to life with an example.

"We sell cotton clothing for kids; Carter's is a national brand and we also have a private brand called Okie Dokie with more of an opening price point," he said. "When we studied the data, we found the core Carter's customer is our current mature customer—the grandmother who is willing pay more money because she is buying it for back-to-school, gifts and holiday. The millennial mom is a disproportionately higher purchaser of Okie Dokie; she's on a tight budget, and she's trying to clothe [her kids] daily, monthly and each season by finding the best value. But our marketing campaign for kids' cotton clothing was marketing to both customers in the exact same way. And those two customers receive data and media very differently. The more mature customer reads the paper and watches TV. The millennial customer is all digital, and her world centers around her mobile devices, and she's on Facebook, Instagram and Twitter. But we were trying to communicate with that customer the traditional way and wondering why we weren't successful. Once we unraveled that, we now understand how to target each brand."

Ellison said making these marketing switches paid off in a big way: JCPenney was able to reduce its total spending on marketing in the first quarter of 2016 by roughly 10 percent, but impressions went up 3 percent in the same time period as the company shifted from traditional to digital and social media for some target groups.

According to Ellison, the "one customer fits all" strategy is partly to blame for JCPenney's struggles, and changing this view has been instrumental in JCPenney's turnaround.

"When we look at the failure of the 2010 to 2013 era, they targeted one core customer, shifting away from the current customer strategy and chasing the new customer," he said. "But by ignoring the existing core customer, they didn't realize the current customer was going to feel neglected and would go to other places. We feel we can serve both customers at the same time. They share common traits of value, convenience and service. The one caveat to all of this is that all our customers fall into the same household income bracket that is a key target, but within that bracket we have two subsets of customers. So we think, with the right assortment and marketing strategy, we don't have to put all our eggs in one basket."

One example of this new strategy: selling a diverse range of appliance brands, including LG and Samsung for younger customers and GE for more mature customers.

Revamping the Store

Ellison has thought a lot about what to do with the hundreds of thousands of square feet JCPenney owns across the country. As he told us, he doesn't see physical stores as a disadvantage if they're harnessed to increase customer convenience.

"We don't see having a thousand retail stores as a disadvantage in our marketplace," he said. "We closed roughly forty stores last year [2015] that weren't productive, and we'll close about seven this year. The key question is now to monetize the key locations and create convenience for our customer fulfillment, from pick-up or brand marketing standpoints. So my idea of convenience is connecting online with brick and mortar."

By this he means initiatives like buy online, pick up in store, ship from store, and in-store returns. Ellison says these initiatives are paying off: in addition to increasing customer loyalty, more than 90 percent of online returns are made in a store, and more than 30 percent of those customers buy something else during the trip. Even more significant is that more than 40 percent of buy online, pick up in store customers buy another item when they come to collect their online purchase, even if they've already paid for it.

"The physical store gives you the ability to solve an immediate problem," Ellison said. "And over 70 percent of our orders are ready in an hour. This is way more convenient than any pure-play e-commerce company can ship it to you. If you can limit the friction and create seamless connectivity to the digital world, the store becomes even more important, especially when you can create reasons to come in."

But retailers not only to have these programs in place, they also have to be efficient to avoid leaking margin.

"We are rolling out a new ship-from-store system," Ellison said. "We are identifying a group of stores that would be the first option for delivery for hard-to-ship-to areas. So we'll have the staffing, equipment and support at these designated stores to make this as efficient as possible. Our goal is to push a significant number of orders to these designated stores with a different type of assortment. So you may walk into a store that traditionally may be a low-volume brick-and-mortar store for us, but because of its geographic location and square footage, you may see a different assortment because that store, in addition to cash-and-carry, is also a distribution point. We have some pretty aggressive plans to expand this into 2017."

Convenience for Ellison also means being a one-stop shop, hence his decision to start selling appliances.

"Carrying major appliances was not initially well received—it wasn't intuitive to most of the leaders here," he said. "But an outside study we commissioned revealed that over one-third of our customers are buying appliances at Sears, which tells me they have no problem buying appliances in the mall. So as Sears goes through its current situation and their future may be in question, why not get into the space to pick up some market share?"

A similar idea runs through JCPenney's partnerships with Empire Flooring and Ashley Furniture, but these cases revolve around the idea of making the department store into a showroom—JCPenney doesn't own most of the inventory.

"These are examples of strategic partnerships we think we can bring on board that won't tie up a lot cash but [will] leverage our physical space to serve our customers in a different way," Ellison said.

Even though JCPenney doesn't own the inventory, Ellison said the company must own the customer relationship and data.

"That's the most important thing," he said. "Our appliances are delivered through a network managed by GE, but when that delivery person shows up, he's in a JCPenney uniform. And when a customer calls our customer service center, it is identified by a JCPenney number. We protect the precious relationship with our customer even with a third-party supplier. We scrutinize potential partnerships to be sure the brand will be equal to, if not superior to, the JCPenney brand."

Finally, to succeed, stores need to provide a compelling experience as well as convenience. Ellison points to significant opportunities in areas where the physical store can provide a better experience than online—like salon services, home decorating and plus-size clothing.

"Our goal is to create a beauty experience connection between Sephora and the rebranded InStyle salons, which drives frequency, because these are physical trips by definition," he said. "There are other things in the store we think we can do that require a physical visit. Other physical trips are home décor and decorating and plus-size clothing. Customers say it's very difficult to buy plus-size online because the fit and style is a challenge, and our customers have said consistently that they want to feel it, touch it and try it on and to be sure it looks right on them. Our new plus-size shop and private brand is partnering with Ashley Nell Tipton, who was the first plus-size designer to win Project Runway."

Another entertaining experience that seamlessly connects the online and in-store worlds: JCPenney's partnership with Pinterest, which placed ten large digital, interactive, in-store Pinterest boards in malls across the country leading up to Mother's Day weekend.

"One of the most successful things we did was a partnership with Pinterest," Ellison said. "Customers pinned different fashions and styles, and then came into the store, and it was an overwhelming success for both brands. We're going to continue to do these kinds of partnerships, and you're going to see us leverage stores as a gathering place for events and activities that will resonate with our customers."

If Ellison can turn stores into a strategic, convenient, entertaining weapon, the increasingly digital retail environment of 2026 may not seem so threatening. We're excited to see what other new ideas he brings to JCPenney.

Leading Through Change

Paul Charron, Chairman of the Board,
Campbell Soup Company

We all know the retail world is changing, but the jury's still out on the type of leadership needed to respond to this accelerating change. To help answer that question, we sat down with Paul Charron, who is certainly no stranger to leadership himself.

Charron is board chair of Campbell Soup Company, and he

previously served as chair and CEO of Liz Claiborne, as well as in senior positions at VF Corporation and the private equity firm Warburg Pincus.

Charron discussed with us the forces driving a new retail landscape during the 250th birthday year of the United States and, more important, how to respond to them.

Charron pointed to several demographic shifts driving rapid change in retail, especially the shift toward urbanization and suburbanization.

"I think it will be very interesting to see how things are going to play out in New York, Boston, Philadelphia, Washington, Chicago, Detroit, Houston, Miami, Atlanta, San Francisco and Los Angeles versus everywhere else," he said. "There's a tremendous difference in mind-set, values, composition of population. I think the gap with [rural] areas will widen."

Many of these cities are filled with millennials, another demographic force to be reckoned with, according to Charron.

"The whole idea of millennials, the segmentation, how demanding they are—if you're a retailer or a CPG firm trying to tailor products to consumer needs, you need to understand all that," he said. "They're concerned about sustainability, global warming."

These demographic shifts are so critical because they're driving changing consumer behavior, and the consumer has to be at the center of everything a brand or retailer does.

Charron said retailers can easily be distracted by new technology, but the consumer has to come first.

"Everything begins and ends with the consumer in my opinion, not with the technology," he said. "Look at consumer behavior, and key factors influencing it, then see how technology impacts it and retail responds. But technology is only a tool."

That said, Charron sees technology as a hugely valuable tool, once it's directed by consumer insights.

"The biggest thing impacting retail is technology," he said. "I see technology as an enabler that gives us more control, choice and convenience. I also see it as a threat that gives us less control and invades our privacy. . . . Technology will help us target our messaging better. For example, CVS already knows everything I buy. I may want to get rid of the CVS app because they send me too many messages and too much information. But I still want the 30-percent-off coupon, because who pays retail?"

Technology also makes it possible to effect rapid changes in every aspect of the business, meaning that any competitive advantage a retailer develops will be fleeting. Especially in the current economy, retailers need to respond to changing dynamics quickly and effectively to stay one step ahead of their competitors.

"We don't have the growth, and any competitive advantage is more temporary," Charron said. "Everyone's taking a good idea and making it better. You're constantly evolving instead of setting and forgetting."

So if constant improvement and innovation are the new competitive mandates, our next question for Charron was, naturally, how do you do that successfully? What will retailing look like in 2026?

First, Charron says, retailers need to seriously rethink their real estate strategy. Everyone in retail knows that the United States is overstored. In fact, a Lazard Freres study showed that in 1980, there was twice as much retail space as demand warranted—and it's been growing at 4 percent per year since then, even after flattening briefly during the Great Recession.

But Charron said that considering which store to keep and which to kill, not all stores should carry the same significance.

"Retailers in the future will have a series of flagships, not outposts, keeping the focus on clicks," he said. "Think of the Wild

West. You had Fort Dodge. It was an impenetrable command post, but the outposts were much more vulnerable to attack."

Specifically, Charron thinks retailers should sell 25 percent or more of their stores so they can invest more time and energy in the highest performers—the flagships. The remaining stores should all have assortments highly tailored to key demographics and location.

For consumer packaged goods companies, Charron recommended shifting focus. Campbell Soup Company, where Charron chairs the board, has gone from having 50 percent of the soup market to just 44 percent, its share slowly eaten away by smaller, newer competitors. But Charron said the company, led by its CEO, Denise Morrison, is fighting back.

"Denise said, 'I'm going to shift my portfolio from soup to well-being,'" Charron related. "To shift the product from the center of the store to the periphery of the store. I'm going to take the profit from soup and redefine how I market and define soup and get into higher-growth categories. I'm going to change the organizational structure to free up $300 million in annual cost savings. She decided to fundamentally alter the way we run the company and choose to compete."

But despite all the change he prescribed for future success, Charron believes the leaders who are successful at taking their companies through it won't be especially fresh faced.

"For revolution, for the most part, you need new leadership," he said. "But you don't need a bunch of thirty-year-olds. They haven't lived enough life. They're full of promise but not perspective. I think you walk into a company, you look at its financials, you look at the world you'll be competing in in five to ten years, and most retailers conclude that it has to be revolution. You need to rethink the interaction with the consumer, the application of consumer insights, the structure of the organization, allocation of data, how much capital, assets—time, dollars, people—the CEO has to rethink that. If you don't, you won't get organizational change, which you need for behavioral change."

So at its core, the future retailing world that Charron envisions—full of more specialized brands, more localized but fewer stores and dominated by technology—will be all about change. But the leaders best positioned to take their companies through this retailing revolution will be a bit more seasoned.

ACKNOWLEDGMENTS

This book would never have been written without the support, encouragement, and active participation of so many friends, advisors, and industry thought leaders.

It all started with our determined agent, Edward Necarsulmer IV, who created the path for our first book, *The New Rules of Retail*. And Emily Carleton, our first editor at St. Martin's Press, had the faith that we could write another great book and led the initial stages of the project to get others on board to consider our ideas. Without her we would not have been able to get this project started. We owe her a big thank-you. Tim Bartlett, our second editor, took on the project with gusto and challenged our argument and logic numerous times, always with the goal of making the book better and more readable. Both Tim and Emily were exceptional in helping us complete this project. And they made the process fun to boot!

Scott Olivet (CEO, Renegade Brands) read the entire manuscript and critiqued it brilliantly, while always providing great encouragement and new ideas.

Our thoughts were influenced in great discussions with

William Lauder (Executive Chairman, Estee Lauder), David Jaffe (CEO, Ascena), Eric Wiseman (former CEO, VF Corporation), Jeff Gennette (CEO, Macy's), Michelle Lam (CEO, True & Co.), Paul Jones (CEO, Payless), Paul Charron (ex-Chairman, Campbell's Soup), Jeremy Liew (partner at Lightspeed Ventures), Mindy Grossman (CEO, Weight Watchers), Karen Katz (CEO, Neiman Marcus), Mark Cohen (Professor of Retail at Columbia Business School), Jane Elfers (CEO, The Children's Place), Blake Nordstrom (President, Nordstrom), Harvey Kanter (CEO, Blue Nile), David Campisi (CEO, Big Lots), Mitchell Modell (CEO, Modell's Sporting Goods), Demos Paneros (CEO, Barnes & Noble), Norman Matthews (Chairman, The Children's Place), Gerry Rittenburg (Chairman, Party City), Will Kussell (Operating Partner, Advent Capital) and Mitchell Klipper (ex-CEO, Barnes & Noble), Jeremy Liew (Partner, Lightspeed Ventures), Claudio Del Vecchio (Chairman and CEO, Brooks Brothers), Michael Gould (former CEO, Bloomingdale's), Tony Spring (CEO, Bloomingdale's), Allen Questrom (former CEO, Federated Department Stores, JC Penney, and Barney's). All provided great insights in our discussions with them which helped us to expand on our thesis.

Michael Massey (former CEO, PetSmart) was very generous with his time in discussing the thesis with Michael Dart, helping to shape the trends and challenges facing a large-scale retailer like Pet Smart, how they need to be addressed, and what is required to lead in these enormously turbulent times.

We owe all of these industry thought leaders tremendous gratitude for sharing their time and knowledge.

Amy Brooks was invaluable in editing many of the ideas by conducting primary research and managing the entire process of putting it all together. We cannot thank her enough for always being there to support us and for pushing the book forward-an incredible job.

Monica Sallouti provided the brilliant graphics that captured the essence of so many of the key points in the book.

NOTES

Chapter 1: The Supply-Demand Imbalance

1. Paul Cashin and C. John McDermott, "The Long-Run Behavior of Commodity Prices," IMF Working Paper, May 2001, https://www.imf.org /external/pubs/ft/wp/2001/wp0168.pdf.

2. "Do TVs Cost More Than They Used To?" Reviewed.com, September 4, 2012, http://televisions.reviewed.com/features/do-tvs-cost-more-than-they -used-to.

3. "Clothing Production in China from March 2016 to March 2017 (in Billion Meters)," https://www.statista.com/statistics/226193/clothing -production-in-china-by-month/.

4. Gladys Lopez-Acevedo and Raymond Robertson, eds., *Stitches to Riches? Apparel Employment, Trade, and Economic Development in South Asia* (Washington, DC: World Bank Group, 2016), https://openknowledge .worldbank.org/bitstream/handle/10986/23961/9781464808135.pdf?sequence =2&isAllowed=y.

5. Zhai Yun Tan, "What Happens When Fashion Becomes Fast, Disposable And Cheap?," *NPR*, April 10, 2016, http://www.npr.org/2016/04/08/473513620 /what-happens-when-fashion-becomes-fast-disposable-and-cheap.

6. Marilyn Geewax, "Why Americans Spend Too Much," *NPR*, December 6, 2011, http://www.npr.org/2011/12/05/143149947/why-americans -spend-too-much.

7. "The Rise in Dual Income Households," Pew Research Center, June 18, 2015, http://www.pewresearch.org/ft_dual-income-households-1960-2012-2/.

8. Tyler Cowen, "Silicon Valley Has Not Saved Us from a Productivity Slowdown," *The New York Times*, March 4, 2016, http://www.nytimes.com /2016/03/06/upshot/silicon-valley-has-not-saved-us-from-a-productivity -slowdown.html?smprod=nytcore-ipad&smid=nytcore-ipad-share&_r=0.

9. Sarah Halzack, "There Really Are Too Many Stores. Just Ask the Retailers," *The Washington Post*, April 5, 2016, https://www.washingtonpost.com /news/business/wp/2016/04/05/there-really-are-too-many-stores-just-ask-the -retailers/.

10. John Kell, "Coach Is Pulling Its Products From Department Stores Across the US," *Fortune*, August 9, 2016, http://fortune.com/2016/08/09/coach -department-stores-discount/.

11. Shelly Banjo, "A Fool's Hope for Retail Resurgence," *BloombergGadfly*, March 2, 2016, https://www.bloomberg.com/gadfly/articles/2016-03-02 /brick-and-mortar-retail-shows-no-sign-of-a-comeback.

12. Manikandan Raman, "Goldman Sachs Cuts Bed Bath & Beyond's Q2 Expectations Following Q1 Report, Says 'Omnichannel is Omnichallenged,'" *Benzinga*, June 23, 2016, https://www.benzinga.com/analyst-ratings/analyst -color/16/06/8144392/goldman-sachs-cuts-bed-bath-beyonds-q2-expectations -foll.

Chapter 2: Dematerialization

1. Kevin Kelly, *The Inevitable* (New York: Penguin, 2016), 111.

2. "US and Global Consumer Spending on Media Content and Technology Continues to Rise," *Digital Content Next*, March 11, 2016, https:// digitalcontentnext.org/blog/2016/03/11/us-and-global-consumer-spending -on-media-content-and-technology-continues-to-rise/.

3. Uptin Saiidi, "Millennials Are Prioritizing 'Experiences' over Stuff," CNBC.com, May 5, 2016, http://www.cnbc.com/2016/05/05/millennials-are -prioritizing-experiences-over-stuff.html.

4. James Hamblin, "Buy Experiences, Not Things," *The Atlantic*, October 7, 2014, https://www.theatlantic.com/business/archive/2014/10/buy-experiences /381132/.

5. Sam Frizell, "The New American Dream Is Living in a City, Not Owning a House in the Suburbs," *Time*, April 25, 2014, http://time.com /72281/american-housing/.

6. Centers for Medicare and Medicaid Services, "National Health Expenditure Factsheet," https://www.cms.gov/research-statistics-data -and-systems/statistics-trends-and-reports/nationalhealthexpenddata /nhe-fact-sheet.html.

7. Bureau of Labor Statistics, US Department of Labor, "Share of Total Spending on Healthcare Increased from 5 Percent in 1984 to 8 Percent in 2014," *The Economics Daily,* http://www.bls.gov/opub/ted/2016/share-of -total-spending-on-healthcare-increased-from-5-percent-in-1984-to-8 -percent-in-2014.htm.

8. "Cracking the Trade Promotion Code," October 2, 2014, Nielsen.com, http://www.nielsen.com/us/en/insights/news/2014/cracking-the-trade -promotion-code.html.

Chapter 3: The Great Demographic Shift

1. Greg Ip, "How Demographics Rule the Global Economy," *The Wall Street Journal,* November 22, 2015, http://www.wsj.com/articles/how -demographics-rule-the-global-economy-1448203724.

2. Arthur C. Brooks, "An Aging Europe in Decline," *The New York Times,* January 6, 2015, http://www.nytimes.com/2015/01/07/opinion/an-aging -europes-decline.html?smprod=nytcore-ipad&smid=nytcore-ipad-share& _r=0.

3. Jacob M. Schlesinger and Alexander Martin, "Graying Japan Tries to Embrace the Golden Years," *The Wall Street Journal,* November 29, 2015, http://www.wsj.com/articles/graying-japan-tries-to-embrace-the-golden -years-1448808028.

4. US Bureau of Labor Statistics, "Consumer Expenditures in 2013," Survey, BLS Reports, US Census Bureau, Report 1053, February 2015, https:// www.bls.gov/cex/csxann13.pdf.

5. US Bureau of Economic Analysis, "Personal Saving Rate," March 1, 2017, available from Federal Reserve Bank of St. Louis, Economic Research, https://fred.stlouisfed.org/series/PSAVERT#0.

6. "Past 65 and Still Working: Big Data Insights on Senior Citizens' Financial Lives," JPMorgan Chase Institute, n.d., https://www.jpmorganchase .com/corporate/institute/document/past-65-and-still-working.pdf.

7. Investopedia.com, "America's Retirement Crisis is Here," http://www .investopedia.com/articles/retirement/060816/americas-retirement-crisis -here.asp.

8. Etienne Gagnon, Benjamin K. Johannsen, and David Lopez-Salido, *Understanding the New Normal: The Role of Demographics,* Finance and Economics Discussion Series 2016-080 (Washington, DC: Board of Governors of the Federal Reserve System, 2016), https://www.federalreserve.gov/econ resdata/feds/2016/files/2016080pap.pdf.

9. Jacob M. Schlesinger and Alexander Martin, "Graying Japan Tries to

Embrace the Golden Years," *The Wall Street Journal*, November 29, 2015, http://www.wsj.com/articles/graying-japan-tries-to-embrace-the-golden -years-1448808028.

10. Mark Bradbury, "The 7 Incredible Facts About Boomers' Spending Power," *The Huffington Post*, March 17, 2015, http://www.huffingtonpost .com/mark-bradbury/the-7-incredible-facts-about-boomers-spending_b _6815876.html.

11. Marina Vornovitsky, Alfred Gottschalck, and Adam Smith, "Distri- bution of Household Wealth in the U.S.: 2000 to 2011," https://www.census .gov/content/dam/Census/library/working-papers/2011/demo/wealth -distribution-2000-to-2011.pdf.

12. Ann C. Foster, "A Closer Look at Spending Patterns of Older Amer- icans," *Beyond the Numbers: Prices & Spending* 5, no. 4 (March 2016), https:// www.bls.gov/opub/btn/volume-5/spending-patterns-of-older-americans .htm. This is a publication of the US Bureau of Labor Statistics.

13. Ip, "How Demographics Rule the Global Economy."

14. The figures provided are averages. Pamela Villarreal, "How Are Se- niors Spending Their Money?" National Center for Policy Analysis, Janu- ary 22, 2014, http://www.ncpa.org/pub/ib135.

15. Ann C. Foster, "A Closer Look at Spending Patterns of Older Amer- icans," *Beyond the Numbers: Prices & Spending* 5, no. 4 (March 2016), https:// www.bls.gov/opub/btn/volume-5/spending-patterns-of-older-americans .htm. This is a publication of the US Bureau of Labor Statistics.

16. Pamela Lockard, "Should You Market to Baby Boomers on Social Media?," DMN3.com, February 19, 2016, https://www.dmn3.com/dmn3 -blog/should-you-market-to-baby-boomers-on-social-media.

17. Schlesinger and Martin, "Graying Japan."

18. John Lanchester, "What the West Can Learn from Japan About the Cultural Value of Work," *The New York Times Magazine*, December 13, 2016, https://www.nytimes.com/2016/12/13/magazine/what-the-west-can-learn -from-japan-about-the-cultural-value-of-work.html?_r=0.

Chapter 4: The Great Fragmentation

1. Brendan Shaughnessy, "Why Abercrombie Is Smart to Drop Its Logo from Its Clothes (and Why Other Retailers Should Follow)," *The Business Journals*, September 18, 2014, http://www.bizjournals.com/bizjournals /how-to/marketing/2014/09/why-abercrombie-smart-to-drop-logo-from -clothing.html.

2. John Kell, "What You Didn't Know About the Boom in Craft Beer,"

Fortune, March 22, 2015, http://fortune.com/2016/03/22/craft-beer-sales-rise-2015/.

3. Eileen Patten and Richard Fry, "How Millennials Today Compare with Their Grandparents 50 Years Ago," Pew Research Center, March 19, 2015, http://www.pewresearch.org/fact-tank/2015/03/19/how-millennials-compare-with-their-grandparents/.

4. Caelainn Blair and Shiv Malik, "Revealed: The 30-Year Economic Betrayal Dragging Down Generation Y's Income," *The Guardian* (UK), March 7, 2016, https://www.theguardian.com/world/2016/mar/07/revealed-30-year-economic-betrayal-dragging-down-generation-y-income.

5. Patten and Fry, "How Millennials Today Compare with Their Grandparents 50 Years Ago."

6. Nadja Popovich, "A Deadly Crisis: Mapping the Spread of America's Drug Overdose Epidemic," *The Guardian* (UK), May 25, 2016, https://www.theguardian.com/society/ng-interactive/2016/may/25/opioid-epidemic-overdose-deaths-map.

7. Gina Kolata, "Death Rates Rising for Middle-Age White Americans, Study Finds," *The New York Times*, November 2, 2015, http://www.nytimes.com/2015/11/03/health/death-rates-rising-for-middle-aged-white-americans-study-finds.html?_r=0.

8. "Tattoo Takeover," The Harris Poll, February 10, 2016, http://www.theharrispoll.com/health-and-life/Tattoo_Takeover.html.

9. Josh Zumbrun, "How Rich and Poor Spend (and Earn) Their Money," *The Wall Street Journal*, April 6, 2015, http://blogs.wsj.com/economics/2015/04/06/how-the-rich-and-poor-spend-and-earn-their-money/; Jacob Goldstein, "How the Poor, the Middle Class and the Rich Spend Their Money," *NPR*, August 1, 2012, http://www.npr.org/sections/money/2012/08/01/157664524/how-the-poor-the-middle-class-and-the-rich-spend-their-money.

10. Lauren Carroll, "Warren: The Average Family in the Bottom 90 Percent Made More Money 30 Years Ago," *PolitiFact*, January 13, 2015, http://www.politifact.com/truth-o-meter/statements/2015/jan/13/elizabeth-warren/warren-average-family-bottom-90-percent-made-more-/.

11. "America's Shrinking Middle Class: A Close Look at Changes Within Metropolitan Areas," Pew Research Center, May 11, 2016, http://www.pewsocialtrends.org/2016/05/11/americas-shrinking-middle-class-a-close-look-at-changes-within-metropolitan-areas/.

12. Ibid.

13. Figures based on A.T. Kearney analysis.

14. Associated Press, "So Much for the American Dream! Fewer Than

Half of Young Adults Will Earn as Much as Their Parents Did at the Same Age—Compared to 92 Per Cent Who Did in 1940," *Daily Mail* (UK), December 9, 2016, http://www.dailymail.co.uk/news/article-4015374/Americans-odds -earning-parents-plunged.html.

15. Figures based on A.T. Kearney analysis.

16. Laura Kusisto, "Influx of Younger, Wealthier Residents Transforms U.S. Cities," *The Wall Street Journal*, June 9, 2016, http://www.wsj.com /articles/influx-of-younger-wealthier-residents-transforms-u-s-cities -1465492762.

17. A.T. Kearney analysis of U.S. Census Bureau data.

18. Josh Sanburn, "U.S. Cities Are Slowing but Suburbs Are Growing," *Time*, May 21, 2014, http://time.com/107808/census-suburbs-grow-city -growth-slows/.

19. David R. Bell, *Location Is (Still) Everything* (New Harvest, 2014), 30.

20. "Current Cigarette Smoking Among Adults in the United States," Centers for Disease Control and Prevention, 2015, https://www.cdc.gov/tobacco /data_statistics/fact_sheets/adult_data/cig_smoking/.

21. Thomas B. Edsall, "How the Other Fifth Lives," *The New York Times*, April 27, 2016, http://www.nytimes.com/2016/04/27/opinion/campaign-stops /how-the-other-fifth-lives.html?mwrsm=Email.

22. National Center for Education Statistics, "Private Elementary and Secondary Enrollment, Number of Schools, and Average Tuition, by School Level, Orientation, and Tuition: Selected Years, 1999–2000 Through 2011–12," *Digest of Education Statistics*, June 2013, https://nces.ed.gov/programs/digest /d13/tables/dt13_205.50.asp; Derek Thompson, "Which Sports Have the Whitest/Richest/Oldest Fans?," *The Atlantic*, February 10, 2014, https:// www.theatlantic.com/business/archive/2014/02/which-sports-have-the -whitest-richest-oldest-fans/283626/.

23. Joe Cortwright, "Young and Restless," City Reports, October 19, 2014, http://cityobservatory.org/ynr/.

24. Tyler Cowen, "The Marriages of Power Couples Reinforce Income Inequality," *The Upshot* (blog), *The New York Times*, December 24, 2015, https://www.nytimes.com/2015/12/27/upshot/marriages-of-power-couples -reinforce-income-inequality.html.

25. "Americans Say They Like Diverse Communities; Election, Census Trends Suggest Otherwise," Pew Research Center, December 2, 2008, http:// www.pewsocialtrends.org/2008/12/02/americans-say-they-like-diverse -communities-election-census-trends-suggest-otherwise/.

26. "USDA Reports Record Growth In U.S. Organic Producers," U.S. De-

partment of Agriculture, April 4, 2016, https://www.usda.gov/media/press
-releases/2016/04/04/usda-reports-record-growth-us-organic-producers.

27. "Small and Independent Brewers Continue to Grow Double Digits," Brewers Association, March 22, 2016, https://www.brewersassociation
.org/press-releases/small-independent-brewers-continue-grow-double
-digits/.

28. Caroline Fairchild, "Does Levi Strauss Still Fit America?" *Fortune*, September 18, 2014, http://fortune.com/2014/09/18/levi-strauss-chip
-bergh/.

29. Jing Cao, "Wal-Mart Close to Acquiring Bonobos for About $300 Million," *Bloomberg*, April 17, 2017, https://www.bloomberg.com/news
/articles/2017-04-17/wal-mart-said-close-to-acquiring-bonobos-for-about-300
-million.

30. Chavie Lieber, "Bonobos and the Brotherhood of the Flattering Pants," *Racked*, June 11, 2015, http://www.racked.com/2015/6/11/8762431
/bonobos-andy-dunn.

Chapter 5: The Technology Catalyst

1. "U.S. E-Commerce Sales Growth by Quarter," https://www.digital
commerce360.com/2017/04/01/u-s-e-commerce-sales-quarter/.

2. Jason Keath, "105 Facebook Advertising Case Studies," Social Fresh, June 19, 2012, https://www.socialfresh.com/facebook-advertising-examples/.

3. Itamar Simonson and Emanuel Rosen, *Absolute Value: What Really Influences Customers in the Age of (Nearly) Perfect Information* (New York; Harper Business, 2014).

4. Hayley Peterson, "Amazon Changed the Price of an Item Eight Times in a Single Day," *Business Insider*, August 1, 2014, http://www.businessinsider
.com/amazon-price-tracking-2014-8; Jason del Rey, "How Amazon Tricks You Into Thinking It Always Has the Lowest Prices," *Recode*, January 13, 2015, http://www.recode.net/2015/1/13/11557700/how-amazon-tricks-you-into
-thinking-it-always-has-the-lowest-prices.

5. "History of APIs," *API Evangelist*, http://history.apievangelist.com/.

6. Andrew Perrin, "One-fifth of Americans Report Going Online 'Almost Constantly,'" *FactTank*, Pew Research Center, December 8, 2015, http://www.pewresearch.org/fact-tank/2015/12/08/one-fifth-of-americans
-report-going-online-almost-constantly/.

7. Manikandan Raman, "Goldman Sachs Cuts Bed Bath & Beyond's Q2 Expectations Following Q1 Report, Says 'Omnichannel is Omnichallenged,'" *Benzinga*, June 23, 2016, https://www.benzinga.com/analyst-ratings

/analyst-color/16/06/8144392/goldman-sachs-cuts-bed-bath-beyonds-q2
-expectations-foll.

Chapter 6: The Story So Far ... Everything Heading to Free
and Volatility

1. Richard Dobbs, Tim Koller, and Sree Ramaswamy, "The Future and
How to Survive It," *Harvard Business Review* (October 2015): 48–56, 58, 60, 62,
https://hbr.org/2015/10/the-future-and-how-to-survive-it.

Chapter 7: Maslow's Hierarchy Revisited

1. Eric Almquist, John Senior, and Nicolas Bloch, "The Elements of
Value," *Harvard Business Review* (September 2016): 46–53, https://hbr.org
/2016/09/the-elements-of-value.

2. Jeremy Quittner, "Why Americans Are Spending More on Experiences
vs Buying Stuff," *Fortune*, September 1, 2016, http://fortune.com/2016/09
/01/selling-experiences/; Uptin Saiidi, "Millennials Are Prioritizing 'Experiences' Over Stuff," *CNBC.com*, May 5, 2016, http://www.cnbc.com/2016/05
/05/millennials-are-prioritizing-experiences-over-stuff.html.

3. Barbara L. Goebel and Delores R. Brown, "Age Differences in Motivation Related to Maslow's Need Hierarchy," *Developmental Psychology* 17,
no. 6 (November 1981): 809–15.

4. A. H. Maslow, "A Theory of Human Motivation," *Psychological Review*
50 (1943): 386.

5. Richard E. Ocejo, *Masters of the Craft: Old Jobs in the New Urban
Economy* (Princeton, NJ: Princeton University Press, 2017).

6. "Millennials: Confident. Connected. Open to Change," Pew Research
Center, February 24, 2010, http://www.pewsocialtrends.org/2010/02/24
/millennials-confident-connected-open-to-change/.

7. Keith Hampton, Lauren Sessions Goulet, Eun Ja Her, and Lee Rainie,
"Social Isolation and New Technology," Pew Research Center, November 4,
2009, http://www.pewinternet.org/2009/11/04/social-isolation-and-new
-technology/.

8. Steve Reed and Malik Crawford, "How Does Consumer Spending
Change During Boom, Recession, and Recovery?" *Beyond the Numbers: Prices
& Spending* 3, no. 15 (June 2014), http://www.bls.gov/opub/btn/volume-3
/how-does-consumer-spending-change-during-boom-recession-and
-recovery.htm#_edn2.

9. Nathaniel Popper, "How Millennials Became Spooked by Credit Cards,"
The New York Times, August 14, 2016, http://www.nytimes.com/2016/08/15
/business/dealbook/why-millennials-are-in-no-hurry-to-take-on-debt.html.

10. Ibid.; Jeanine Skowronski, "More Millennials Say 'No' to Credit Cards," Bankrate.com, http://www.bankrate.com/finance/credit-cards/more -millen'ials-say-no-to-credit-cards-1.aspx.

11. Cary Funk and Lee Rainie, "Chapter 6: Public Opinion About Food," Pew Research Center, July 1, 2015, http://www.pewinternet.org/2015/07/01 /chapter-6-public-opinion-about-food/.

12. Eric Almquist, John Senior, and Nicolas Bloch, "The Elements of Value," *Harvard Business Review* (September 2016): 46–53, https://hbr.org /2016/09/the-elements-of-value.

13. Caroline Webb, *How to Have a Good Day* (New York: Crown Business, 2016).

14. Gordon Foxall, *Interpreting Consumer Choice* (New York: Routledge, 2010).

15. Zeynep Tom, "Why Good Jobs are Good for Retailers," *Harvard Business Review* (January–February 2012), https://hbr.org/2012/01/why-good-jobs -are-good-for-retailers.

Chapter 8: The New Consumer Value

1. Scott Magids, Alan Zorfas, and Daniel Leemon, "The New Science of Customer Emotions," *Harvard Business Review* (November 2015): 66–74, 76, https://hbr.org/2015/11/the-new-science-of-customer-emotions.

2. Daniel Batson, *Altruism in Humans* (New York: Oxford University Press, 2011), 33.

3. Andrew Cave, "'Don't Buy This Racket': Patagonia to Give Away All Retail Revenues on Black Friday," *Forbes*, November 21, 2016, http://www .forbes.com/sites/andrewcave/2016/11/21/dont-buy-this-racket-patagonia -to-give-away-all-retail-revenues-on-black-friday/#6af32085230c.

4. J. B. MacKinnon, "Patagonia's Anti-Growth Strategy," *The New Yorker*, May 21, 2015, http://www.newyorker.com/business/currency/patagonias -anti-growth-strategy; Nick Paumgarten, "Patagonia's Philosopher-King," *The New Yorker*, September 19, 2016, http://www.newyorker.com/magazine/2016 /09/19/patagonias-philosopher-king.

5. Belinda Parmar, "The Most (and Least) Empathetic Companies," *Harvard Business Review* (November 27, 2015), https://hbr.org/2015/11/2015 -empathy-index.

Chapter 9: The Future of Stores

1. Frank W. Elwell, "Robert Putnam on the Decline of Communities," in *Industrializing America: Understanding Contemporary Society Through Classical Sociological Analysis* (Westport, CT: Praeger, 1999), http://www.

faculty.rsu.edu/users/f/felwell/www/Theorists/Putnam/Community
.html.

2. https://www.census.gov/topics/families/families-and-households
.html.

3. SI Wire, "National NFL TV Ratings Continue Decline," *Sports Illustrated*, October 25, 2016, http://www.si.com/nfl/2016/10/25/tv-ratings-decline
-primetime-games.

4. Molly Driscoll, "Why the Definition of a 'Hit' TV Show Has Changed," *The Christian Science Monitor*, September 21, 2016, http://www.csmonitor
.com/The-Culture/TV/2016/0921/Why-the-definition-of-a-hit-TV-show
-has-changed.

5. David W. McMillan and David M. Chavis, "Sense of Community: A Definition and Theory," *Journal of Community Psychology* 14 (January 1986): 9, https://pdfs.semanticscholar.org/e5fb/8ece108aec36714ee413876e61b0510
e7c80.pdf.

Chapter 10: Generation Z and the Future

1. Amanda Cox, "How Birth Year Influences Political Views," *The New York Times*, July 7, 2014, http://www.nytimes.com/interactive/2014/07/08
/upshot/how-the-year-you-were-born-influences-your-politics.html?rref
=upshot&_r=1.

2. Peter Aspden, "Were the Hippies Right?" *Financial Times*, August 12, 2016.

3. "Taking Stock with Teens—Spring 2015: A Collaborative Consumer Insights Project," Piper Jaffray, 2016, http://www.piperjaffray.com/2col.aspx
?id=3444.

4. Kate Taylor, "Millennials Spend 18 Hours a Day Consuming Media—And It's Mostly Content Created by Peers," *Entrepreneur*, March 10, 2014, https://www.entrepreneur.com/article/232062; "Generation Z Media Consumption Habits," Trifecta Research, 2015, http://trifectaresearch.com/wp
-content/uploads/2015/09/Generation-Z-Sample-Trifecta-Research
-Deliverable.pdf.

5. The Kids Are Alright: TYF2016 Generations Survey, Institute for the Future.

6. U.S. Census Bureau 2014 National Population Projections.

7. Northeastern University, Black Youth Project at the University of Chicago with the Associated Press-NORC Center for Public Affairs Research.

8. Simon Mainwaring, "Sustainability Storytelling: How Levi's Inspires Engagement to Scale Impact," *Forbes*, October 3, 2015, http://www
.forbes.com/sites/simonmainwaring/2015/10/03/sustainability-storytelling

-how-levis-inspires-engagement-to-scale-impact/#4297a8906e83;   Jessica Knoblauch, "Ten Eco-friendly Retailers," *Mother Nature Network*, February 4, 2010, http://www.mnn.com/money/green-workplace/stories/10-eco-friendly -retailers.

9. The Kids Are Alright: TYF2016 Generations Survey, Institute for the Future.

10. Ibid.

11. Robert Half: Get Ready for Generation Z, https://www.roberthalf .com/workplace-research/get-ready-for-generation-z.

Chapter 11: The New Retail Landscape

1. Allison Arieff, "Rethinking the Mall," *Opinionator* (blog), *The New York Times*, June 1, 2009, https://opinionator.blogs.nytimes.com/2009/06 /01/rethinking-the-mall/.

2. Alyssa Abkowitz, "Plaza Fiesta!" *Creative Loafing*, June 21, 2006, http://www.clatl.com/news/article/13020869/plaza-fiesta.

3. Lisa Brown, "Pace Proposes $79 Million Retail, Residential Expansion at the Boulevard," *St. Louis Post-Dispatch*, December 3, 2015, http://www.stltoday .com/business/local/pace-proposes-million-retail-residential-expansion-at -the-boulevard/article_b07e09d4-e2f1-5278-89b2-085334a2f800.html.

4. Jeremy Adam Smith, "Won't You Be My Neighbor?" *Shareable*, October 26, 2009, http://www.shareable.net/blog/wont-you-be-my-neighbor.

5. Richard Dobbs, Tim Koller, and Sree Ramaswamy, "The Future and How to Survive It," *Harvard Business Review* (October 2015): 48–56, 58, 60, 62, https://hbr.org/2015/10/the-future-and-how-to-survive-it.

Chapter 12: Small Is Beautiful

1. Yahoo Finance, https://finance.yahoo.com/.

2. Daniel Roberts, "Here's What Happens When 3G Capital Buys Your Company," *Fortune*, March 25, 2015, http://fortune.com/2015/03/25/3g-capital -heinz-kraft-buffett/.

3. Maggie McGrath, "TJX Companies Continues Run as Retail's Out-lier, with Healthy Sales Growth," *Forbes*, August 16, 2016, http://www.forbes .com/sites/maggiemcgrath/2016/08/16/with-second-quarter-sales-growth -tjx-companies-continues-its-run-as-retails-outlier/#23f3c77e32dc.

4. Krystina Gustafson, "Target Is Chasing Wal-Mart with Its Smaller Stores but Using a Different Playbook," CNBC.com, October 5, 2016, http:// www.cnbc.com/2016/10/05/target-is-chasing-wal-mart-with-its-smaller -stores-but-using-a-different-playbook.html.

5. Matthew Townsend, "Lowe's Struggles to Catch Home Depot in

Store Locations," *Bloomberg*, February 24, 2016, https://www.bloomberg
.com/news/articles/2016-02-24/lowe-s-sales-top-estimates-as-home
-improvement-boom-continues; John Kell, "Lowe's Renovates Retail Strategy
with New Manhattan Stores," *Fortune*, August 5, 2015, http://fortune.com
/2015/08/05/lowes-renovates-retail-strategy-manhattan/.

6. "Office Depot Set to Close 300 More Stores But Increase New Format
Locations," *Retail TouchPoints*, August 3, 2016, http://www.retailtouchpoints
.com/features/news-briefs/office-depot-set-to-close-300-more-stores-but
-increase-new-format-locations.

Chapter 13: Becoming a Brand

1. http://www.theworldin.com/.

2. Kevin Kelly, *The Inevitable* (New York: Penguin, 2016), 8.

3. Cesar Hidalgo, *Why Information Grows:The Evolution of Order, from
Atoms to Economics* (New York: Basic Books, 2015).

4. Jason Ankeny, "What Retailers Can Learn from J.C. Penney's
Turnaround—and Lands' End's Turn for the Worse," *RetailDIVE*, October 3,
2016, http://www.retaildive.com/news/lessons-for-retailers-from-jc-penney
-lands-end-turnarounds/427394/.

5. Ibid.

Chapter 14: The Liquefied Organization

1. Miles Kohrman, "How Google's Flexible Workspace Ignites Creative
Collaboration (on Wheels)," *Fast Company* (newsletter), September 26, 2013,
https://www.fastcompany.com/3017824/work-smart/how-googles-flexible
-workspace-ignites-creative-collaboration-on-wheels.

2. Jennifer Reingold, "How a Radical Shift Left Zappos Reeling," *Fortune*,
March 4, 2016, http://fortune.com/zappos-tony-hsieh-holacracy/.

3. Alicia Fiorletta, "Collaboration Becomes Key to Success for Retailers
and Suppliers," *Retail TouchPoints*, September 2, 2014, http://www.retailtouch
points.com/topics/inventory-merchandising-supply-chain/collaboration
-becomes-key-to-success-for-retailers-and-suppliers.

4. Ibid.

5. Figures based on A.T. Kearney analysis.

Chapter 15: Amazon and the Distribution Century

1. Eugene Kim, "Leaked documents show Amazon is making a big play
to bypass UPS and FedEx," *Business Insider*, February 9, 2016, http://www
.businessinsider.com/leaked-documents-about-amazons-global-logistics
-business-2016-2.

2. Robin Lewis, "Amazon's Shipping Ambitions Are Larger Than It's Letting On," *Forbes*, April 1, 2016, https://www.forbes.com/sites/robinlewis /2016/04/01/planes-trains-trucks-and-ships/#2c602ade6d39.

3. Robin Lewis, "Amazon's Shipping Ambitions Are Larger Than It's Letting On," *Forbes*, April 1, 2016, https://www.forbes.com/sites/robinlewis /2016/04/01/planes-trains-trucks-and-ships/#2c602ade6d39.

Chapter 16: Platforming

1. Geoffrey G. Parker and Marshall W. Van Alstyne, *Platform Revolution: How Networked Markets Are Transforming the Economy—And How to Make Them Work for You* (New York: W. W. Norton, 2016).

2. Phil Wahba, "How Macy's New CEO Plans to Stop the Bleeding," *Fortune*, March 22, 2017, http://fortune.com/2017/03/22/macys-ceo-plan/.

3. David Gelles and Rachel Abrams, "Macy's to Buy Bluemercury Spa and Beauty Chain," *Dealbook* (blog), *The New York Times*, February 3, 2015, https:// dealbook.nytimes.com/2015/02/03/macys-to-acquire-bluemercury/?_r=0.

4. Adam Levine-Weinberg, "J.C. Penney Is Leaning on Sephora to Lead Its Comeback," *The Motley Fool*, March 22, 2016, http://www.fool.com /investing/general/2016/03/22/jc-penney-is-leaning-on-sephora-to-lead-its -comeba.aspx.

5. Mike Hower, "Timberland and VF: A Tale of Merging Two Sustainability Programs," *GreenBiz*, February 24, 2016, https://www.greenbiz.com /article/timberland-and-vf-tale-merging-two-sustainability-programs.

6. "Ascena Retail Group, Inc. to Acquire Ann Inc. for $47 per Share in Accretive Transaction," *PR Newswire*, May 18, 2015, http://www.prnewswire .com/news-releases/ascena-retail-group-inc-to-acquire-ann-inc-for-47-per -share-in-accretive-transaction-300084673.html.

Chapter 17: Making Change Practical

1. Josh Constine, "Facebook Beats in Q4 with $8.81B revenue, Slower Growth to 1.86B Users," *TechCrunch*, February 1, 2017, https://techcrunch .com/2017/02/01/facebook-q4-2016-earnings/.

2. Fareeha Ali, "How Chubbies Uses Social Media to Build its Brand," *Internet Retailer*, June 15, 2016, https://www.digitalcommerce360.com/2016 /06/15/how-chubbies-uses-social-media-build-its-brand/.

3. Barry Schwartz, *The Paradox of Choice: Why More Is Less* (New York: HarperCollins, 2004).

4. Denise Lee Yohn, "Trader Joe's, Where Less Is More," *Business Insider*, May 31, 2011, http://www.businessinsider.com/trader-joes-where-less-is-more -2011-5.

5. Leonie Barrie, "VF Corp's Third Way Shores Up Key Supplier Partnerships," *Just-Style News and Comment*, December 14, 2015, http://www.just-style.com/analysis/vf-corps-third-way-shores-up-key-supplier-partnerships_id126825.aspx.

Chapter 18: Industry Ideas

1. "Myths, Exaggerations and Uncomfortable Truths," http://www-935.ibm.com/services/us/gbs/thoughtleadership/millennialworkplace/.

2. Lydia Saad, "The '40-Hour' Workweek Is Actually Longer—by Seven Hours," Gallup.com, August 29, 2014, http://www.gallup.com/poll/175286/hour-workweek-actually-longer-seven-hours.aspx.